Feminist Thought

Twentieth-Century Social Theory

Series Editor: Charles C. Lemert

Twentieth-Century Social Theory invites authors respected for their contributions in the prominent traditions of social theory to reflect on past and present in order to propose what comes next. Books in the series will consider critical theory, race, symbolic interactionism, functionalism, feminism, world systems theory, psychoanalysis, and Weberian social theory, among other current topics. Each will be plain to read, yet provocative to ponder. Each will gather up what has come to pass in the twentieth century in order to define the terms of social theoretical imagination in the twenty-first.

Titles in the series include:

Feminist Thought

Desire, Power, and Academic Discourse

Patricia Ticineto Clough

BLACKWELL
Oxford UK & Cambridge USA

First published 1994
Reprinted 1995

Blackwell Publishers Inc.
238 Main Street
Cambridge, Massachusetts 02142
USA

Blackwell Publishers Ltd
108 Cowley Road
Oxford OX4 1JF
UK

Library of Congress Cataloging-in-Publication Data
Clough, Patricia Ticineto
    Feminist thought: desire, power, and academic discourse /
  Patricia Ticineto Clough.
        p.   cm. – (Twentieth-century social theory)
    Includes bibliographical references and index.
    ISBN 1–55786–485–3. – ISBN 1–55786–486–1 (pbk.)
    1. Feminist theory.   2. Social sciences – Philosophy.   I. Title.
  II. Series: Twentieth-century social theory (Cambridge, Mass.)
HQ1190.C55   1994   93-51072
305.42′01 – dc20   CIP

Designed by Emma Gotch

Typeset in 10 on 12 pt Sabon by Best-set Typesetter Ltd., Hong Kong
Printed in Great Britain by Hartnolls Ltd., Bodmin

This book is printed on acid-free paper

*For Women Around the World Resisting Oppression,
Domination, and Exploitation*

Contents

Series Editor's Preface

One might assume that a book under the title *Feminist Thought* would be of primary interest to feminists. Though it is expected that the readers of Patricia Clough's book will in fact include a good number of feminists, I propose that it is well past time to denaturalize the assumption that *only* feminists ought to read such a book.

These few prefatory words are addressed, most particularly, to those who might have taken up this book – even inadvertently – in spite of having a personal relation to feminism that is indefinite, uncertain, or non-existent. I urge you not to put this important book down too hastily. It, and a very great deal of feminism, speaks well beyond the concerns of what is thought to be feminism, in ways outsiders to the enterprise itself might not imagine possible.

Feminism, as Clough makes clear, is now too important and complex a phenomenon to be ignored by anyone. It is not just that women are increasingly among the movers of power in world politics. Certain issues which are commonly considered feminist (though they are sharply contested among feminists) are among the more salient topics of public discourse – reproductive freedom, domestic violence, and sexual abuse being obvious instances. Nor is it the somewhat less obvious fact that many of the most troubled aspects of social life – health care, education, crime and violence, drugs, AIDS, the well-being of children – are addressed rather considerably in language heavily shaped by feminist consciousness. These are important facts of our times that form the context for any book in or about feminist thinking. But beyond them, and more precisely, feminist thought itself has emerged in the last generation as *the* single most creative and challenging source of social thought there is. Most of what the next generations of social theorists will take as their working assumptions about the nature and effects of class, race and ethnicity, sex and sexuality, post-coloniality, among other subjects, have already been redefined by recent debates in feminism.

Yet, feminist thought is not any one thing. This exactly is what makes it so important. It may be that those who are not feminist fear this field of social theory because they understand, perhaps intuitively, that it presents challenges and demands unlike the usual rigors incumbent upon the learning of that of which one is ignorant. This is true, but it is, I suppose, equally true to those who have lived within feminism for a long time.

Feminist thought is, thus, just one of the expressions of a constantly changing, tumultuous world in which, it is fair to say, nearly all of the most important debates of the day make some reference to considerations of feminist thinking. But feminist thought can no longer be thought of as though it were preoccupied exclusively with women's interests. Rather, it is that loosely organized domain of cultural work and intellectual activity that concerns itself just as much with questions of the wider complexity of social forces like race, class, and post-colonial history as with those more commonly thought of as women's issues.

This is a time when thinking people – whether academics, intellectuals, or those who read simply because they care to read – remain ignorant of the issues debated among feminists at a considerable risk. There is not yet any so well developed a political and intellectual culture from which one can so immediately understand the social thought of those of varied social circumstances who, after centuries of exclusion, are now increasingly the most provocative and powerful voices in both public and academic life.

Patricia Clough's *Feminist Thought: Desire, Power, and Academic Discourse* is a brilliant and clear introduction to that culture. Her book, therefore, can be justifiably compared to earlier efforts to describe and analyze the state of feminist thought, in particular Alison Jaggar's *Feminist Politics and Human Nature* and Sandra Harding's *The Science Question in Feminism*. These earlier books – appearing respectively in 1983 and 1986 – were invaluable interpretations of the state of feminist thought as it then was. Jaggar's clearly diagnosed the emergence of feminist thought from marxism, just as Harding's was one of the first to outline the emergence of a postmodern feminism. In the short interlude since Harding's 1986 book, feminist thought has changed as much as, or more than, it had changed in the even shorter interval between hers and Jaggar's. Clough's *Feminist Thought* describes and interprets these most recent changes.

Patricia Clough's *Feminist Thought* is not, however, merely a presentation of the ideas of others. Like her predecessors, Jaggar and Harding,

Clough brings an explicit theory of the recent history of feminist theory. She argues, with convincing evidence, that from its first classic work (Kate Millett's *Sexual Politics* in 1970), academic feminism has always been at definite, if sometimes concealed, odds with academic discourse. The actual history of feminist thought since Millett's *Sexual Politics* has been the history of thinking that forced itself to move again and again against the unspoken authority of mainstream social thought. But the culture of feminist theory is not simply a counter-authority. In large measure, it is a rethinking of authority itself in ways that require examination of the degradations and promises of social life experienced by those who bear the realities – of racial and sexual oppressions, of the different conditions of life in decolonized regions of the world, as well as of gender-based discriminations.

Though Clough puts this differently, and more exactly, this is why feminist thought has moved from the early classic works of literary theorists like Millett, poets and writers like Adrienne Rich, and sociologists like Dorothy Smith to its current, sometimes awkward relations with those other social theories that cannot leave feminism alone, just as now feminism cannot treat Black and post-colonial feminisms, or queer theory, as though they were separate enterprises. This is how, and why, feminist theory today is not any one thing and why, accordingly, it is so intimidating to those who have read it just a little or not at all.

Few writers are as uniquely prepared as Patricia Clough to guide readers through such a complex intellectual terrain. She is a film and communications theorist, ethnographer, musician, and sociologist, among all the other things a feminist intellectual and woman is called upon to be (in and outside the academy). She brings from these aspects of her background not just expertise, but a capacity to tolerate and appreciate variety and differences. This most rare of human gifts is what makes *Feminist Thought* such a readable, demanding, and entertaining account of one of the most important fields of social theory today.

Charles Lemert

Acknowledgements

Writing a book about feminist thought has afforded me the opportunity to work closely with the writings of feminist theorists whose brilliant and risk-taking efforts have changed and are changing what it means to do social theory; I especially want to thank them for their courage and determination in shaping feminist thought. Each has challenged me and in some way changed the way I read and write, think, and imagine – just as I hope this book about them will provoke others to do.

I also want to thank Simon Prosser at Blackwell for the care he took with my manuscript; and Charles Lemert who, as editor of this series in Twentieth-Century Social Theory, is contributing substantially to the development of a social theory that will shape the future with the voices of those who often have been silenced in and by the academy. I gladly contribute the voices of feminists to such a project. And thanks to Barbara Heyl, Anne Hoffman, Norman Denzin, Zali Gurevitch, Virginia Olesen, Joseph Schneider, Steven Seidman, Charles Smith, Alan Shelton, Stanley Aronowitz and colleagues at Fordham for reading parts of the manuscript; and also to all of you, along with Jill Herbert, Ann Galligan, Elizabeth Harriss, Geri Thoma, Vincent Barry, Barry Goldberg, Ellen Rosenthal, and Anahid Kassabian, I send thanks for being good friends. I thank my family for their usual but unusually generous support – especially my son, Christopher, whose quick mind and delicious sense of humor always get me through. Finally, I especially send my love to my father and mother whose encouragement and love for me made it inevitable that I would become a feminist thinker, unwilling to accept oppression, domination, and exploitation, especially of women.

Introduction

On the cover of the January 1993 volume of *Ms.* magazine, Gloria Steinem, the founder of various feminist organizations and of *Ms.* magazine, is pictured with bell hooks, the African-American feminist theorist, Urvashe Vaid, the former director of the National Gay and Lesbian Task Force, and Naomi Wolf, the author of *The Beauty Myth* – all under the headline, "NO, FEMINISTS **DON'T** ALL THINK ALIKE (Who Says We Have To?)." To underscore the point, the copy at the bottom of the cover promises that in the dialogue among these feminists, there will be "No Rules, No Limits, No Holds Barred!"[1] Thus, even while publicizing the differences among feminists, the *Ms.* cover suggests that it still is a bold, if not a provocative, act for feminists to reveal their differences; it seemingly requires letting down defenses, letting it all hang out, perhaps even challenging the long-standing dictum that "sisterhood is powerful."[2]

Indeed, the dialogue among the four feminists does reveal that the differences among feminists have been muted in feminist debates, not only "for fear of being misconstrued by our critics," but also because a "bourgeois white feminism" has "steered the movement in a certain direction," and therefore not all feminist theorists have had access to the mass media from which "most people learn about feminism."[3] Thus, these feminists do agree that if a grass-roots feminist politics is to be revived, now is the time to allow the diversity among feminists to gain a public forum and, thus, to shape the images of feminism which the mass media project.

Of course, none of this is news for feminist theorists in the academy. After all, academic feminist thought increasingly has been marked by debates, often difficult but profoundly productive, about how to articulate the differences among feminists and therefore how to theorize a feminist politics characterized by diversity. But if the *Ms.* dialogue especially focuses the discussion of diversity on the relationship of feminist politics and the images which the mass media authorize, the recent debates among academic feminist theorists also have focused on the relationship of diversity and the authority of academic discourse.

This book traces the development of these debates among academic feminist theorists by offering close readings of various texts that have shaped academic feminist thought since the early 1970s, especially: Kate Millett's *Sexual Politics* (1970), Adrienne Rich's *Of Woman Born* (1976), Dorothy Smith's *The Everyday World as Problematic* (1987), Nancy Hartsock's *Money, Sex and Power* (1985), Patricia Hill Collins's *Black Feminist Thought* (1990), Gloria Anzaldúa's *Borderlands/La Frontera* (1987), Trinh T. Minh-ha's *Woman, Native, Other* (1989), and Judith Butler's *Gender Trouble* (1990). Taken together, these texts suggest that feminist theorists always have been engaged in a struggle over the authority of academic discourse. But, especially throughout the 1980s, feminist theorists have developed a powerful social criticism that takes disciplinary knowledges as a point of departure, thereby making visible the hitherto suppressed links between disciplinary knowledges and the political, economic, and ideological arrangements in which the academy is embedded and which the academy often promotes. Over this period, then, feminist theorists have made the academy itself a site of feminist politics.

Reinventing the Literary, Reinventing the Social

Surely as early as Kate Millett's *Sexual Politics* (1970) and Adrienne Rich's *Of Woman Born* (1976), feminist thought was characterized by its encounter with the authority of disciplinary knowledges. Both texts made evident that the disciplines themselves were an obstacle to feminist theorizing, given that the disciplines either had denied the relevance of women's lives or profoundly misrepresented them. But while *Sexual Politics* and *Of Woman Born* pointed to the masculinist bias of traditional social science and literary criticism, thereby at least suggesting the need for a more general feminist criticism of the authority of all disciplinary knowledges, neither Millett nor Rich fully elaborated a feminist criticism that would take the very distinction of social science from literary criticism as a point of departure.

Indeed, even in the late 1970s and the early 1980s, as feminist theorists developed a more systematic criticism of disciplinary authority, they further problematized but they still did not fully deconstruct the distinction of social science from literary criticism. In social science, Dorothy Smith would subject sociology to a feminist revision and Nancy Hartsock would take on political science. Both argued that the interpretations usually offered by traditional social science reflected a male-dominated organization of the production of disciplinary knowledges; they therefore developed "standpoint epistemologies" that revised sociology and political science by making women's experiences the point of departure for the production of social scientific knowledge. But, in demanding a social science that takes its starting point from women's experience instead of men's, Smith and Hartsock all but left intact those understandings of experience, subjectivity, identity, and agency that have characterized traditional social science.

In the humanities, however, feminist theorists were developing a criticism of literary texts as well as mass media communication technologies that, in challenging modern literary canons and privileged traditions of cultural interpretation, would deconstruct understandings of experience, subjectivity, identity, consciousness, and agency that especially characterize modern, Western discourse. While feminist theorists such as Elaine Showalter, Carolyn Heilbrun, Elizabeth Abel, and Judith Kegan Gardiner criticized modern literary criticism for only reflecting the literary practice of male writers, other feminist theorists such as Laura Mulvey, Kaja Silverman, and Teresa De Lauretis harnessed the "crisis of representation," instigated by deconstruction, semiotics, and psychoanalysis, for a more general feminist criticism of the narrative logic of modern Western discourse; they made use of these critical approaches to elaborate the way modern forms of representation privilege masculinity in the construction of discursive authority.

Uncovering in Western, modern discourse the operation of forms of representation that exceed the individual's intentionality, feminist theorists in the humanities opened the criticism of knowledge to an analysis of a mass-mediated, intertextual network of fictions that permit the ideological deployment of unconscious fantasies in the discursive construction of the authorial subject. Thus, rather than focus on interpretation only as an effect of a male-dominated production of disciplinary knowledges, feminist theorists in the humanities located the problem of discursive authority at the level of literary practice – at the level of a political unconscious, which the narrative logic of Western, modern discourse puts into play. Feminist theorists in the humanities focused on the way narrativity elicits the participation of readers and writers in the practices of dominant forms of knowledge, thereby showing how a male-dominated production of knowledge is linked to modern practices of reading and writing – practices of meaning construction generally.[4]

But in focusing their criticism primarily on literary texts and mass media communication technologies, feminist theorists in the humanities did not explicitly extend their criticism of discursive authority to the assumptions and methodological orientations of social science. Like feminist theorists in social science, they did not deconstruct the distinction of social science from literary criticism, although their criticisms often pointed to how the hegemony of modern science generally makes feminist theorizing difficult; that is, the hegemony of modern science maintains certain oppositions that privilege masculinity as well as factuality, historicity, and "reality" over femininity, fiction, unconscious desire, fantasy, and polemic – oppositions that necessarily must be challenged by feminist theory.[5]

Thus, while throughout the late 1970s and the early 1980s, feminist theorists urged a general self-consciousness about how disciplinary knowledges promote, even as they disavow, their own cultural, political, and authorial vantage points, nonetheless, feminist theorists did not fully deconstruct the distinction of social science from literary criticism. Thus, by the late 1980s and the early 1990s, when faced with the challenges of Black feminist theorists, feminist post-colonial critics, Third World feminist theorists, and queer theorists, feminist thought already was troubled by debates over essentialism, identity, textuality, subjectivity, unconscious desire, agency, and experience – debates that might best be understood in terms of the as yet unresolved differences between feminist theorists in social science and feminist theorists in the humanities.[6] And while the challenges of African-American feminists, feminist post-colonial critics, Third World feminist theorists, and queer theorists seem only to have more profoundly troubled feminist thought, exacerbating the differences among feminist theorists, it is these challenges, I would propose, that now are furthering the deconstruction of the distinction of social science from literary criticism.

Indeed, in criticizing feminist thought itself for the way it has focused on gender differences at the exclusion of other differences, African-American feminists, Third World feminists, feminist post-colonial critics, and queer theorists also have become engaged in deconstructing the authority of academic discourse but in order to question the disciplinary deployment of certain definitions of race, class, sexuality, ethnicity, nationality, as well as gender. Thus, these feminist theorists are reformulating the notions of subjectivity, identity, experience, unconscious desire, intentionality, and agency but by revising the notions of nationality, sexuality, race, class, ethnicity, and gender.

These feminist theorists, therefore, are extending feminist theory developed in the humanities to rewriting the constitutive elements of social science. Because their writings negotiate across a number of languages, reclaiming previously assimilated cultural histories as well as revising notions of fantasy and unconscious desire, African-American feminist theorists, feminist post-colonial critics, Third World feminist theorists, and queer theorists necessarily are theorizing across the border of social science and literary criticism. They therefore are sharpening the aim and enlarging the scope of a general feminist criticism of disciplinary knowledges.

Indeed, Trinh T. Minh-ha's *Woman, Native, Other* (1989) and Gloria Anzaldúa's *Borderlands/La Frontera* (1987) refer to film-making and poetry to criticize and reformulate the conventions of social science and literary criticism; indeed, in their criticism of disciplinary knowledges, they treat both traditional social science and literary criticism as one – the human sciences. In *Black Feminist Thought* (1990), Patricia Hill Collins revises the standpoint epistemologies theorized by Smith and Hartsock and criticizes social science by making use of the literary criticisms of, among others, bell hooks, Hazel Carby, Barbara Smith, and Barbara Christian. In *Gender Trouble* (1990), Judith Butler deconstructs an earlier lesbian literary criticism as well as feminist revisions of psychoanalysis, as she criticizes the heterosexism of all sociological and philosophical treatments of identity.

Thus, even more than the feminist theorists they challenge, African-American feminists, Third World feminists, feminist post-colonial critics, and queer theorists are reinventing the literary by making clear how the literary is not merely a matter of fiction. Indeed, they are showing how the literary, especially its modern narrative form, has a political or ideological content and, therefore, how narrative form provides the logic or the ideologics by which social relationships are made intelligible. Thus, African-American feminists, feminist post-colonial critics, Third World feminist theorists, and queer theorists also are reinventing the social by making clear that reading and writing are not merely about the verbal or written text. Rather, they are about contentions over hegemony and counterhegemonies, shaping and reshaping the forms of intelligibility by which social reality is constituted.

Hence, more than the feminist theorists they challenge, African-American feminists, Third World feminists, feminist post-colonial critics, and queer theorists are connecting the deconstruction of the authority of academic discourse to grass-roots political movements. Indeed, they are reformulating the very meaning of the political in showing how political movements are themselves contentions over authority, over the authorized forms of making social reality intelligible. These feminist theorists are rearticulating both social science and literary criticism, making feminist theory a self-reflective social criticism that not only focuses on the contending modes of reading and writing the social but also enables grass-roots political movements. Thus, African-American feminist theorists, Third World feminist theorists, feminist post-colonial critics, and queer theorists also are giving new meaning to the dictum that sisterhood is powerful.

Indeed, while not all feminist theorists now think alike, nonetheless feminist theorizing is still marked by a desire for sisterhood, by a desire for the power that sisterhood might afford against oppression, domination, and exploitation. Indeed, it is both the differing among feminist theorists and their desire for a politics that might alleviate oppression, domination, and exploitation that not only enlarges and emboldens feminist thought but allows it to profoundly affect the academy. It is in articulating a desire for sisterhood, while demanding recognition of differences, that feminist theorizing has rewritten, is still rewriting, the relationship of desire, power, and academic discourse.

Reading and Writing Feminist Texts

Without understanding how feminist theory since the early 1970s has been about its differing with the disciplines – about its deconstructing the oppositions that disciplinary knowledges maintain, of fantasy and reality, fiction and history, polemic and academic discourse, it would be hard to grasp, not to mention appreciate, how and why feminist theorizing necessarily has been, and increasingly becomes even more blatantly, nothing more than a political writing shaped by a poetic, evocative, performing language of desire. It would be hard to grasp that feminist theorizing is a *writing* to save lives. And if it is the writer's life that is especially to be saved in writing, nonetheless the soaring of its poetry, the passion of its evocations, the power of its performances allow feminist theorizing always to lift up others as well.

In proposing, then, to offer close readings of various feminist texts, I would treat feminist theorizing as writing, especially focusing on the composition of each text: how each text made theorizing itself problematic and in ways never before imagined; how each text raised questions of narrative form that had not yet been raised as questions about doing theory; how each responded to a particular intertextual context. My readings, then, focus on the effort that each theorist expends in making academic feminist theory possible in the first place, and only then on what each theorist theorized. My readings also focus on the authorial desire of each text, its particular expression, usually culminating in the author's autobiographical framing of her writing. And while each text has left me with a lasting impression of the passion and wisdom each woman brought to bear on a struggle against oppression, exploitation, and domination, it will be clear that I prefer some variations of feminist theorizing more than others.

Thus, I have written *Feminist Thought: Desire, Power, and Academic Discourse* as a social critic, trained as a sociologist, who advocates feminism, especially various articulations of feminist theorizing by African-American feminists, feminist post-colonial critics, queer theorists, and Third World feminists. But more specifically, my readings of feminist theorizing are informed by a feminist materialist approach, especially one which takes both the deconstruction of hegemony and the critical reassessment of counterhegemonies as its primary focus.

Although I will be discussing the development of a feminist materialism throughout the various readings that follow, here I at least want to indicate that a feminist materialism was first developed in the works of feminist theorists, who in struggling against the limitations of a marxist analysis of women's oppression, would incorporate analyses of the discursive construction of subjectivity and experience in the production of hegemony and counterhegemonies. Thus, a feminist materialism not only refers to an analysis of political economy which focuses on the ideologies that constitute hegemony; it therefore also refers to an analysis of the materiality of language, that is, an analysis of the material inscription of ideology on the body, the subjective, the everyday.

Thus, a feminist materialism is focused on the material effects of discourse and political economic relations on the lived experience of the subject; it is especially concerned with the construction of hegemony in relationship to the oppression of women as well as with counterhegemonic resistances. In this sense, a feminist materialism refuses the incommensurability of the differences among women or between men and women in the construction of a feminist politics. That is, although a feminist materialism recognizes differences of race, class, ethnicity, nationality, gender, and sexuality, it works within the horizon of possible alliances against oppression, domination, and exploitation and therefore a feminist materialism somewhat de-emphasizes the reader's positionality.

My inclination toward a materialist feminism, then, allows me to de-emphasize without denying my position as a reader; I therefore present my readings of various feminist texts in something like a third-person narrative form. But, my inclination toward a materialist feminism also is characterized by a strong interest in those versions of it which explore fantasy and unconscious desire in relationship to hegemony and counterhegemonies. Thus, de-emphasizing my own reader's positionality also has to do with my sense that my identifications with feminism and the variations of feminist theorizing that I will be considering are more unconscious and ideological than an autobiographical accounting of my lived experiences would or even could reveal. In other words, I think that one's reader's positionality has everything to do with how one reads and writes but not all is explained by autobiographical accounts of the sociological aspects of identity.[7]

Thus, while I am white, heterosexual, a single head of household, raising a son in a suburb of New York City, a tenured Professor of Sociology and Media Studies, having been educated and having taught only in non-elite universities or colleges, I think of these limitations of identity, as well as the dis-identifications these limitations make necessary, as giving shape to but also being shaped by my unconscious grasp of my experience and the experience of others. For me, finer autobiographical readings increasingly open up to the instability of unconscious desire, in whatever terms it is conceived. Indeed, this is one of the points I will be exploring in the various articulations of feminist theorizing I will be considering.

But there is, then, the possibility of finer autobiographical readings of my ethnic, racial, and class background, having grown up in an Italian-American, Roman Catholic home, with a mother who had but a few years of schooling, a father who was the first in his family to attend college, and my older sister. Though I began to live something more like a middle-class lifestyle only when I was a teenager, ethnicity, class, and catholicism long had their effect; long enough that they still do. Certainly I could double back to them, connecting my long-lasting ambivalence toward schooling and my profound attraction to reading and writing and studying music, even though as a girl, in fact as a young woman, these always seemed to be activities I should not be doing.

After all, was not my desire to read, write, and make music a desire to get away from my background to something more sophisticated, something more controlled, something less crowded than the three-room apartment in which I was growing up? Was not my desire to read, write, and make music informed with a desire to be other? To make all identifications, identifications with difference? But, what of my desire to have no background at all; to be normal? Was this not really a desire to change nothing, to never change at all? To make all identifications, identifications with the same? Unconscious desire urges only variations; there is no original scenario. Not that I do not know something about which scenarios predominate in me, and at least I can say that that family is with me in every bit of reading and writing I do. In some sense, reading and writing is how I keep those whom I love and who have loved me, with me, at a critical distance.

But it was not only that family, but what that family determined as the world beyond it which entered my reading and writing, at the same time the family did. How I wanted to be in the world, and always it seemed that I thirsted for the world as a space/time outside family. And it would be that thirst for self in the world, guilt-ridden and pleasure-seeking, that led me to becoming a Catholic nun, because I somehow knew that nuns were in the world in a very particular way; nuns did not marry or have family and did that not mean to me – being in the world? But at the same time, becoming a nun was a way to punish myself for wanting to get away from my family but also wanting a family, a husband, a child and music, books, reading and writing. Too much; so, I could only get out by cloistering myself, leading to the first stirring of an understanding of unconscious desire, of the psyche's confusing one image with another, of transferring one figure onto another, of making one's position seem like some other's – the stubbornness of unconscious desire to play itself into every representation, however it can, even in reversals of reversals. Freedom for cloisters, cloisters for freedom. The autobiography loses control; the autobiography is in the control of unconscious desire.

And it was the stirring of unconscious desire that led me out of the convent but to new identifications that allowed for more living – mine and others'; at least, I still hope so. But, what multidirectional identifications were these that led to my community organizing in "poor" neighborhoods of African-American and Puerto Rican men and women, political protesting, underground newspaper writing, consciousness raising, and being a leftist, even before being sure what it was to be one and certainly before I thought I could read and write Marx. But I did read and write Marx and then Freud – Marx for making politics the bottom line; Freud for mirroring back to marxism the eroticization of power that marxism could only assume and ignore. And along the way, also a marriage, a Ph.D. in sociology, a son, a teaching position in an undergraduate college, a divorce, and a psychoanalysis. And then, suddenly, I was reading something else: feminist theories.

My autobiography transmuted itself onto pages of marxist feminism, psychoanalytically oriented feminism, radical feminism, post-structural feminism, African-American feminism, post-colonial criticism, queer theory, Third World feminism. Making itself anew again and again, my autobiography ends and begins in the recognition of how it cannibalizes/celebrates others' autobiographies. But, reading and writing invite that! Feminist theorizing invites that, stirring identifications, even while rendering the limitations of identity, demanding dis-identifications, demanding courage to go on reading and writing.

After all, it is reading and writing that allows the feminist theorist to make public her self-reflection on her own processes, even to reflect on the limitations of her reflection; it is reading and writing that allows the theorist to perform theory, that is, as much as possible to bare the device for constructing the object of knowledge, to experience and re-experience the labor. But it is reading and writing which also always escapes the control of the reader and the writer, escapes the control of the autobiograph. And that which escapes me in what follows, I await the return in the reading and the writing of some others, in some other time and place.

Notes

1 See *Ms.*, 4:2 (1993).
2 The often repeated dictum "sisterhood is powerful" appeared as the title of an early collection of essays written by feminists; see Robin Morgan (ed.), *Sisterhood Is Powerful: An Anthology of Writings From the Women's Liberation Movement* (New York: Vintage Books, 1970).
3 *Ms.* Editor, "Let's Get Real about Feminism, the Backlash, the Myths, the Movement," *Ms.*, 4:2 (1993), pp. 34–43.
4 I will be discussing the development of feminist literary criticism throughout the following chapters; however, especially in chs 2 and 3, I focus on the feminist criticism developed in the works of Elaine Showalter, Elizabeth Abel, Judith Kegan Gardiner, Laura Mulvey, Kaja Silverman, and Teresa De Lauretis, among others.
5 Sandra Harding offered an early statement of the influence of feminism on science that only begins to thematize the differences between sociologically oriented studies of the organization of science and analyses of the authority of disciplinary knowledges, thereby reflecting the need of feminist theory to integrate the criticisms of feminist theorists in social science and in the humanities; see Sandra Harding, *The Science Question in Feminism* (Ithaca: Cornell University Press, 1986).
6 Indeed, feminist social scientists have noted that even though there has been a substantial amount of work done by feminist social scientists, a feminist revision of social science discourse has lagged behind the feminist revision in the humanities; see Judith Stacey and Barrie Thorne, "The Missing Feminist Revolution in Sociology," *Social Problems*, 32 (1985), pp. 301–17 and Marilyn Strathern, "An Awkward Relationship: The Case of Feminism and Anthropology," *Signs*, 12 (1987), pp. 276–92. While Stacey, Thorne, and Strathern have offered various explanations for the failure of a feminist revision of social science discourse, more recently Anna Yeatman, building on their explanations, has made clear that "social science in general and sociology in particular are proving refractory" to a feminist revision precisely because social scientists refuse to recognize that "the ruling modernist fiction" both organizes social science discourse and legitimizes a certain reading of the social; see Anna Yeatman, "A Feminist Theory of Social Differentiation," in Linda Nicholson (ed.), *Feminism/Postmodernism* (New York: Routledge, 1990), pp. 281–99. While Yeatman points to the necessity of criticizing the narrative and rhetorical strategies deployed in social science, few such criticisms have been elaborated, especially by social scientists. I have reviewed

these few treatments in social science of the narrative logic of social science discourse in *The End(s) of Ethnography: From Realism to Social Criticism* (Newbury Park: Sage Publications, 1992). Because these treatments have not usually been feminist in orientation, in *The End(s) of Ethnography* I especially make use of feminist theory developed by feminist theorists in the humanities in order to trace the operation of a dominant narrative fiction especially in sociology's practice of ethnography.

7   For a treatment of materialist feminism, see Rosemary Hennessy, *Materialist Feminism and the Politics of Discourse* (New York: Routledge, 1993). For my discussion of the development of feminist materialism, especially in relationship to psychoanalytic treatments of the unconscious, see chs 2 and 3.

1

The Hybrid Criticism of Patriarchy

Although in 1970 Kate Millett's *Sexual Politics* would be hailed in the popular press for providing a theoretical foundation to the newly organized women's liberation movement, what now seems so remarkable about *Sexual Politics* is that it also is a book of literary criticism – the first book of academic feminist literary criticism.[1] And perhaps it was for its unique form of criticism that *Sexual Politics* also was described in the popular press as "a polemic suspended in academic traction."[2] Academic literary critics too focused on Millett's polemical style, often finding it inappropriate for literary scholarship. As Patricia Meyer Spacks would put it, Millett "constructed an elaborate exercise in political rhetoric, and for it she got a Ph.D. in English."[3] Even Millett describes the kind of criticism she elaborates in *Sexual Politics* as "something of an anomaly, a hybrid, possibly a new mutation altogether."[4]

Of course, it would be some years after the publication of *Sexual Politics* before feminist theorists would become deeply engaged in the epistemological and methodological questions that have characterized debates in many academic disciplines throughout the 1970s and 1980s, questions concerning writing style and the discursive authority of the disciplines. Still, I would suggest that in making the argument that the sexual is political, *Sexual Politics*, although often unintentionally, raises the very same questions that have been the focus of these debates. *Sexual Politics* initiates a revision of the relationship of reality and fantasy, history and fiction, polemic and academic discourse, literary criticism and social science.

Composing the Politics of Sex

Sexual Politics is an awkward book. After all, it not only treats as a matter of politics what long had been taken to be a matter of nature, thereby forcing a hybrid of the sexual and the political. It also proposes to do so by means of a criticism of literary texts, which Millett describes as "a criticism which takes into account the larger cultural context in which literature is conceived and produced."[5] Indeed, the very composition of *Sexual Politics* models such a criticism, giving new meaning not only to the literary text but to the cultural context as well.

Thus, while feminist literary critics claim *Sexual Politics* as the first book of academic feminist literary criticism, feminist social scientists claim *Sexual Politics* as "one of the first major attempts to provide a thorough theoretical examination of the oppression of women using the concept of patriarchy."[6] Indeed, while Millett does offer analyses of literary texts, the primary goal of *Sexual Politics* is, as Millett describes it, to sketch "notes toward a theory of patriarchy."[7] It might be argued, then, that it is Millett's aim to turn questions of literary criticism into questions about patriarchy, while at the same time, moving the reader from a view of the sexual as natural to a view of it as socially constructed and, therefore, political.

Indeed, Millett's intention to make literary criticism an analysis of patriarchy is established in Part One of *Sexual Politics*. Made up of two chapters, one focused on literary texts and the other on social science research, Part One proposes that to make literary criticism an analysis of patriarchy, that is, to make visible the links between patriarchy and literary texts, a certain relationship between social science and literary criticism is required.

Thus, in "Instances of Sexual Politics," the first chapter of Part One, Millett reproduces scenes of sexuality from Henry Miller's *Sexus* (1965), Norman Mailer's *An American Dream* (1964), and Jean Genet's *The Thief's Journal* (1964). Both Miller's and Mailer's scenes focus on coitus, involving anal intercourse or intercourse from the rear (of the female), which, for Millett, suggests the overall tone of the scenes – a mastering humiliation and degradation of the female, who seemingly finds pleasure in the deadly passivity of a nearly complete objectification by the phallic male. Millett argues that as Miller and Mailer would have it, the female's pleasure is a matter of her natural passivity, even while it is her passivity which allows for the spectacularization of various other natural characteristics of her sexuality: lustfulness, lewdness, and wantonness.[8] The dominance of the male is also a matter of nature.

While commenting that these scenes are presented as "masculine fantasies," from the "point of view" of "one male relating an exploit to another male in the masculine language,"[9] Millett, however, does not explore, as feminist theorists later would, questions about fantasy, the textual construction of a point of view, and its authority. She does not ask: what are the mechanisms by which a text both projects onto and elicits from the reader and the writer identification with an authorized point of view? What is a masculine point of view; is there a feminine one and who can identify with which? In other words, what is the relationship of fantasy, the literary, and how anyone comes to identify themselves as masculine and/or feminine in the first place?[10]

Instead Millett treats the literary text as a transparent reflection of reality that therefore provides evidence of sex in patriarchal society; she assumes an identification between the masculine point of view and the male reader or writer. As for the female reader, Millett can only imagine her as being put off altogether by those very aspects of the scenes that mark them as fantasy or fiction. In commenting on Miller's description of a woman character in nothing but "a silk bathrobe and a pair of silk hose," Millett proposes:

> The female reader may realize that one rarely wears stockings without the assistance of other paraphernalia, girdle or garters, but classic masculine fantasy dictates that nudity's most appropriate exception is some gauzelike material, be it hosiery or underwear.[11]

More like Andrea Dworkin's readings of pornography, Millett's readings might be described as "ultra-thematic," focusing only on the content of the scenes of sexuality, at the exclusion of any exploration of their form, of the literariness of texts and their construction of authority.[12] And if ultra-thematic readings only emphasize the brutishness of the scenes of sexuality, it is this brutishness which most makes the scenes seem shockingly real, simply reflecting actual sex in patriarchal society.

Indeed, Millett finally turns to Genet's scene of sexuality in which the "criminal homosexual world" he presents mirrors "with brutal frankness" the brutishness of heterosexuality in male-dominated society. But, although Millett notices that it is Genet's "identification with the feminine position" that allows him to reveal that in male-dominated society, being feminine is being "ravished and subjugated by the male,"[13] she does not explore, as feminist theorists later would, how his writing style is productive of a feminine identification or how such a writing style itself might be critical of male domination.[14]

If, then, Millett, like the female reader she describes, is less interested in analyzing the literary or the play of fantasy in the literary text, it is in order to make representations of coitus stand in for coitus itself – to make the sex act truthfully reveal itself and thereby speak the truth about patriarchy. Although not quite taking the position Dworkin later would, that is, that heterosexual intercourse is both symptom and root cause of male domination, Millett does seem to want to make coitus the very test of a feminist politics, that is, to make it the test case of a feminist transformation of the natural into the political, the personal into the political. As Millett puts it:

> Coitus can scarcely be said to take place in a vacuum; although of itself it appears a biological and physical activity, it is set so deeply within the larger context of human affairs that it serves as a charged microcosm of the variety of attitudes and values to which culture subscribes. Among other things, it may serve as a model of sexual politics on an individual or personal plane.[15]

Thus, while Millett suggests that coitus is a charged microcosm that speaks the truth of sex and therefore the truth about patriarchy, she nonetheless proposes that in order to hear this truth, an understanding of literature's larger cultural context is needed; and for this, theory is needed. If, then, the literary text is to be used to evidence the brute facts of sexuality in patriarchal society, theory is to be used for providing a true or correct view of that evidence. To put it another way, if the literary text offers a politically incorrect view of sexuality as natural, theory offers a correct or true view of it as political.

Thus, in "Theory of Sexual Politics," the second of the two chapters that make up Part One of *Sexual Politics*, Millett turns to social science. Beginning with the suggestion that "the relations between the sexes," like "the relations between the races," would better be understood as a matter of politics rather than in terms of a "rule by birthright,"[16] Millett then reviews research in the fields of political science, history, sociology, economics, anthropology, and psychology in order to present evidence of a seemingly trans-historical, cross-cultural sexual politics of male domination – what Millett calls patriarchy.

Thus, making use of a history of civilizations and an anthropology of myth and religion, Millett not only unsettles any rationalization of patriarchy in terms of the physical differences between men and women. She also argues that consent for a male domination of women, therefore, is necessarily ideologically obtained. Then, drawing on political science and sociology, Millett connects the ideology of male domination with the patriarchal family and its "socialization" of both males and females into "the basic patriarchal politics with regard to temperament, role, and status."[17] Millett turns to psychology to suggest further that the myths that have long sustained woman-hating continue to inform modern society but as internalized psychological orientations which turn women to self-doubt and self-hatred.

In "Theory of Sexual Politics", then, Millett does not exactly define patriarchy. Without questioning the adequacy of the term, as feminist theorists later would, Millett simply includes in the description "patriarchal" those situations of male domination which actually differ from patriarchy, that is, situations in which descent is neither defined nor controlled exclusively by the father or situations in which the father is no longer absolute head of the family, financially, legally, or politically. In attempting to identify all male domination with patriarchy, Millett can pay little attention to the contradictory practices likely to arise when male domination is more diffuse than the notion of patriarchy would imply; nor can she pay much attention to the interrelation of male domination and the differences of class, race, ethnicity, nationality, and sexuality.

In other words, Millett does not theorize male domination as it is deployed by various representational structures of the state outside the family. She never makes explicit the relationship of the ideological deployment of male domination, representation, literature, and discursive authority. Therefore, Millett also does not notice that social science is itself a form of representation, a form of discursive authority; instead, Millett employs social science in order to reject a view of the sexual as natural, physical, or biological. Millett simply makes use of social science to show that what first appears to be the "rule by birthright" is in truth a system of domination which is socially, culturally, economically, and politically structured. It is social science, then, which provides a view of the sexual as political by giving patriarchy the status of reality and truth.

Thus, in Part One of *Sexual Politics*, the literary text and social science research are brought into close proximity and perhaps it is this that makes the criticism which *Sexual Politics* offers "altogether new." Still, the use to which Millett puts literature in "Instances of Sexual Politics" is itself limited, as is the use to which she puts social science research in "Theory of Sexual Politics." That is to say, literature is not merely a reflection of reality; nor does social science merely offer dispassionate or disinterested explanations of the larger cultural context that ground the truth of that reality.

Of course, it would not be until after the publication of *Sexual Politics* that feminist theorists would shift the focus of criticism from the content of the literary text to the literary form itself and to processes of reading and writing, thereby challenging a view of the literary text as a mere reflection of reality. It would be even later that a criticism of social science would be initiated that also would focus attention on the discursive forms of scientific authority – its fictional or textual forms of facticity, objectivity, and truth. Still, even though it would be only after the publication of *Sexual Politics* that feminist theorists would directly challenge the distinction of fact and fiction, reality and fantasy, polemic and academic discourse, literary criticism and social science, nonetheless, it is these very distinctions that would be made to tremble in Part Two of *Sexual Politics*.

That is to say, if in Part One of *Sexual Politics* Millett brings together social science research and the literary text, while maintaining their distinctiveness, in Part Two of *Sexual Politics* their distinctiveness will be troubled, as will the possibility of viewing both literature as a mere translation of sexuality and social science as a disinterested explanation of patriarchy. Part Two will make ready for Part Three of *Sexual Politics* in which finally it will become clearer that it is not only the social that is at the heart of the literary but the literary that is at the heart of the social.

Writing and Rewriting Revolution

If in Part One of *Sexual Politics*, then, it is the literary text that is made to evidence the brute facts of the sexual in a patriarchal society, in Part Two of the book, the function of the literary text, indeed, of writing more generally, becomes more complicated. Thus, in Part Two of *Sexual Politics*, Millett first discusses what she describes as the sexual revolution from 1830 to 1930 and its counterrevolution from 1930 to 1960. Each of the reviews of these two periods is an odd mix of historical accounts of the changing relationship between men and women, analyses of literary texts, interpretations of philosophical tracts, and critical treatments of social scientific theories.

In discussing the sexual revolution, Millett first turns to the historical accounts of the changing relations between the sexes, especially focusing on the first wave of the women's movement: the changes it wrought in education,[18] the way its political organization developed,[19] and how it supported women's struggle for employment.[20] But the readings of various texts which Millett then offers suggest that literary, philosophical, and social scientific writing, rather than merely reflecting or explaining reality, instead play an important part in shaping it.

Although still focusing on the content of these texts, Millett treats them more as productions of meaning – sites of struggle, sites of contention over polemical and ideological ground. Her readings of Thomas Hardy's *Jude the Obscure* (1895), George Meredith's *The Egoist* (1879), and Charlotte Brontë's *Villette* (1853) do not depend on social science to establish a larger cultural context of meaning; these texts are treated more for the way they themselves shape the cultural context, of which the first wave of the women's movement was a part. No less than the women's movement itself, no less than John Stuart Mill's *The Subjugation of Women* (1869) and John Ruskin's "Of Queen's Gardens" (1865), which Millett also discusses at length, the novels are understood in interaction with other texts, to be producing the common-sense thinking about the relationship between men and women.

And if none of the novels, although *Villette* nearly, are quite as revolutionary as Millett would like, each of them is recognized by her as literally giving life to a woman's struggle with femininity, as it is defined in terms of a chivalrous understanding of the family. But Millett is less concerned with the struggle than she is with success; indeed, so much so that she takes *Villette*'s resistance to the chivalrous understanding of the family to be more a victory than most feminist literary critics later would.[21] But perhaps Millett's reading of *Villette* reflects more her general approach to the sexual revolution. That is to say, according to Millett, what the sexual revolution did accomplish was to lift the veil of chivalry from the family, revealing the family as a historically specific institution of patriarchy.

For Millett, then, *Jude the Obscure*, *Villette*, and *The Egoist* each resonate and revolve around the centerpiece of her account of the sexual revolution, what she describes as "the revolutionary theory" of Friedrich Engels' *The Origin of the Family: Private Property and the State* (1884). While Millett's treatment of social science in the first part of *Sexual Politics* functions to explain the truth of patriarchy, her engagement with Engels' theory suggests something different; it suggests that not all social science is on the side of revolutionary change, and even social science that is, is not always on the side of the revolutionary change of the relationships between men and women. Social science is also a site of contention, a site of struggle for polemical and ideological ground.

Thus, as many feminist theorists later would, Millett finds Engels' thought important because it demonstrates that the patriarchal family is a historical development and therefore not immutable. Engels' argument is that as historically specific conditions strengthen men's ability to accumulate productive wealth, men begin to hold women and the product of their work as private property; it becomes especially important to control women's reproduction in order to ensure an undisputed paternity, necessary to the passing of private property from father to son. Thus, Engels' theory proposes that male domination predates capitalism and therefore it is at least intimated that male domination, even in capitalism, may be relatively autonomous of economic exploitation.

But of course, in the end, Engels would argue that the male domination of the patriarchal family would wither away when private property did, that is, Engels would slip back into assuming that the sexual division of labor is a natural phenomenon and that it is only the capitalist exploitation of it that needs to be revolutionized. Thus, feminist theorists would criticize Engels for closing down the very possibility his theory at first seemed to propose – that is, to theorize male domination in relationship to political economy without reducing one to the other. Millett similarly criticizes Engels for his "victorian views" of sexuality that led him to accept Bachofen's notion that women's surrender to male domination in monogamous marriages is due to their nature and the resulting desire to be rid of "the burden of too much sex."[22]

But, unlike feminist theorists who would continue to struggle to articulate a relationship between marxism and feminism,[23] Millett simply would turn from marxism, only making use of Engels' theory in order to establish the historicity of the patriarchal family and the relative autonomy of male domination from capitalist exploitation. Instead Millett shifts her focus to the sexual counterrevolution in order to show it as an ideological effort to restore the chivalrous view of the patriarchal family which Engels' theory at least had destabilized. And it is in focusing more specifically on the ideological that Millett begins to shape a theory of male domination that is not reducible to political economy. It also is then that the distinction of the literary text and social science research which Millett maintains in the first part of *Sexual Politics* increasingly becomes blurred; the possibility of sexuality speaking its truth also is increasingly undermined.

Thus, in the history of the sexual counterrevolution from 1930 to 1960, Millett discusses the Soviet Union but more specifically Nazi Germany as examples of "state-sponsored and legally enforced sexual counterrevolution."[24] Rehearsing the long list of efforts to control women's reproduction that played a primary role in the maintenance of a fascist ideology, Millett argues that "the overriding reason for the flagrantly patriarchal and male-supremacist character of the Nazi state seems to be temperamental."[25] Insisting on what Engels' theory only proposed, Millett concludes that:

> Sexual politics, while connected to economics and other tangibles of social organization, is, like racism, or certain aspects of caste, primarily an ideology, a way of life, with influence over every other psychological and emotional facet of existence.[26]

But Millett does not make clear what relationship there is between the psychological and the ideological; she does not explore what feminist theorists later would theorize as the relationship of the state, psychic processes, and the ideological construction of subject-identity. She does not make use of the psychoanalytic processes of displacement, projection, and introjection in the analysis of ideology; instead, Millett places

Freud's theory right beside fascist ideology as a counterrevolutionary production.[27]

Millett's criticism of Freud focuses on his treatment of femininity, especially the connection he proposes of femininity with narcissism, masochism, and passivity.[28] As other feminist theorists would be, Millett is especially critical of the Freudian notion of penis envy which seems to her not only to conflate sexuality and anatomy, biology, and nature but in doing so to serve as a way of disciplining women who insist on their dissatisfaction with the social, economic, and political position in which the relationship between the sexes places them.[29] Rather than treat Freud's remark that "what constitutes masculinity or femininity is an unknown characteristic which anatomy cannot lay hold of," Millett focuses on that other remark of Freud, in which anatomy is claimed to be destiny.[30]

And this is because what is central to Millett's criticism of Freud's theory is her recognition of the way it moves from describing to prescribing a certain view of sexuality – for the way it establishes a discourse that restricts sexuality to the terms of normalcy and abnormalcy. Indeed, for Millett, Freud's theory only more clearly exemplifies what can be argued for all social science. Thus, suggesting that the sexual revolution failed because it only dealt with "the superstructure of patriarchal policy" and not with "the socialization processes of temperament," Millett proposes that the counterrevolution only further conserves these processes of socialization, as social science provides subtle and, therefore, more effective ideological mechanisms to maintain patriarchy in "the mind and heart."[31]

Millett therefore proposes that, even more than religion and that version of piety put forth by the New Criticism of literature, it is science, especially social science, that offers the counterrevolution the possibility of an authoritative reformulation of patriarchy. As she puts it:

> The new formulation of old attitudes had to come from science and particularly from the emerging social sciences of psychology, sociology, and anthropology – the most useful and authoritative branches of social control and manipulation. To be unassailable, there should be some connection, however dubious, with the more readily validated science of biology, mathematics, and medicine. To fill the needs of conservative societies and a population too reluctant, or too perplexed to carry out revolutionary changes in social life, even to the drastic modification of basic units such as the family, a number of new prophets arrive upon the scene to clothe the old doctrine of the separate spheres in the fashionable language of science.[32]

Offering as examples the Freudian and post-Freudian thought of psychology, as well as the structural functionalism of sociology and anthropology, Millett suggests that social science be understood as an ideological deployment of the sexual counterrevolution.

Thus, in the second part of *Sexual Politics*, Millett argues that the ideology of male domination is made increasingly effective throughout the first half of the twentieth century because it is deployed through social science, the authority of which also is greatly enhanced in this same period. But, of course, this argument only calls into question the function proposed for social science in Part One of *Sexual Politics*. Surely, Part Two of *Sexual Politics* makes it all but impossible to treat social science as simply offering a dispassionate or disinterested explanation of the sexuality evidenced in the literary text. It also makes it increasingly difficult to treat the literary text as simply reflecting sexuality in patriarchal society.

The Return of the Literary

Indeed, although Millett titles the third and final part of *Sexual Politics* "The Literary Reflection," it has become quite uncertain that literature merely provides a transparent reflection of the reality of sex, if any reality at all. Indeed, Millett's return to literary texts in Part Three of *Sexual Politics* further elaborates what Part Two only implies, that is, that the literary text is more an inflection of various other literary, philosophical, as well as social scientific texts. Thus, the more extensive treatments of Miller and Mailer's texts, which Millett presents in the final part of *Sexual Politics*, show these texts to be ideological promotions of fascist, totalitarian, and/or Freudian thought – mass publications of the sexual counterrevolution. Rather than merely giving evidence of sexuality in patriarchal society, these texts inherit and further elaborate the ideological construct which Millett refers to as the sexual counterrevolution.

So, while in the final part of *Sexual Politics* Millett will return to the writings of Miller, Mailer, and Genet, she also will insert a discussion of the writings of D. H. Lawrence. Not at the beginning of *Sexual Politics*, however: Lawrence's writings are made to appear at the beginning of the end of *Sexual Politics* because his writings are, for Millett, the last attempt of literature to veil the sexuality of patriarchal society in sentiment and chivalry. Stubbornly framed with "the tenderness of romantic love," Lawrence's descriptions of sexuality are, for Millett, more a nineteenth-century soft pornography which Miller and Mailer will turn into the hard core porn of the twentieth-century American novel.

Therefore, in Lawrence's writings, there are previews of what Miller and Mailer will elaborate. Indeed, Millett suggests that when the surface of Lawrence's sentimentality is broken through, as it is especially in his later works, what is seen is his racism, his fascistic adoration of "the superior male," his homophobia, and his sadistic imagining of the woman. Beneath the surface of Lawrence's seeming tenderness, Millett thus concludes, is the heart of Lawrentian sexuality – "coitus as killing."[33] For Millett then, Miller and Mailer's texts only give full exposure to the violent degradation of the woman, often still diffuse in Lawrence's view of heterosexuality.

Thus, Millett argues that Miller removes the veil of sentimentality and romanticism from heterosexuality – both reducing the woman to an object and coitus to "a biological event between organs."[34] As she puts it:

> Lawrence had turned back the feminist claims to human recognition and a fuller social participation by distorting them into a vegetative passivity calling itself fulfillment. His success prepared the way for Miller's escalation to open contempt. Lawrence had still to deal with persons; Miller already feels free to speak of objects. Miller simply converts woman to "cunt" – thing, commodity, matter. There is no personality to recognize or encounter, so there is none to tame or break by the psychological subtleties of Lawrence's Freudian wisdom.[35]

If, for Millett, Miller's insistent exposure of the sexual organs is meant to reduce sexuality to what he describes as "organ grinding" and "the utter impersonality" of the "perfect fuck," Mailer's scenes of sexuality are meant to reveal men's hatred for women as the primary motivation of having sex with them.

For Mailer, not only is war like sex but sex is war – the expression of the male's destiny to be "the hunter-fighter-fucker."[36] Thus, more than in Miller's scenes of sexuality, the "dirtiness" of sex in Mailer's scenes refers to his insistence on guilt and confession, the "wrestling" of his "sexistentialism," which for Millett only means to rationalize the violence to be meted out on "dirty" women who seemingly deserve it and find it satisfying. As Millett puts it:

> While Mailer found he could appreciate the "mythology" of Lady Chatterley, the manner in which it encouraged the notion that "sex could have beauty," he found it sadly ignorant of "the violence which is part of sex," and later came to prefer the more amenable context of filth which he so enjoys in Miller, arguing that actually, "most people don't find sex that pure, that deep, that organic." Instead, they find it "sort of partial and hot and ugly." Best to keep it this way, for sex is really "better off dirty,

damned, even slavish! than clean and without guilt." Guilt, he would persuade us, constitutes "the existential edge of sex," without which the act is "meaningless."[37]

If Mailer argues that masculinity is not "something you're born with but something you gain," he also proposes that violence is the only means of gaining it. Thus, Millett points out that since for Mailer masculinity presupposes violence and war, then femininity and homosexuality necessarily become what prevent masculinity; that is, femininity marks all that prevents the realization of masculinity, especially in battles for men's honor, which is, for Mailer, the honor of America itself.

Thus to counter the sexual counterrevolution which the writings of Lawrence, Miller, and Mailer give full expression, Millett finally turns to Genet's writings. For Millett, Genet's writings not only make clear that, in patriarchy, the feminine has been made to mean being ravished by and subjugated to the male. But, as a feminine-identified homosexual, Genet also elaborates in his writings the specifically homophobic aspects of heterosexuality – that is, the equation of homosexuality with a degraded femininity.

Thus, by detaching the feminine and the masculine from "their usual justification in an assumed biological congruity," Genet's writings necessarily reveal "the arbitrary and invidious nature of sex role;" masculine and feminine therefore "stand out as terms of praise and blame, authority and servitude, high and low, master and slave."[38] But perhaps what is most important to Millett is that Genet, especially in his final works, suggests that sex roles are not only arbitrary rather than natural but that they, therefore, must be politically enforced. Thus, Genet finally proposes that the enforced hierarchy of masculine over feminine in patriarchal society ought not simply be reversed but revolutionized.

If, then, Millet would have Genet's writings provide a revolutionary end for *Sexual Politics*, it is nevertheless Genet's writing which, in the end, troubles *Sexual Politics*, suggesting as it does that the masculine and the feminine are fictions, positions which the reader and the writer are offered. Indeed, his writing even suggests that the literary is primarily a provision of subject positions for reading and writing the social, for reading and writing what Millett refers to as literature's larger cultural context. To put it another way, Genet's writing collapses the distinction of literary text and cultural context; it collapses the distinction of sexual fantasy and the play of sexual identification in reading and writing. Profoundly questioning the distinction of fantasy and reality, fact and fiction, his writing raises the question as to whether writing can deliver the truth of sexuality.

By the end of *Sexual Politics*, then, much of what enabled it ironically has been called into question. That is to say, Millett's effort was to isolate coitus as a symptom of patriarchal society by retracing literary texts which also try to isolate it, and in both cases the effort fails. As even Millett suggests in commenting on Miller, "Paradoxically, this attempt to so isolate sex only loads the act with the most negative connotations."[39] Indeed, by the end of *Sexual Politics*, it becomes clear that coitus can not be separated from the fantasy condensed in the scenic elements by which the act is framed and by which the act is projected onto the reader whose fantasy is simultaneously being elicited. That is, there can be no simple reduction of literary form to the content of literature; there can be no simple reduction of the content of literature to the facts of reality. Hence, there can be no simple reduction of male domination to the sexual act, to sexuality generally.

Thus, finally, the distinction of literary text and social science is questioned. Indeed, by the end of *Sexual Politics*, it seems that the literary text, more than reflecting reality, organizes scenes to stage what can count as reality. Social science also seems more like the literary text, to authorize as reality what, in the interest of social science, it would define as the norm or the normal. Thus, it is only at the end of *Sexual Politics* that it becomes clearer that, rather than a criticism of sexuality in patriarchal society, *Sexual Politics* is a monumental intertextual production which brilliantly cuts across the disciplines and the various distinctions the disciplines maintain. As such, *Sexual Politics* founds academic feminist criticism as a social criticism of a knowledge-formation which is informed with a sexual politics of representation that privileges masculinity and with which feminist criticism, ironically but necessarily, becomes deeply engaged.

In this sense, *Sexual Politics* at least suggests that not only do literature and social science interpenetrate each other but, even more importantly, they both are interpenetrated by a certain eliciting of the truth of sexuality. *Sexual Politics* intimates that not only through sociology, anthropology, psychology, and psychoanalysis but through the fictional productions of culture, there has been what feminist theorists later would describe as the implantation in knowledge of a desire for maximum visibility that specifically engages a sexual politics of representation that privileges masculinity. Indeed, this implantation occurs during that historical period from the second half of the nineteenth century to the beginning of the twentieth century, not only when the sexual revolution was being disciplined into the counterrevolution and the authority of social science gaining power, but also when the mass media, especially motion pictures, were being developed.

If, then, feminist theorists later would argue that it was mass-mediated productions of culture, especially motion pictures, that first mass marketed the notion that knowing is seeing and that seeing more is knowing better, they also would propose that it was these mass-mediated productions of culture which insistently make "the woman's body" the object of knowledge's quest. Thus, if motion pictures first equate objectivity with a disembodied envisioning, they nonetheless guarantee that objectivity with a depersonalizing fetishization of the woman's body. The woman's body, that is, is made the site of a struggle in which it is made to give up its secrets, by making more and more visible that which is always partially hidden – feminine sexuality and feminine pleasure. In this sense, the feminine becomes the figure of a nature to be explored and revealed in order to be understood and controlled; the masculine becomes the figure of a disembodied, objective, and authorized knowledge.[40]

If, then, some feminist theorists also would connect this knowledge-formation with the development of hard core pornography, it is because the utter passivity of the woman, her being forced into sex without her consent, are, for hard core, "the genre's proof of sincerity," offering "not a voluntary performance of feminine pleasure, but its involuntary confession."[41] Thus, hard core porn reveals, perhaps in an exaggerated form, the sexual fantasy that animates this knowledge-formation. It makes clear that the installment into knowledge of a desire for maximum visibility carried by a sexual politics of representation is the installment into knowledge of a desire for a vision of the thing itself, in which the envisioning or framing of what is known finally is disavowed or denied. By the twentieth century, then, this desire for an objective, disinterested, factual, or truthful envisioning informs all literary, mass media, and social scientific texts as does the sexual politics of representation that carries that desire into reading and writing.

Indeed, it is this knowledge-formation that *Sexual Politics* uncovers, although only inadvertently, and perhaps this is why *Sexual Politics* itself often is complicit with this form of knowing. Not only is this the case in the first part of the book, where Millett makes uncritical use of both social science research and the literary text. But as even Mailer points out, in his otherwise defensive and sexist response to *Sexual Politics*, Millett makes use of data, Masters and Johnson's data for example, seemingly without concern that the techniques and mechanisms of this research are not radically different from those figured in the literary texts which Millett criticizes.[42] Thus, even though Millett claims to use such data only to counteract "patriarchal myths" about women's sexuality and to uncover "its true character,"[43] still the question is raised as to whether the very methods of doing so, the very research methods of various academic disciplines, are not already invested with the eliciting of the truth of sex which requires a sexual politics of representation that privileges masculinity.

Women's Writing at the End of *Sexual Politics*

Indeed, it only is after the publication of *Sexual Politics* that questions about how to uncover the true character of women's sexuality or of women's experience become central for feminist theorists. Then, feminist theorists, especially those in social science, would turn their efforts not only to representing the reality of women's experiences but also to revising epistemology in order to establish the truth of that reality. However, at this same time, feminist theory would find its greatest institutional support in the humanities, as feminist theorists turned from a criticism focused on male-authored texts to a criticism focused on women's writings. This shift in feminist literary criticism would occur just as it was becoming more apparent in literary studies generally that literary texts are their own larger cultural context, that literary form has a content and that, therefore, literary form is itself a cultural production. That is to say, increasingly, the cultural context of literature no longer is conceived as extrinsic to literary texts, but rather intrinsic to their intertextuality.

Thus, in the years after the publication of *Sexual Politics*, feminist literary criticism was able to gain institutional support not only because feminist literary critics turned to women's texts which had been largely ignored by the literary establishment but also because feminist literary critics increasingly directed their attention to the literariness of literature, that is, to representation, writing, and discursive authority. Feminist literary criticism therefore benefitted from, while profoundly influencing, a transformation of literary criticism from New Criticism to social criticism. Yet, if in this time feminist literary critics increasingly would make reference to "critical theory" in the construction of social criticism, they no longer mean social science theory but literary theory itself.

Indeed, in her now well-known essay of 1981, "Feminist Criticism in the Wilderness," Elaine Showalter retroactively dates this shift of focus among feminist theorists to a criticism of women's writings at about 1975. She also names this criticism "gynocriticism."[44] Although describing gynocriticism as a critical method based on the reality of women's experience, Showalter nonetheless discusses how various critical theories such as post-structuralism, semiotics, deconstruction, psychoanalysis, and cultural linguistics might enable the new purpose of feminist literary criticism.[45] Thus, Showalter appropriates the various critical theories that had undermined New Criticism in order to refind the matrix of feminist literary criticism in a denied tradition of women's writings about women. Indeed, as a proposal to establish a matrilineage of literary authority, gynocriticism would make the mother–daughter relationship central to feminist theorizing, and then it seems that *Sexual Politics* would be all but forgotten.

Indeed, in her 1975 *The Female Imagination*, Patricia Meyer Spacks introduces her book about women's writings about women with a criticism of Millett's *Sexual Politics*. Millett not only is criticized because she focused *Sexual Politics* primarily on male writers; she also is criticized for her style. For Spacks, Millett's style fails to integrate her personal anger about "the limitations imposed on women," so that it frequently disturbs "the impersonal, sexless voice of twentieth century politics" with which Millett delivers *Sexual Politics*.[46] But, Spacks's criticism is not so much that Millett's anger is inappropriate. Rather, it is that her style fails to integrate the personal and the political.

Of course, the integration of the political and the personal already had been announced as the goal of the women's movement, which *Sexual Politics* was claimed to have helped develop. But the integration of the personal and the political would take on special meaning in feminist literary criticism focused on women's writing about women. That is, after the publication of *Sexual Politics*, the integration of the personal and the political would lead to recovering identity and voice – the recovering of a uniquely feminine voice, a uniquely feminine "imaginary," a uniquely feminine writing.

That Millett would lose her place in this project is both ironic and sad, especially since after the publication of *Sexual Politics*, or perhaps because of it, Millett suffers in print the struggle to integrate her personal life with the politics of the women's movement. In her autobiographical writings, especially *Flying* (1974) and *Sita* (1976), Millett gives form to the dailiness of a woman's life in a non-linear documentation of moment-to-moment thought and activity – a form that feminist theorists later would describe as the interruption of a feminine voice or imagination in the linear form of the masculine point of view. Nonetheless, if the personal documentation of a woman's daily life could not easily find its way into *Sexual Politics*, Millett's autobiographical writing shows that neither could "sexual politics" easily be placed in the daily life of this woman.

Thus, in a 1990 introduction to *Flying*, Millett describes it as "her first book" because it is "written in my own voice" instead of the "mandarin mid-Atlantic to propitiate a committee of professors of English" – the voice of *Sexual Politics*.[47] But *Flying* is not only a life story in a personal voice. While it does tell of Millett's early life with an abusive father, as well as describe her everyday experiences in the eighteen months after the publication of *Sexual Politics*, experiences with her husband and her women lovers and friends, *Flying* is just as often a reflective justification for her "treat[ing] my own existence as documentary."[48]

Although a self-conscious justification for writing autobiography increasingly characterizes much autobiographical writing especially in the twentieth century,[49] Millett is concerned specifically with justifying her focus on her own personal life against the political demands of the women's movement. If, then, at the beginning of *Flying*, the reader is introduced to Millett's struggle with her women lovers, friends, and colleagues who want "*Sex Pol* to be anonymous so it can be the whole movement talking,"[50] even at the end of *Flying*, Millett still will appear torn between her desire to voice herself and her wanting to fulfill her obligations as a leader in the women's movement.

Thus, at the beginning of *Flying*, Millett complains:

> It's all a mistake. The nightmare months of folly. Microphones shoved into my mouth. . . . Tired and I don't know any answers. The whole thing is sordid, embarrassing, a fraud. The same questions always. Boring. Repetition of old stuff, no new work. Have I lost faith? If I am bored am I a traitor? They ought to shoot me. Made into a leader. We're not supposed to have leaders. . . . The whole bloody system is sick: the very notion of leadership, a balloon with a face painted upon it, elected and inflated by media's diabolic need to reduce ideas to personalities.[51]

But, as her position of leadership continues to instigate the mass media publication of her private life, Millett comes to believe that *Flying* must document this loss of self in order to get back a self:

> The confessional should wait upon one's ripe old age. But it was apparent to me that I might have no ripe old age, was sure not to have one, if I did not take some steps towards recovering my being. . . . You may well ask how I expect to assert my privacy by resorting to the outrageous publicity of being one's actual self on paper. There's a possibility of it working if one chooses the terms, to wit: outshouting image-gimmick America through a quietly desperate search for self. And being honest enough. Of course it is impossible to tell the truth. For example, how does one know it? I will not belabor the difficulty by telling you how hard I have tried. And if compulsion forces me to tell the truth, it may also lead me into error, or invention.[52]

Still, the effort to write the truth of self threatens to turn into fiction, a literary convention, perhaps even an invention of an unconscious compulsion – a lying in the place of the "I." Indeed, all through *Flying*, Millett tells about a film she is making about herself and her women friends – a political project. The film, a reflection of *Flying* itself, finally is rejected by "the movement" because it is not political. Although Millett insists that the politics of the film is in telling about women's lives – telling about "ordinary women" who are "usually ignored,"[53] eventually she herself becomes convinced and "suddenly" realizes that "it's just a movie."[54]

So too, for the reader, there is always the sudden realization that *Flying's* obsessive self-conscious focus on moment-to-moment thought and action is, in the end, just writing – a writing which never succeeds in giving the reader the fullness of Millett's self, nor in giving Millett her self in full; after all, there will be more autobiographical writings after *Flying*. Nor is the tension between the politics of the women's movement and the desire for voicing the self fully resolved for Millett or the reader. Thus, in the last pages of *Flying*, Millett reports watching a father with his daughter, who after a certain difficulty between them, embrace one another – the father treating the daughter with a gentleness and care that Millett's father never expressed.

And if "in their two bodies hugging" Millett proposes that she has "overwhelmed my childhood, free of its pattern finally,"[55] nonetheless, in the very last words of the book, there are splits and breaks still threatening what appears at last to be held together:

> Gulls so many of them I try to count them but they split and break I cannot place and order them in the sky. Flying in a haze of wings noises cries. Chaos and serenity together.[56]

Thus, in calling into question whether writing the self can truly integrate the personal and the political, *Flying* already shows the complications, the splits and breaks, that finally would disturb the effort of gynocritics to ground a uniquely feminine voice or imaginary in a fixed or unified feminine identity. Nonetheless, *Flying* also writes the shift in feminist literary criticism to gynocriticism by shifting its readers from the two bodies of father and daughter to what Millett describes as the ideal vision "of two beautiful women in ecstasy,"[57] which at least for Millett is "hardly as simple as sex," but more:

> . . . a strange communion of spirit looking in her eyes those endless seconds while we touched each other's center, perfectly, just the fingertip upon the clitoris moving more and more slowly, our eyes steady on each other and the delicate pressure fine and more fine until all motion stopped in one still point remembered always, a vision. And then I did not know her pleasure

from mine, my body from hers. We fell into and became each other. Then we slipped over the edge, entered and made love.[58]

Afterwords

It would seem now that what was most important about *Sexual Politics*, at least at the time of its publication, was that it generalized women's oppression by naming its cause, patriarchy. As Vivian Gornick and Barbara Moran would argue in the introduction to one of the first anthologies of feminist writings, *Woman in Sexist Society* (1971): "to name the thing by its rightful name is instantly to begin to alter its power. To *recognize* the political nature of woman's condition, to see that it constitutes one-half of a binding relationship of power to powerlessness . . . is vital to any understanding of women's liberation and of the women's liberation movement."[59] *Sexual Politics* not only gave a name to women's powerlessness but it sought to demonstrate the intimate relationship of it to men's power – the dependence of men's power on women's powerlessness.

But in naming patriarchy as the cause of women's powerlessness, *Sexual Politics* would raise problems for feminist theorists. Indeed, in 1974, a group of Black feminists, calling themselves the Combahee River Collective, would begin meeting, and in 1977 would offer a statement of their politics in which they would argue:

> We believe that sexual politics under patriarchy is as pervasive in Black women's lives as are the politics of class and race. We also often find it difficult to separate race from class from sex oppression because in our lives they are most often experienced simultaneously.[60]

Proposing that "this focusing upon our own oppression is embodied in the concept of identity politics,"[61] the Combahee River Collective insist that they had expanded "the feminist principle that the personal is political," going beyond "white women's revelations," by "dealing with the implications of race and class as well as sex."[62]

If, then, feminist theorists eventually will raise the question of the adequacy of the notion of patriarchy or, more importantly, ask whether excluding the differences of race, class, ethnicity, nationality, and sexual preference does not make it possible to argue that all women are oppressed by patriarchy, still, *Sexual Politics* models what will characterize most feminist theorizing that follows it: that is, the critical activity of showing that what appears as natural is rather socially constructed and therefore political. Thus, in naming the sexual political, *Sexual Politics* initiates a reinvention of the social.

That is to say, in investing the notion of the social with the political intent of feminism, *Sexual Politics* initiates the deconstruction of the notion of the social, at least as it first was defined from the eighteenth through the nineteenth centuries in the discourse of Western, modern, industrial capitalism. Indeed, after *Sexual Politics*, feminist theorizing increasingly would question the opposition of nature and the social, the private and the public, the political and the economic, the individual and society – oppositions that delimit the notion of the social, at least in the modern West. Feminist theorizing also would recall what had been cut off from the social by these oppositions. That is to say, it would recall the force of fantasy or unconscious desire, only intimated in *Sexual Politics* in Millett's effort to connect a sexual politics with a literary imagination.

Thus, in naming the sexual political, *Sexual Politics* also initiates a reinvention of the literary. Insisting that literature is socially constructed or culturally produced, *Sexual Politics* would orient feminist theorists to raise such questions as: whose literature is it; whose culture is it; whose imagination is it; whose desire is it? Questions about authority and tradition, about styles of writing and discursivity, would be made political questions – questions of ideology.

Thus, not only would feminist theorists increasingly challenge the distinction between reality and fantasy, history and fiction, polemic and academic discourse; but the distinction of literary criticism and social science also would be called into question. And if feminist theorizing even would trouble the epistemological grounding of the Western discourse of modern, industrial capitalism, feminist theorists themselves also would have to face that the "West" has been constituted in an erasure of difference, and although it is the feminine figure that bears the trace of that erasure, the feminine figure also inscribes the erasure of differences other than sexual difference – differences of race, class, ethnicity, nationality, and sexual preference as well.

Notes

1   Jane Gallop makes this claim in *Around 1981: Academic Feminist Literary Theory* (New York: Routledge, 1992), p. 78.
2   "Who's Come a Long Way, Baby?" *Time Magazine*, August (1970), p. 16.
3   Patricia Meyer Spacks, *The Female Imagination* (New York: Alfred Knopf, 1975), p. 29.
4   Kate Millett, *Sexual Politics* (New York: Ballantine Books, 1970), p. xvi.
5   Ibid., p. xiv.
6   See Roisin McDonough and Rachel Harrison's discussion of early theories of patriarchy, especially their remarks about *Sexual Politics*: "Patriarchy and Relations of Production," in Annette Kuhn and Ann Marie Wolpe (eds),

Feminism and Materialism (London: Routledge and Kegan Paul, 1978), p. 12. See also Rosalind Coward's *Patriarchal Precedents: Sexuality and Social Relations* (London: Routledge, 1983).

7 Millett, *Sexual Politics*, p. 32.
8 Ibid., p. 6.
9 Ibid., p. 5.
10 See chs 2 and 3 for a fuller discussion of the relationship of feminist literary criticism and sexual identification.
11 Millett, *Sexual Politics*, p. 5.
12 Susan Sulieman uses the term "ultra-thematic" in discussing Andrea Dworkin's works: Susan Sulieman, *Subversive Intent: Gender, Politics and the Avant-Garde* (Cambridge: Harvard University Press, 1990), pp. 73–87. For other discussions of pornography and feminist theory also see Jane Joe Frug, *Postmodern Legal Feminism* (New York: Routledge, 1992); Susan Gubar, "Representing Pornography: Feminism, Criticism, and Depictions of Female Violation," *Critical Inquiry*, 13 (1987), pp. 712–41; Linda Williams, *Hard Core: Power, Pleasure, and the "Frenzy of the Visible"* (Berkeley: University of California Press, 1989). See also Andrea Dworkin, *Pornography: Men Possessing Women* (New York: Perigee Books, 1979) and *Intercourse* (New York: Free Press, 1987).
13 Millett, *Sexual Politics*, p. 24.
14 The feminist theorists referred to as "French feminists" often mention Jean Genet in discussing the possibility of a feminine identification constructed in the text regardless of the author or reader's gender; for a fuller discussion of "French feminism" see chs 2, 5, and 6.
15 Millett, *Sexual Politics*, p. 31.
16 Ibid., p. 33.
17 Ibid., p. 35.
18 Ibid., pp. 103–6.
19 Ibid., pp. 111–19.
20 Ibid., pp. 119–24.
21 See, for example, Sandra Gilbert and Susan Gubar, *The Madwoman in the Attic: The Woman Writer and the Nineteenth-Century Literary Imagination* (New Haven: Yale University Press, 1979), pp. 399–440) and Spacks, *The Female Imagination*, pp. 32–5.
22 Millett, *Sexual Politics*, p. 163.
23 For a fuller discussion of the relationship of feminist theorizing and marxist theory, see ch. 3.
24 Millett, *Sexual Politics*, p. 238.
25 Ibid., p. 237.
26 Ibid., p. 237.
27 For a fuller discussion of the use of psychoanalytic theory in relationship to a feminist analysis of ideology, see ch. 3.
28 Millett, *Sexual Politics*, pp. 274–9.
29 Ibid., pp. 253–9.
30 See Sigmund Freud's "Femininity," in *The Standard Edition of the Complete*

Works of Sigmund Freud, vol. 22, edited by James Strachey (London: Hogarth Press, 1955), p. 114.

31 Millett, *Sexual Politics*, p. 250.

32 Ibid., p. 251.

33 Ibid., p. 411.

34 Ibid., p. 420.

35 Ibid., p. 416.

36 Ibid., p. 458.

37 Ibid., p. 453.

38 Ibid., p. 480.

39 Ibid., p. 421.

40 For a fuller discussion of the relationship of the feminine figure and the knowledge-formation referred to here, see ch. 3.

41 Williams, *Hard Core*, p. 52.

42 See Norman Mailer, "Prisoner of Sex," *Harper's Magazine*, March (1971), pp. 41–92.

43 Millett, *Sexual Politics*, p. 165.

44 Elaine Showalter, "Feminist Criticism in the Wilderness," (in Elizabeth Abel (ed.), *Writing and Sexual Difference* (Chicago: University of Chicago Press, 1981), pp. 9–35. For a fuller discussion of gynocriticism, see ch. 2.

45 It is of some interest to note that Elaine Showalter more recently has returned to the study of male-authored texts but suggests reading them not as "documents of sexism and misogyny but as inscriptions of gender and 'renditions of sexual difference'." See Elaine Showalter (ed.), *Speaking Gender* (New York: Routledge, 1989), p. 5.

46 Spacks, *The Female Imagination*, p. 29.

47 Kate Millett, *Flying* (New York: Ballantine Books, 1974), p. ix.

48 Ibid., p. 81.

49 For a discussion of autobiography and self-consciousness about writing, see Paul Jay, *Being in the Text: Self Representation from Wordsworth to Roland Barthes* (Ithaca: Cornell University Press, 1984). For a discussion of Kate Millett's autobiographical writing, see Suzanne Juhasz, "Towards a Theory of Form in Feminist Autobiography: Kate Millett's *Flying* and *Sita*; Maxine Hong Kingston's *The Woman Warrior*," in Estelle Jelinek (ed.), *Women's Autobiography* (Bloomington: Indiana University Press, 1980), pp. 221–37 and Annette Kolodny, "The Lady's Not For Spurning: Kate Millett and the Critics," in Estelle Jelinek (ed.), *Women's Autobiography*, pp. 238–59.

50 Millett, *Flying*, p. 59.

51 Ibid., pp. 12–13; p. 23.

52 Ibid., p. 83.

53 Ibid., p. 365.

54 Ibid., p. 412.

55 Ibid., p. 546.

56 Ibid., p. 546.

57 Ibid., p. 153.

58 Ibid., p. 158.

59 Vivian Gornick and Barbara Moran (eds), *Woman in Sexist Society: Studies in Power and Powerlessness* (New York: Basic Books, 1971), pp. x–xi.
60 The Combahee River Collective, "A Black Feminist Statement," republished in Zillah Eisenstein (ed.), *Capitalist Patriarchy and the Case for Socialist Feminism* (New York: Monthly Review Press, 1979), p. 365.
61 Ibid., p. 365.
62 Ibid., p. 366. It should be noted that even earlier than "A Black Feminist Statement," Black women's critical writings appeared in Toni Cade (ed.), *The Black Woman* (New York: Penguin, 1970).

2

The Matrix of Feminist Criticism

If, in 1970, Kate Millett would call for a sexual revolution that "would bring the institution of patriarchy to an end," and establish in its place "a permissive single standard of sexual freedom,"[1] in 1976, Adrienne Rich would resubmit patriarchy to critical analysis but in order to valorize the distinctive experiences of women. Without abandoning the goal of sexual freedom, Rich nevertheless focuses on releasing sexuality from the grip of patriarchy, so to return it to the matrix of feminine desire – the maternal body. Thus, no less than Millett's *Sexual Politics*, Rich's *Of Woman Born: Motherhood as Experience and Institution* treats as political what long had been taken to be a matter of nature; that is, *Of Woman Born* treats motherhood as "an institution" under male control, "defined and restricted under patriarchy."[2] But it also gives value to motherhood as an "experience" involving "the potential relationship of any woman to her powers of reproduction and to children."[3]

And if making the sexual a matter of politics made it necessary that *Sexual Politics* have a certain style – a weaving together of polemic and academic discourse, fantasy and reality, history and fiction, social science and literary criticism, the style of *Of Woman Born* also is a weave of what usually had been kept separate, even in Kate Millett's writings – that is, academic discourse and the autobiographical account of one's own experience. As Rich puts it:

> It seemed to me impossible from the first to write a book of this kind
> without being often autobiographical, without often saying "I." Yet for
> many months I buried my head in historical research and analysis in order
> to delay or prepare the way for the plunge into areas of my own life which
> were painful and problematical, yet from the heart of which this book has
> come. I believe increasingly that only the willingness to share private and

sometimes painful experience can enable women to create a collective description of the world which will be truly ours.[4]

Not the awkward book that *Sexual Politics* seems to be, *Of Woman Born* is more, as Rich describes it, "a vulnerable book," marked with the feminine voice, with the vulnerability of its newly born authority.

Indeed, *Of Woman Born* not only makes the autobiographical account of experience a means of remembering the mother. It also proposes that feminist criticism, especially gynocriticism, be grounded in remembering – remembering women's experience of mothering. But, in shifting the focus of feminist theorizing to mothering, *Of Woman Born* also leads feminist theorists back to psychoanalysis and to a revision of Freud's treatment of the mother–child relationship. Yet, the feminist revision of psychoanalysis, I would suggest, not only makes psychoanalysis more useful for feminist theorizing, furthering the deconstruction of the distinction of fantasy and reality, history and fiction, polemic and academic discourse, social science and literary criticism. The feminist revision of psychoanalysis also finally calls into question what at first psychoanalysis was only meant to authorize – that is, a way of knowing that is "truly ours," truly grounded in women's experience, especially women's experience of mothering. Not only will psychoanalysis finally trouble gynocriticism, disturbing the notions of a unified feminine identity and a unique women's experience especially by articulating a division or difference of desire within a woman; but gynocriticism also will come to be troubled by differences among women, differences of race, class, ethnicity, nationality, and sexuality.

Authorizing Women's Voices, Autographing Women's Experiences

If Rich suggests that women's voices can only be authorized by sharing private and sometimes painful experience, it is because women's experiences otherwise would continue to be excluded from the history of culture; only pain can give a sense of the specificity of women's experiences, the specificity of their exclusion from the collective description of the world. Indeed, having finally permitted herself to plunge back into her own experiences of mothering, Rich notices the difference between her pain-filled memories and academic scholarship:

> I soon began to sense a fundamental perceptual difficulty among male scholars (and some female ones) for which "sexism" is too facile a term. It is really an intellectual defect, which might be named "patrivincialism" or

"patriochialism": the assumption that women are a subgroup, that "man's world" is the "real" world, that patriarchy is equivalent to culture and culture to patriarchy, that the "great" or "liberalizing" periods of history have been the same for women as for men, that generalizations about "man," "humankind," "children," "blacks," "parents," "the working class" hold true for women, mothers, daughters, sisters, wet nurses, infant girls, and can include them with no more than a glancing reference here and there, usually to some specialized function like breast-feeding.[5]

Of Woman Born, then, is an effort to unsettle patriochialism and thereby to recover the experiences of women buried under the history of patriarchal culture. Thus, if it is not until the penultimate chapter of *Of Woman Born* that Rich actually focuses on the mother–daughter relationship, which she describes as the "core of my book," she nonetheless prepares for going to the core of a woman's history by going again and again to the core of the history of patriarchal culture where the power of the mother is limited and bound exclusively to the needs of the fathers. She also goes again and again to her own experience of the private and sometimes painful relationship of mother and child.

Thus, at the start of *Of Woman Born*, Rich presents eleven entries from her journal, beginning with one from November 1960, one year after the birth of the third of her three sons. All the entries, like the first, detail an ambivalence between "anger and tenderness" and thus also tell of guilt, exhaustion, even despair and death.

My children cause me the most exquisite suffering of which I have any experience. It is the suffering of ambivalence: the murderous alternation between bitter resentment and raw edged nerves, and blissful gratification and tenderness. Sometimes I seem to myself a monster of selfishness and intolerance. . . . And I'm weak sometimes from held-in rage. There are times when I feel only death will free us from one another. . . . *I love them.* But it's in the enormity and inevitability of this love that the sufferings lie. . . . For it is really death that I have been fearing – the crumbling to death of that scarcely-born physiognomy which my whole life has been a battle to give birth to – a recognizable, autonomous self, a creation in poetry and in life.[6]

If Millett begins *Sexual Politics* with literary texts meant to offer transparent reflections of sex in patriarchal society, Rich seemingly abandons all literary device. She would offer her experience of mothering; she would present mothering as she experienced it. But in doing so, there is the return of the literary; in publishing the journal entries, something is made of them that is more than one's own experiences. There is the hope that comes from sharing one's experiences and, in doing so, finding that they are "not unique." As Rich puts it, "Only in shedding the illusion of my uniqueness could I hope, as a woman, to have any authentic life at all."[7]

But, to face the illusion of the uniqueness of one's experience also is to refuse any sense in which "this interpenetration [in mothering] of pain and pleasure, frustration and fulfillment" is only part of "the human condition."[8] For Rich, then, what puts the woman beyond the illusion of the uniqueness of her experience is its historical specificity – the truth of patriarchy. Like Millett's literary texts, Rich's journal entries, having been made public, become evidence in need of contextualization. And again social science will be employed to provide that context in offering an account of patriarchy.

But Rich's historical review of patriarchy will differ from Millett's. While, like Millett, Rich does not directly question the discursive authority or the narrative voice of social science upon which she draws, she nonetheless continues to voice her "I," to tell of her experiences, even as she rehearses the arguments of various academic disciplines. And there also is the recurring movement of her own text – the movement from uncovering the history of patriarchy to recovering the power of the mother which patriarchy suppresses. This move to recovering women's experience also is an indication of the shift in Rich's understanding of patriarchy, a shift from Millett's initial understanding of it.

For Rich, "the history of patriarchy is yet to be written – I do not mean the history of men, but of an idea which arose, prospered, had its particular type of expression, and which has proven self destructive."[9] Not only does Rich recognize the historical specificity of patriarchy but she recognizes that in post-industrial capitalist society the "substance" of the father's "old practical authority" is lost.[10] Patriarchy is now a matter of an idea; drawing on Mitscherlich, Rich suggests that patriarchy is a matter of "magical thought"[11] – something of the mind and heart, as finally even Millett came to describe it.

Thus, in the second chapter of *Of Woman Born*, Rich positions herself and the reader in relationship to the separation of the private and public spheres, which first arose with modern, Western, industrial capitalism. Rich proposes that it is in this historical period that "female consciousness" is especially "underemployed" by restricting it to the support of "the morality and the emotional life of the human family."[12] Focusing on a historical period which already had become a primary concern for feminist historians and political economists, Rich sketches the woman's life in modern, Western, industrial capitalism as a combination of isolation, powerlessness, loneliness, and the drudgery of unending housework and child care. While recognizing the benefits to capital of the separation of the private and the public spheres, Rich claims that the "sacred calling" of domesticity is more about men's suppression of the woman's reproductive powers.

Therefore, in the third chapter, "The Kingdom of the Fathers," and in the fourth chapter, "The Primacy of the Mother," Rich makes use of historical studies and anthropological analyses of myths to discuss the proposal of a universal matriarchy which preceded patriarchy and which patriarchy suppressed. Although Rich is unable to conclude with certainty that such a matriarchy existed, if by matriarchy is meant the opposite of patriarchy, that is, the control of the fathers by the mothers, nonetheless, her reconsideration of this proposal reminds the reader of the mythical proportions of the power of reproduction – the power of the mother. It also gives a more certain sense of social formations in which at least "female creative powers" were pervasive and respected, even though women did not dominate men.

Finally then, the discussion of the relationship of patriarchy and matriarchy suggests that, like patriarchy, matriarchy refers to the history of an idea, an inner longing of the heart and the mind. As Rich puts it:

> In other words (and this was Freud's view) each woman and each man has once, in earliest infancy, lived under the power of the mother, and this fact alone could account for the recurrence of dreams, legends, myths, of an archetypal powerful Woman, or of a golden age ruled by women. Whether such an age, even if less than golden, ever existed anywhere, or whether we all carry in our earliest imprinting the memory of, or the longing for, an individual past relationship to a female body, larger and stronger than our own, and to female warmth, nurture, and tenderness, there is a new concern for the *possibilities* inherent in beneficent female power, as a mode which is absent from the society at large, and which, even in the private sphere, women have exercised under terrible constraints.[13]

For Rich, the patriarchal cosmogony gives a certain shape to this longing for the mother; it does so by distorting and thereby controlling women's reproductive capacities, representing them only in terms of "darkness, unconsciousness, and sleep."[14] Thus, Rich proposes that it is necessary to discuss motherhood in close connection to women's reproductive capacities not only to liberate the birthing process itself from the institutionally alienating forms of modern obstetrics. It also is to liberate a female consciousness – a matriarchal cosmogony. More focused on the recovery of female consciousness, Rich's analysis of modern obstetrics allows her only to initiate what would be developed later by feminist theorists as a general criticism of scientific authority.

Thus, in the sixth and the seventh chapters, Rich frames a discussion of the shift from midwifery to obstetrics with a history of the introduction of forceps into the birthing process. Only doctors used forceps and since it was not until the mid-nineteenth century that doctors knew about asepsis or bacterial infection, they did not properly prepare and, as a result, they often carried infection directly from operations and other medical procedures to the birthing mother. Midwives, whose only function was to aid in the birthing process, were less likely to infect the woman. Therefore the introduction of forceps and a male-dominated obstetrics brought with it a plague of puerperal fever. From the seventeenth century until the second half of the nineteenth century, then, the increasing death-fantasies of the pregnant and birthing woman had "a literal unassailable basis in statistical fact."[15]

But, even since the nineteenth century, throughout the twentieth century, childbirth, Rich proposes, has remained a matter of "alienated labor." During this period, the birthing process has become the site of another struggle over the medical profession's resistance to women's efforts to ensure that the birthing process will be theirs. Drawing on cross-cultural data about childbirth and discussing methods of "natural childbirth," Rich insists that modern obstetrics makes every effort to make birthing "an experience of passively handing over our minds and our bodies to male authority."[16] Thus, for Rich, the liberation of the birthing process is as much about the rebirth of the woman herself, the re-envisioning of her authority, a matter which Rich will describe as a restoration of the mother–daughter relationship. Indeed, in the midst of leveling criticism at the medical profession, Rich conjures up the image, or better, the fantasm or ghost, of the birthing mother's mother. As Rich describes it:

> A woman who has experienced her own mother as a destructive force –
> however justified or unjustified the charge – may dread the possibility that
> in becoming a mother she too will become somehow destructive. The
> mother of the laboring woman is, in any case, for better or worse, living or
> dead, a powerful ghost in the birth-chamber.[17]

Thus, Rich moves closer to the core of her book; but before discussing the mother–daughter relationship, she takes up the relationship of mother and son seemingly in order to situate the destructiveness attributed to the mother in the context of patriarchal culture. Beginning chapter 8, "Mother and Son, Woman and Man," with a reconsideration of Jocasta and Gertrude and ending it with a criticism of Freud, Rich argues that the fantasm of the destructive mother is man's creation – more precisely, the son's recreation of the mother. As she puts it, "By far, the majority of men have written of women out of the unexplored depths of their fears, guilt, centered on our relationship to them, that is, to women perceived as either mothers or antimothers."[18]

Thus, Rich sketches what will be detailed as a critical assumption of gynocriticism – that is, that in the productions of culture, the woman-figure has been cast primarily by men. Or to put this another way, in the productions of culture the child of the mother–child relationship is assumed to be male. The woman, then, is made to figure men's displaced fear and hostility; it is through men's displacements that she becomes the enemy. As Rich puts it, the woman is made the one "who tries to prevent the child from being born; she is the birth trauma."[19]

If, then, Rich finally turns to the mother–daughter relationship only after having shifted the conditions of its possible destructiveness onto patriarchal culture, it is in order to restore to the daughter both the mother's mind and the mother's body freed of the distortions of patriar-chal culture. But this restoration turns out to be no easy task. Starting with Susan Griffin's quote at the head of the chapter, "Motherhood and Daughterhood," in which Griffin asks her mother to "give me my body back," there is an intimation of confused bodily boundaries that seems inevitably destructive to both mother and daughter and to be not only a condition of patriarchal culture.

And there also is the unmarked shift of Rich's perspective, a shift of the gaze, of the voice, which will come to characterize feminist theory itself – a shift from the woman in the figure of the mother, as Rich is at the beginning of *Of Woman Born*, to the woman in the figure of the daughter in search of a mother, as Rich is at the end of her book. Indeed, this chapter on the mother–daughter relationship begins with Rich's gaze on her mother's body but also with her awareness of some-one else's gaze, someone else's voice – her father's. Telling of reading about Helen of Troy with whom she identified her mother Helen, Rich comments:

> She was Helen my mother, *my* native shore of course; I think that in that poem I first heard my own longings, the longings of the female child, expressed by a male poet, in the voice of a man – my father.[20]

Identified with the father, even in competition with him, the female child desires the mother: "For years I felt my mother had chosen my father over me, had sacrificed me to his needs and theories."[21] Thus, as Rich approaches the mother–daughter relationship, there are "old, smoldering patches of deep-burning anger,"[22] which she tries to explain as a condi-tion of patriarchal culture.

> Few women growing up in patriarchal society can feel mothered enough; the power of our mothers, whatever their love for us and their struggles on

our behalf, is too restricted. And it is the mother through whom patriarchy early teaches the small female her proper expectations.[23]

But the female child's loss of the mother to the father or to the mother's desire for the other is not easily reduced to the woman's loss of power in patriarchal society. Thus, there remains until the very end of "Motherhood and Daughterhood" a deeply felt ambivalence. There is the woman's "matrophobia," the fear "of becoming one's mother, . . . the one through whom the restrictions and degradations of a female existence were perforce transmitted."[24] But, there also is "the girl-child still longing for a woman's nurture, tenderness, and approval, a woman's power exerted in our defense, a woman's smell and touch and voice, a woman's strong arms around us in moments of fear and pain."[25] Finally the terrifying anger and the fierce longing are drawn together in the very last chapter of *Of Woman Born*, "Violence: The Heart of Maternal Darkness," as Rich ends her recovery of motherhood and daughterhood by pleading the case of a distraught mother who decapitated and chopped up the bodies of the two youngest of her eight children.

So in the end of *Of Woman Born*, it becomes clear that the ambivalence between tenderness and anger, love and hate, sweetness and violence, which Rich describes herself to experience as a mother, are the same ambivalences she experiences as a daughter. No matter how much the woman tries to borne herself, the ghost of the mother continues to haunt not only the woman's self-imaging of herself but her imaging of her experience of reality. Thus, the mother also haunts the authority of a woman's writing. That is to say, in the displacements and projections from mother to her daughter, from the daughter to her daughter, the boundaries are made increasingly permeable; as in dreams, all the figures are always each other, all the figures are always of the other, and what is, is folded in on itself.

Indeed, by the end of *Of Woman Born*, the accounts of Rich's experiences of motherhood and daughterhood move beyond a historical analysis of patriarchy's suppression of the power of the mother, uncovering the poet's voice, the voice of remembered, even imagined loss. If, for Rich, "the energy of poetry comes from the unconscious and always will,"[26] it might be argued that it is the voice of the unconscious that finally arises out of *Of Woman Born*, the voiced unconscious desire of the female child for the mother, inextricably mixed in the woman's experience of reality. Thus, in raising the question of the unconscious, *Of Woman Born* finally makes tremble the very meaning of women's experience – how to read it, how to write it, without losing what Rich describes for the poetic as the force of the sensuousness of form – "that burning gauze in a poem which flickers over words and images, through the energy of desire, summoning a different reality."[27] Therefore, the question is raised as to what the autobiographical account of experience actually evidences, if not unconscious desire.

The Return to Freud, the Return of the Literary

Indeed, it is this question of the daughter's relationship to the mother as well as the question of the distinctiveness of women's experience, that returns feminist theorists to Freud. After almost nothing but rejection of Freudian psychoanalysis for its seeming exploitation and denigration of women, feminist theorists would turn to the task of revising psychoanalysis for feminist criticism. Thus, in *The Reproduction of Mothering: Psychoanalysis and the Sociology of Gender* (1978), Nancy Chodorow would argue that the desire to mother and the way a woman does mother can not adequately be explained by biological arguments or socialization theories of role learning; an understanding of the unconscious processes of parenting is necessary. In an effort to deliver psychoanalysis from a biologism on one hand, and on the other hand, to reinsert unconscious processes into socialization theories, Chodorow makes *The Reproduction of Mothering* a revision of the Freudian oedipal drama, especially drawing attention to the preoedipal relationships both of mother and son and of mother and daughter.

But, while Chodorow draws on the object-relations school of psychoanalysis in order to return Freudian psychoanalysis to the preoedipal mother, other feminist theorists, who would come to be referred to as "French feminists," draw instead on Jacques Lacan's rereading of Freud for their revision of the preoedipal mother–daughter relationship. While their understanding of preoedipality would differ from Chodorow's, not much would be made of the difference, at least not at first. Instead, both versions of feminist psychoanalysis would be made to inform gynocriticism; both versions would be understood to give voice to the difference between the masculine and the feminine rather than voice the difference or division of unconscious desire within both the masculine and the feminine.

Thus, at first, the turn to preoedipality in feminist revisions of psychoanalysis brings psychoanalysis into the service of feminism; it makes psychoanalysis function to revalorize a full and unified feminine identity. If in *The Reproduction of Mothering*, psychoanalysis is made to serve feminism by turning preoedipality into an explanation of the social relations of gender, in French feminist theory, psychoanalysis is made to serve feminism by making preoedipality the basis of a unique feminine

imaginary or language. In both versions of psychoanalysis, the displacement of the father, begun with Rich's *Of Woman Born*, is further
elaborated; psychoanalysis is made to focus on the figure of the mother,
seemingly displacing the father as the central figure of that discourse.

Thus, in *The Reproduction of Mothering*, Chodorow argues that
except for object-relations theory, psychoanalysis has paid insufficient
attention to the preoedipal phase when the infant is becoming differentiated, developing both an inner sense of bodily integrity and an inner
sense of psychological separateness – an ego-boundedness. It is in this
phase, then, that the infant is beginning to establish a sense of basic
relatedness. For Chodorow, psychoanalysis is to be used to demonstrate
that girls and boys come to have radically different senses of basic
relatedness.

Focusing on the historically specific situation of Western, modern,
industrial capitalist society, in which the mother usually is solely responsible for early infant care, Chodorow emphasizes what even object-
relations theory fails to notice, that is, that the infant's differentiation
is from the mother – from a woman. By introducing the variable of
gender, Chodorow is able to conclude that the mother's sense of her own
gender, and that of her infant, informs the process of separation. Thus,
Chodorow argues that in the earliest stages of infancy, the mother begins
to recognize the distinctiveness of the male infant, perceiving him as
different from her, that is, differently gendered. At an earlier stage of
the male's infancy, then, the mother "may push her son out of his
preoedipal relationship to her, into an oedipally toned relationship
defined by its sexuality and gender distinction."[28] The boy's gender
identity thereby becomes "intertwined," as Chodorow puts it, "with
supposedly nongender-differentiated object relational and ego issues
concerning the creation of a sense of separate self."[29]

Whereas the male child's sense of a separate self develops as a sense of
masculinity which is defensively defined as not-mother or not-woman, it
seems that for the female child, coming to any clearly defined sense of a
separate self is never accomplished fully. That is to say, because the
female child is not urged by her mother into a relationship with her,
which is oedipally toned and defined by sexuality, the girl remains more
attached to her mother, even throughout her oedipal complex. Thus,
Chodorow suggests that when the girl "rejects" her mother in developing
an oedipal relationship with her father, it does not "mean the termina-
tion of the girl's affective relationship to her mother."[30] Indeed,
Chodorow proposes that although the girl develops "important oedipal
attachments to her mother *as well as* to her father," while probably

becoming heterosexual, "these attachments and the way they are internalized, are built upon, and do not replace, her intense and exclusive preoedipal attachment to her mother and its internalized counterpart."[31] The girl's intrapsychic relational structure thereby remains triadic: "her relationship of dependence, attachment, and symbiosis to her mother continues and her oedipal (triangular, sexualized) attachments to her mother and then her father are simply added."[32]

For Chodorow, what then becomes evident is that a woman becomes a mother precisely because her heterosexual relationship to a man is never as satisfying as the intensity of her intrapsychic relationship to her preoedipal mother would have it be. In other words, becoming a mother in the context of a relationship with a man allows the woman to reproduce the symbiotic relationship that she had with her mother and which remains part of her intrapsychic relational structure; it allows the woman "to reimpose intrapsychic relationship structure on the social world, while at the same time resolving the generational component of her oedipus complex as she takes a new place in the triangle – a maternal place in relationship to her own child."[33]

Arguing that woman's identity is a condensation of her desire for her mother and for her child, Chodorow also elaborates Freud's notion of penis envy in terms of the mother–daughter relationship. That is to say, while recognizing that "a girl's wish to liberate herself from her mother engenders penis envy,"[34] Chodorow nonetheless argues that the girl does not only wish for a penis as a phallic symbol of power, that is, as a means of freedom from dependence on the mother. The girl also desires the phallus for the mother – to have what the mother seemingly lacks and desires. Thus, Chodorow is willing to follow Gayle Rubin in arguing that castration anxiety is not inevitable;[35] the girl only suffers castration anxiety or the devaluation of her genitals in confrontation with her already oedipalized, heterosexual mother who has also suffered castration anxiety and the devaluation of her genitals.

By focusing attention on the assumed heterosexuality of the mother, Rubin means to problematize heterosexuality and to raise questions about unconscious processes in relationship to sexual preference and sexual identification. For Chodorow, however, these questions are subsumed by the question of why women mother. Thus, Chodorow restricts the psychoanalysis of preoedipality to a sociology of gender in order to explain why and how women mother, at least when women have the sole responsibility to mother as they usually do in Western, modern, industrial capitalist society. In other words, Chodorow explains gender by assuming sexual identity; at least she assumes that the father and mother always unconsciously identify themselves as masculine and feminine, respectively, and that they always unconsciously identify their male and female children as masculine and feminine, respectively.

Thus, in the end, Chodorow shifts the focus to preoedipality only to put it in the service of a girl and boy's "positive" oedipal resolutions. That is to say, Chodorow makes use of psychoanalysis only to complicate the girl's positive oedipal resolution in an effort which otherwise means to explain how the girl becomes heterosexual and feminine. Indeed, in her discussion of a woman's desire for a baby, Chodorow will assume a woman's internalized taboo against homosexuality in proposing that the woman only desires a baby in the context of her less satisfying heterosexual relationship to a man.[36]

Thus, Chodorow risks restricting psychoanalysis to a normalizing account of heterosexuality and motherhood. Indeed, Rich would criticize Chodorow not so much for failing to see motherhood as a political institution but for failing to see heterosexuality as such. Thus, in what has become a classic essay, "Compulsory Heterosexuality and Lesbian Existence" (1980), Rich proposes that Chodorow fails to recognize the lesbian existence which Rich defines in terms of a "continuum," that is:

> a range – through each woman's life and throughout history – of woman-identified experience; not simply the fact that a woman has had or consciously desired genital sexual experience with another woman. If we expand it to embrace many more forms of primary intensity between and among women, including the sharing of a rich inner life, the bonding against male tyranny, the giving and receiving of practical and political support . . .[37]

While this definition of lesbian existence would long be debated by feminist theorists, for Rich, the lesbian continuum is not proposed in order to define lesbianism. Rather, it is proposed as another way to uncover the history of patriarchy and thereby recover the history of woman-identified experience. That is to say, it is to make the task of feminist theory not only a matter of making women's experience visible but of making visible what in women's experience has been and is resistant to patriarchy, what is and has been "a rejection of a compulsory way of life."[38] Indeed, in her normative and stereotypical treatment of male homosexuality, Rich ironically winds up proposing that the lesbian continuum is meant to ally lesbian and heterosexual women against patriarchy, rather than lesbians and gay males against compulsory heterosexuality.[39] Thus, Rich's criticism of Chodorow's heterosexism is troubled by Rich's limiting view of male homosexuality.

In fact, Chodorow's argument is more complicated than Rich would have it. That is to say, in *The Reproduction of Mothering*, Chodorow draws on psychoanalysis not to argue that heterosexuality or mother-hood are not ideologically imposed but to argue that even if they are ideologically imposed, ideology can only be effective if men and women's unconscious desires are elicited in engaging them in identifications.[40] Still, by harnessing a psychoanalysis of preoedipality to a sociology of gender, Chodorow seems finally to unmake her case about unconscious pro-cesses. That is to say, Chodorow seems to trivialize the ongoing produc-tivity of unconscious desire in sexual identifications; she seems only to focus on the relevancy of the unconscious in fixing sexual identity for the infant, seemingly once and for all.

Thus, the feminist literary critics who would draw on Chodorow's *The Reproduction of Mothering* to inform a gynocriticism of women's writing do not do so in order to explore the relationship of writing and the ongoing play of unconscious desire in the construction of sexual identifications. Instead, they make Chodorow's treatment of the mother and daughter's preoedipal relationship a model of women's friendship. Women's writing often is explored only for providing case studies of women's experience, especially women's experience of each other. Thus, Elizabeth Abel's "(E)Merging Identities: The Dynamics of Female Friend-ship in Contemporary Fiction by Women" (1981) studies women's rela-tionships as elaborated in five twentieth-century novels written by women about women. Reading Doris Lessing's *The Four-Gated City* (1969) and *The Golden Notebook* (1973), Christa Wolf's *The Quest for Christa T.* (1970), Ruth Prawer Jhabvala's *Heat and Dust* (1977), and Toni Morrison's *Sula* (1975), Abel suggests:

> Women friends, as well as children, play a crucial role in relaxing ego boundaries and restoring psychic wholeness. Identification, especially with a woman who is older or who is perceived as either older or wiser, is essential in these novels to the achievement of the central figure's full identity.[41]

Thus, Abel makes use of Chodorow's revision of psychoanalysis both to shift the focus of literary criticism to woman-identified experience and to establish a relationship between women's shared experience and the woman's development of a full identity. Just as Carroll Smith-Rosenberg's "The Female World of Love and Ritual: Relations between Women in Nineteenth-Century America" (1975) had shifted the focus of feminist history to women's experience, making feminist history a study of women's indifference, if not resistance, to the world of men,[42] Abel's study of the novels of contemporary women writers shifts the focus of feminist literary criticism to the development of women's identities in relationship to women's shared experience, especially of each other. For Abel, then, women's writings about women elaborate how a woman finds her identity in commonality with another woman; a woman's identity is "a collaborative construction of meaning from experience."[43]

Abel even proposes that Chodorow's revision of psychoanalysis provides a way of understanding a tradition of women writers, that is, a theory of women's literary history that adjusts Harold Bloom's influential oedipalized history of male literary authority. Thus, while Bloom's argument emphasizes an oedipalized "anxiety of influence," urging the author to originality that will distinguish him from a dominant and powerful precursor,[44] Abel suggests instead that the woman writer's relationship to the male tradition may be more like an oedipal struggle but her relationship to other women writers is more likely a self-differentiation through merging, informed by the preoedipal mother–daughter relationship which Chodorow's psychoanalytic account describes.

After all, in *The Madwoman in the Attic* (1979), Sandra Gilbert and Susan Gubar already had shown that in relationship to the male tradition, the woman writer's struggle was less a matter of an anxiety of influence and more a matter of "an anxiety of authorship" – a struggle not so much with the dominant powerful precursor but with the images male authors had created – images of women, limiting, even damaging, any sense of female authority.[45] Thus, Abel concludes that in such a situation, the woman writer's relationship to other women writers is more likely a matter of differentiation through merging, a collaborative interaction toward self-definition. "Once again a triadic female pattern emerges: the relationship to the male tradition reflects women's oedipal issues, the relationship to the female tradition reflects the preoedipal."[46]

Thus, even though Chodorow had not proposed that women's experience of each other is free of ambivalence – after all, they experience castration anxiety in relationship to each other – nonetheless, *The Reproduction of Mothering* was read by literary critics to support a characterization of women's relationships, especially their relationships with each other, as supportive, cooperative, nurturing, noncompetitive, and personally oriented. Indeed, it is this reading of Chodorow's revision of psychoanalysis that is made to inform a feminist literary collectivity – not only of women writers but of gynocritics as well.

And if all of this is only to further the project of recovery that Rich's *Of Woman Born* initiated – that is, to more clearly differentiate women's experiences from patriarchal culture, it also subsumes into a unified or full feminine identity the ambivalences of love and hate, tenderness and anger, sweetness and violence which, in *Of Woman Born*, Rich at least suggests are within a woman – a difference or division of unconscious desire within feminine identity. That is to say, focusing on women's writing in order to recover women's relationships from the distortions of patriarchal culture, gynocritics not only elide the difference within femininity of unconscious desire. They therefore also do not focus on the play of unconscious desire in writing and reading.

Indeed, Judith Kegan Gardiner would criticize Abel for making too little of the fact that in the novels Abel interprets, one woman of each of the pairs of women friends is the narrator of the novel and all but one of the narrators are characterized in the novels as writers who actually only find their identities by *writing* about the other friend and only after she is dead. If, as Gardiner argues, the narrating woman "finds herself not by merging with another woman but by writing about another woman," then it may be that "each fictional relationship mirrors the author's relationship to her characters and our relationship to both."[47] Thus, the preoedipal relationship of mother and daughter is not to be found as much in the content of women's writings as in its form; that is, the form is shaped by an authorial desire for the preoedipal relationship. Gardiner's remarks therefore suggest that focusing on writing places the question of the authority of women writers in a different light than Abel proposes. As she puts it:

> As we have seen, then, the relationships between women in these books are not entirely reciprocal. One woman in each pair is more of a knower; the other one is to be known. The knower also seeks the love of the other woman. This loving contains elements of both freedom and constraint. Abel stresses the idealization of identification in female friendship. However, the intense ambivalence between mother and daughter colors the emotional dynamics of all these relationships between women.[48]

If in women's writing the relationship between women, "with its exhilarating fusions and frightening threats to autonomy," is written as a recreation "in imagination and memory,"[49] as Gardiner would have it, then the question is raised as to the relationship of writing and unconscious desire; that is, what is the relationship of writing and the transference onto the text of an authorial desire for the preoedipal mother–daughter relationship? Indeed, it is the French feminists who would make visible the relationship of unconscious desire, femininity, and writing, even though their revisions of psychoanalysis also focus on the preoedipal mother and even though they, like gynocritics, insist only on giving voice to that shift from the ambivalence of the mother–daughter relationship to the fullness of feminine identity.

Indeed, it is for their voice that Luce Irigaray's essays would become so influential. Both in "And the One Doesn't Stir without the Other," first published in the 1981 special issue of *Signs* on "French Feminist Theory," and in "When Our Lips Speak Together," published earlier in the 1980 special issue of *Signs* on "Women – Sex and Sexuality," Irigaray seeks to give voice to all that Chodorow implies has been silenced in, if not by, Freudian psychoanalysis. Thus, Irigaray gives voice to the preoedipal daughter, a voice already full of confusion, anger, and desperation – the voice Rich could hear and desired to make speak:

With your milk, Mother, I swallowed ice. And here I am now, my insides frozen. . . . You've prepared something to eat. You bring it to me. You feed me/yourself. But you feed me/yourself too much, as if you wanted to fill me up completely with your offering. You put yourself in my mouth and I suffocate.[50]

But always distracted, you turn away. Furtively, you verify your own continued existence in the mirror, and you return to your cooking.[51]

With your milk, Mother, you fed me ice. And if I leave, you lose the reflection of life, of your life. And if I remain, am I not the guarantor of your death? Each of us lacks her own image; her own face, the animation of her own body is missing. And the one mourns the other. My paralysis signifying your abduction in the mirror. And when I leave, is it not the perpetuation of your exile? And when it's my turn, of my own disappearance? I, too, a captive when a man holds me in his gaze; I too am abducted from myself. Immobilized in the reflection he expects of me.[52]

Ending "And the One Doesn't Stir Without the Other," Irigaray wishes that both the daughter and mother might live separate lives; to this end, Irigaray proposes that the symbiosis of mother and daughter may be transvalued to model a feminine imagination of difference, a differing from the "sameness" of phallocentricism which only prescribes masculinity. Thus, in "When Our Lips Speak Together," Irigaray counters phallocentricism, in which the mother–daughter relationship is deformed, in order to free a feminine imaginary, connected both to the woman's body – her two lips, and to the possibility of a language outside phallocentricism, a language only spoken between women – only between their lips.

If we continue to speak the same language to each other, we will reproduce the same story.[53]

We are luminous. Beyond "one" or "two". I never knew how to count up to you. In their calculations, we count as two. Really, two? Doesn't that make you laugh? A strange kind of two, which isn't one, especially not one. Let them have oneness with its prerogatives, its domination, its solipsism: like the sun. Let them have their strange division by couples, in which the other is the image of the one, but an image only.[54]

Erection doesn't interest us; we're fine in the lowlands. We have so many spaces to share. Because we are always open, the horizon will never be circumscribed. Stretching out, never ceasing to unfold ourselves, we must invent so many different voices to speak all of "us," including our cracks and faults, that forever won't be enough time. Don't make yourself erect, you abandon us. The sky isn't up there: it's between us.[55]

Although we can be perfect dissemblers within their system, we relate to each other without simulation. Our resemblance does without semblances: in our bodies, already the same. Touch yourself, touch me you'll "see."[56]

If Irigaray's writing itself proposes a certain intimacy of the poetic, the voicing of a feminine imaginary and the deconstruction of phallocentricism, it is because for the French feminists generally, preoedipality not only is situated at the moment that the child is bound up with the mother's body but it also refers to the preverbal; therefore a revaluation of preoedipality can provide a counterposition to what the law or the structure of language fixes – a counterposition in the name of the preoedipal mother. But this focus on language has much to do with Jacques Lacan's rereading of Freud, upon which Irigaray, but also Julia Kristeva and Hélène Cixous draw. In other words, French feminists return to preoedipality as a counterposition to oedipality, but specifically in relationship to Lacan's proposal that the primary function of the oedipal complex is to construct the subject of language through the imposition of sexual identity, a fixing of sexual difference as an opposition of masculine and feminine.

After all, what Lacan's rereading of Freud makes more visible is that the oedipal complex not only deploys the incest taboo, but in doing so, it also deploys the privilege of white, propertied, heterosexual masculinity as a privilege related to subjectivity, language, and discursive authority. That is to say, for Lacan the infant finally enters the symbolic order and becomes subject to the law or the structure of language through the imposition of the *nom du père* or the oedipal deployment of the paternal prerogative. Thus, the final separation of the infant from the preoedipal relationship with the mother is imposed in terms of a sexual difference which privileges masculinity.

It is in the name of the father, then, that the oedipus complex aims to fix the child's sexual identity, in subjugating the child to the symbolic order, which figures the subject as masculine or paternal ("having" the phallus), while figuring that which is lost and therefore lacking in the subject as feminine or maternal ("being" the phallus, albeit the male's missing one). Sexual identity, then, is fixed through the oedipal logic of a sexual difference which privileges the phallic and devalues the non-phallic. Indeed, it is against the privilege of the phallus that French feminists return psychoanalytic discourse to the preoedipal; Irigaray especially offers a preoedipal feminine imaginary, a feminine desire spoken through the preoedipal mother/daughter's body, seemingly free of the imposition of oedipus altogether.

Thus, French feminists take little notice of Lacan's insistence that since both male and female are subjugated to the symbolic in becoming subjects of language, then neither male nor female actually can ever possess the phallus or the paternal function that constitutes the symbolic. After all, Lacan did propose that the imposition of sexual identity or sexual difference always fails and therefore sexual identity remains unconsciously divided or split by a resistance to subjugation, an unconscious resistance that is at play in the fantasies or "fantasmatic scenes of unconscious desire."[57]

That is to say, for Lacan any sexual identity is informed with (post)oedipal fantasies, which rather than being distortions of actual experience, function instead to constitute the subject and the reality of experience as an ongoing process. While some of these fantasies function to disavow oedipality by denying the imposition of sexual difference in a persistent bisexuality, others disavow oedipality in a defensive insistence on a unified, fixed sexual identity, seemingly appropriating the phallic function by disavowing the non-phallic or feminine altogether. Therefore, all fantasies that constitute both the subject and experience necessarily reconstruct preoedipality; that is to say, preoedipality is only grasped in a (post)oedipal fantasmatic construction.

Indeed, in these terms, French feminism might better be understood as itself a (post)oedipal fantasmatic reconstruction of the preoedipal mother–daughter relationship. After all, it surely should be noticed that Irigaray makes use of words to account for what is described as preverbal; that is to say, it is only with writing that the space-time of preoedipality can be made visible. Perhaps, then, it is best to read Irigaray's account against its incipient essentialism – that is, its slippage between a feminine imaginary and female anatomy – as being informed with the unconscious desire to make speak what can not speak without a poetic framing, without a fantasmatic evocation of desire.

And if all this is to say that there is no direct conscious access to the preverbal, preoedipal relationship of mother and infant, as both French feminism and gynocriticism suggest there is, it also is to propose that the discourse of the mother within feminist theory generally is itself informed with fantasy and unconscious desire – the daughter's longing for the mother which Rich speaks of and which is overdetermined in male-dominated, Western, modern industrial capitalism. Thus, French feminism marks, albeit inadvertently, the return in the discourse of the mother, of the literary – the return of textuality and to an understanding of it as the vehicle by which condensations or displacements of unconscious desire are projected onto and elicited from readers and writers.

Therefore, it also marks the turn to a different understanding of psychoanalysis than the one gynocritics have made of Chodorow's *The Reproduction of Mothering*, perhaps even suggesting a return to those aspects of *The Reproduction of Mothering* that have been all but ignored – that is, Chodorow's reflections on the psychoanalytic method of interpretation. Thus, while Chodorow's account of preoedipality is read to fix women's unconscious relational structure and therefore to account for the experience of women, Chodorow nonetheless argues that "psychoanalysis is not in the first instance a psychological theory about behavior."[58] Rather it is a method of interpretation, developed through "a particular kind of behavior in the analytic situation – talk."[59]

Thus, Chodorow recognizes that there is "no one-to-one correspondence between unconscious processes or structure and the content of consciousness and intended activity."[60] The point is that "a particular unconscious process, affect (an idea, wish, preoccupation), or structural form can express itself in almost endless behavioral as well as conscious psychological modes."[61] In other words, as a method, psychoanalysis can not produce interpretations or readings that are separable from the "analytic talk" or from the transference and countertransference of unconscious desire in reading and writing. The fundamental contribution of psychoanalysis, then, is not so much in reproducing the "true contents" of the unconscious, if that at all; as Chodorow puts it, "the fundamental contribution of psychoanalysis lies in its demonstration of the existence and mode of operation of unconscious mental processes."[62]

Thus, other feminist theorists, who draw on Lacan, but differ with the French feminists as well as with gynocritics, feminist theorists such as Juliet Mitchell, Jacqueline Rose, Annette Kuhn, Kaja Silverman, and Constance Penley, instead insist on the persistence of unconscious desire in the ongoing construction of the subject and experience; they also insist on the ongoing play of unconscious desire or fantasy in reading and writing the reality of experience.[63] They suggest that a psychoanalytically oriented feminist criticism unsettles, even deconstructs, those gender-based generalizations such as "woman's experience," or "feminine desire" or "feminine imaginary." That is to say, while on the one hand, they argue that a woman's identification with femininity is never unconsciously fixed, on the other hand, they also argue that femininity therefore can only be fixed through unconscious fantasy that defends against failed sexual identity. Just as a full and unified masculine identity is only a fantasmatic construction, so too is a full and unified feminine identity a fantasmatic construction.

Still, just as the deconstruction of the authorial figure of a unified and full masculine identity is a necessary step for a feminist criticism, the desire for a full and unified feminine identity must also be recognized as a trace of desire within femininity, a desire that plays an essential(izing) part in shaping and motivating feminist practice with notions of every woman or all women. As Kaja Silverman puts it:

> The pre-Oedipal tableau comes into play only as an after-the-fact construction that permits the subject who has already entered into language and desire to dream of maternal unity and phenomenal plenitude. It is a regressive fantasy, that is, through which the female subject pursues both the Oedipal mother and the wholeness lost to her through symbolic castration. . . . It, in fact, represents one of the governing fantasies of feminism, a powerful image both of women's unity and of their at time necessary separatism. I would even go so far as to argue that without activating the homosexual-maternal fantasmatic, feminism would be impossible . . .[64]

The Differences Within Gynocriticism

If, then, the difference of desire within femininity would finally trouble gynocriticism, it also would be troubled by the differences among women – that is, the differences of race, class, nationality, sexuality, and ethnicity. Indeed, it would be something like the return of the repressed which seemingly would throw Rich into remembering the "other" women of feminist discourse. Thus, at the very end of her chapter on motherhood and daughterhood, Rich suddenly tells of "my black mother," the woman who for four years "fed me, dressed me, played with me, watched over me, sang to me, cared for me tenderly and intimately."[65] Recounting the loss and confusion in "discovering that a woman one has loved and been cherished by is somehow 'unworthy' of such love after a certain age," Rich suggests that it is "the double silence of sexism and racism" that intended that her black caretaker "be utterly annihilated."[66]

And the reader, too, might be thrown back to Rich's introductory remarks in which she speaks not only of the pain of mothering but of another painfulness, "a painful consciousness" in becoming aware of the limitations, the absences, constitutive of the discourse of mothering, as it develops within what Rich describes as "my own Western cultural perspective," but also in relationship to differences of class, race, ethnicity, nationality, and sexuality even within Western culture – differences which a psychoanalytically oriented criticism so often elides as well. And if, for Rich, the painfulness of this awareness is "because it says so much about how female culture is fragmented by the male cultures . . . in which women live,"[67] feminist theorists notice that there is some resistance to recognizing differences among women in this claim that only male cultures divide women, a resistance to recognizing that women themselves have been and are divided against each other in relations of power/ knowledge.

While eventually it is in the figure of the "other" mother – the domestic, that the questions of class, race, nationality, and ethnicity are raised against a "white" feminism such as gynocriticism, nonetheless, the desires expressed by women of color to recover other traditions of women's literary authority often also are articulated in relationship to the maternal. Thus, in the same years of the development of gynocriticism, there were a number of novels written by African-American women about African-American women that would urge African-American literary critics to found a Black women's literary tradition – a project that from the start is just as troubled by difference as gynocriticism became.

Indeed, *Conjuring, Black Women, Fiction, and Literary Tradition* (1985), one of the first anthologies of African-American literary criticism and the first edited by a white woman and a Black woman, begins with an introduction by Marjorie Pryse that suggests a correspondence between a Black woman's recovering her relationship with her mother and the recovering of a Black women's literary tradition. But in the end, in the afterword, Hortense Spillers unsettles the very notion of literary tradition – and not without reference to the same critical theories that both supported but finally troubled gynocriticism.

Thus, in the end, Spillers argues that to establish a tradition of Black women writers against the canonical tradition "not only redefines tradition but also disarms it by suggesting that the term itself is a critical fable intended to encode and recircumscribe an inner and licit circle of empowered texts."[68] She therefore further proposes "that 'tradition' for black women's writing community is a matrix of literary *discontinuities* that partially articulate various periods of consciousness in the history of an African-American people."[69] Like Hazel Carby, who would argue that a

Black women's literary tradition be taken "as a problem, not a solution, as a sign that should be interrogated, a locus of contradictions,"[70] Spillers too focuses on discontinuities to ward off essentialism and ahistoricism or what Carby describes as the reduction of criticism to a presupposed identity of writers, characters, and readers based on experience.[71]

Carby problematizes tradition in order to return feminist criticism to the question of the relationship of Black women and white women, especially in terms of the nineteenth-century ideology of the sacred calling of domesticity. Spillers also problematizes the relationship of white women and Black women and by emphasizing discontinuities of tradition; but she would situate Black women writers in relationship to the academy and to the fact that "the American academy, despite itself, is one of the enabling postulates of black women's literary community simply because it is not only a source of income for certain individual writers, but also a point of dissemination and inquiry for their work."[72] Thus, it is in the context of the interrelationships of power/knowledge not only between African-American women and men but also between African-American women and white women – back through the academy to the captivity of African-American women, that the folk tradition, which Pryse means to elaborate, also might be seen as "a critical fable," an enabling fiction of a matrilineage of Black women writers.

Thus, Pryse would speak of Black women writers as drawing on:

> ... their common literary ancestors (gardeners, quilt makers, grand-
> mothers, rootworkers, and women who wrote autobiographies) and to
> name each other as a community of inheritors. By their combined recogni-
> tion and mutual naming, based on magic, oral inheritance and the need to
> struggle against oppression, black women writers enlarge our conventional
> assumptions about the nature and function of literary tradition. Focusing
> on connection rather than separation, transforming silence into speech,
> and giving back power to the culturally disenfranchised, black women
> writers affirm the wholeness and endurance of a vision that, once articu-
> lated, can be shared – though its heritage, roots, survival, and intimate
> possession belong to black women alone.[73]

While celebrating connection rather than separation or discontinuity, Pryse could be read, however, at least to suggest a differing in the similarity between conjuring and unconscious fantasy or desire.

That is, if unconscious fantasy informs and therefore fractures the authorial intention of the writer by subjecting the author's full and unified identity to the instabilities of unconscious desire, conjuring, as Pryse explains it, is itself a magical knowing that also raises the question of literary authority by drawing on, while undermining, a long-standing protestant tradition in which male writers can author but only in the name of God's authority.[74] Drawing on Alice Walker's description of herself as a "medium" – not for God but for the characters of her novels, Pryse suggests that for the conjuring Black woman writer, the identity of the author is never unified; nor is the author's intention in writing fully possessed by the author. Literary authority is always already collective – a collective in the place of God, a collective of women-identified women, or as Walker would have it, "womanish women."[75]

For Pryse, then, the notion of the author as the medium for other women's voices also gives sense to how the lesbian comes to figure the womanish woman writer, as she does in much of Black women's writings in the early 1980s. That is, if the womanish woman writer is one who in "getting man out of her head changes her form of address," thereby changing "the direction of black women's fiction,"[76] she also is the one who puts the woman's body in touch with another woman's body – not just a matter of heads – but always a work of conjuring, as if writing beyond heads, back to the mother.

Thus, if together conjure-criticism and gynocriticism can be understood to counter patriarchal culture, it is not so much by their recovering a unique experience shared by all women but more by their claiming authority for women, which while not reducible to a unique woman's experience, is fantasmatically related to women's experiences. Indeed, all through the 1980s, the relationship of women's experiences and women's authority will continue to shape the problematic of feminist theory, if not in the elaboration of standpoint epistemologies, then in the elaboration of a feminist materialist deconstruction of mass-mediated, hegemonic forms of discursive authority. As both will continue to focus on reproduction, neither will move far from the desire for the mother, for a mothering tradition of women's authority – either to confirm authority figured as feminine or to deconstruct phallocentric authority, without privileging a unique femininity. And for a time, white literary critics would invoke Black women writers' texts in order to legitimate gynocriticism against a deconstructive criticism; but sometimes, too, Black women writers would be read by white feminist critics as prefiguring a deconstructive criticism.[77]

Afterwords

Following the journal entries with which she begins *Of Woman Born*, Rich tells of having been asked, "Don't you ever write poems about your children?"[78] She also tells why her reply always was no: "For me, poetry was where I lived as no-one's mother, where I existed as myself."[79] If, then, Rich seems to suggest that the journal entries of *Of Woman Born* are not poetry, that they only report rather than enact the split between being a mother and existing as an autonomous self, it only makes clear the difficulties encountered in recovering women's experience of mothering through writing – the difficulties of splits and breaks, of lives and genres.

Indeed, what now seems so important about *Of Woman Born* is not that it teaches us about the unique experience of all women as mothers or daughters. It is that it teaches us that in modern, industrial, capitalist society, mothering was made to figure what can neither be easily forgotten nor easily remembered. Thus, it is only with the poetic harnessing of unconscious desire that there can be remembering. Thus, in connecting the woman's recovery of the mother with the founding of a tradition of women's authority, feminist theorists do not simply immortalize those women who have gone before and who have gone unnoticed. Rather, feminist theorists suggest that the past is not remembered but rememoried; memories are not found, they are invented; they are installed as new descriptions, new words, new desires, in what Rich describes as "the dream of a common language."[80]

The discourse on mothering, then, politicizes mothering by making visible that memory itself is a social construction. Thus the discourse of mothering furthers the reinvention of the social by investing it with a will to remember the repressed maternal. But in doing so it also furthers the reinvention of the literary, further collapsing the opposition of reality and fantasy, history and fiction, polemic and academic discourse, social science and literary criticism. Indeed, the discourse of mothering urges a criticism of all knowledge, of science in particular, focusing on how knowledge is produced, by whom and for whom; the discourse of mothering even urges feminist theorists to construct a feminist or women's standpoint epistemology.

But if the construction of a feminist or women's standpoint epistemology would make women's experiences, especially women's experiences of mothering, the starting point for a more adequate knowledge of reality, there also would be responses to that construction that would challenge the dream of a common language. Not only would the difference within femininity, the play of unconscious desire in the failure of sexual identity, again assert itself against standpoint epistemologies. But the differences of race, ethnicity, class, nationality, and sexuality also would be asserted, destabilizing a certain feminist theorizing which, it would be argued, had been based all along on the experiences of white, middle-class, heterosexual women.

Notes

1 Kate Millett, *Sexual Politics* (New York: Ballantine Books, 1970), p. 86.
2 Adrienne Rich, *Of Woman Born: Motherhood as Experience and Institution* (New York: Norton, 1976), pp. 13–14.
3 Ibid., p. 13.
4 Ibid., p. 16.
5 Ibid., p. 16.
6 Ibid., pp. 21–9.
7 Ibid., p. 40.
8 Ibid., pp. 33–4.
9 Ibid., p. 73.
10 Ibid., p. 57.
11 Ibid., p. 57.
12 Ibid., p. 57.
13 Ibid., p. 73.
14 Ibid., p. 109.
15 Ibid., p. 166.
16 Ibid., p. 185.
17 Ibid., pp. 161–2.
18 Ibid., p. 191.
19 Ibid., p. 187.
20 Ibid., p. 220.
21 Ibid., p. 222.
22 Ibid., p. 221.
23 Ibid., p. 243.
24 Ibid., p. 235.
25 Ibid., p. 224.
26 Barbara Charlesworth Gelpi and Albert Gelpi (eds), *Adrienne Rich's Poetry* (New York: Norton, 1975), p. 113.
27 Adrienne Rich, *What Is Found There: Notebooks on Poetry and Politics* (New York: Norton, 1993), p. 242. Also see Adrienne Rich, "Power and Danger: Works of a Common Woman," in *On Lies, Secrets, and Silence: Selected Prose 1966–1978* (New York: Norton, 1979), p. 248.
28 Nancy Chodorow, *The Reproduction of Mothering: Psychoanalysis and the Sociology of Gender* (Berkeley: University of California Press, 1978), p. 107.
29 Ibid., p. 107.
30 Ibid., p. 126.
31 Ibid., p. 127.
32 Ibid., p. 129.
33 Ibid., p. 201.
34 Ibid., p. 123.
35 Chodorow refers specifically to Gayle Rubin, "The Traffic in Women: Notes on the 'Political Economy' of Sex," in Rayna Reiter (ed.), *Toward an*

Anthropology of Women (New York: Monthly Review Press, 1975), pp. 157–210.

36   Chodorow, *The Reproduction of Mothering*, pp. 203–4.

37   Adrienne Rich, "Compulsory Heterosexuality and Lesbian Existence," *Signs*, 5 (1980), pp. 648–9. For further discussion of the relationship of feminist theorizing and lesbian criticism, see ch. 6.

38   Rich, *Of Woman Born*, p. 649.

39   Ibid., pp. 649–50.

40   Chodorow, *The Reproduction of Mothering*, pp. 33–4.

41   Elizabeth Abel, "(E)Merging Identities: The Dynamics of Female Friendship in Contemporary Fiction by Women," *Signs*, 6 (1981), p. 418.

42   Carroll Smith-Rosenberg, "The Female World of Love and Ritual: Relations between Women in Nineteenth-Century America," *Signs*, 1 (1975), pp. 1–30.

43   Abel, "(E)Merging Identities: The Dynamics of Female Friendship in Contemporary Fiction by Women," p. 419.

44   Harold Bloom, *The Anxiety of Influence* (New York: Oxford University Press, 1973).

45   Sandra Gilbert and Susan Gubar, *The Madwoman in the Attic: The Woman Writer and the Nineteenth-Century Literary Imagination* (New Haven: Yale University Press, 1979).

46   Abel, "(E)Merging Identities: The Dynamics of Female Friendship in Contemporary Fiction by Women," pp. 433–4.

47   Judith Kegan Gardiner, "The (Us)es of (I)dentity: A Response to Abel on '(E)Merging Identities,'" *Signs*, 6 (1981), p. 437.

48   Ibid., p. 441.

49   Ibid., p. 441.

50   Luce Irigaray, "And the One Doesn't Stir without the Other," translated by Helene Vivienne Wenzel, *Signs*, 7 (1981), pp. 60–1.

51   Ibid., p. 61.

52   Ibid., p. 66.

53   Luce Irigaray, "When Our Lips Speak Together," translated by Carolyn Burke, *Signs*, 6 (1980), p. 69.

54   Ibid., p. 71.

55   Ibid., pp. 75–6.

56   Ibid., p. 78.

57   The notion of the "fantasmatic," which I will discuss further in ch. 3, is taken from J. Laplanche and J.-B. Pontalis, *The Language of Psychoanalysis*, translated by Donald Nicholson-Smith (New York: Norton, 1973).

58   Chodorow, *The Reproduction of Mothering*, p. 41.

59   Ibid., p. 41.

60   Ibid., p. 41.

61   Ibid., p. 41.

62   Ibid., p. 41.

63   For a fuller discussion of these feminist theorists, see ch. 3.

64   Kaja Silverman, *The Acoustic Mirror: The Female Voice in Psychoanalysis*

and Cinema (Bloomington: Indiana University Press, 1988), p. 124.

65 Rich, *Of Woman Born*, p. 254.

66 Ibid., pp. 254–5.

67 Ibid., p. 17.

68 Hortense Spillers, "Cross-Currents, Discontinuities: Black Women's Fiction," in Marjorie Pryse and Hortense Spillers (eds), *Conjuring, Black Women, Fiction, and Literary Tradition* (Bloomington: Indiana University Press, 1985), p. 251.

69 Ibid., p. 251.

70 Hazel Carby, *Reconstructing Womanhood: The Emergence of the Afro-American Woman Novelist* (New York: Oxford University Press, 1987).

71 Ibid., p. 16.

72 Spillers, "Cross-Currents, Discontinuities: Black Women's Fiction," p. 250.

73 Marjorie Pryse, "Zora Neale Hurston, Alice Walker, and the 'Ancient Power'," in Marjorie Pryse and Hortense Spillers (eds), *Conjuring, Black Women, Fiction, and Literary Tradition*, p. 5.

74 Ibid., pp. 9–12.

75 Ibid., p. 8.

76 Ibid., p. 19. In 1977, Barbara Smith already had argued that Black women's writing was "innately lesbian" in character because of the importance of the relationships between women characters. Smith's 1977 article was republished in 1982; see Barbara Smith, "Toward a Black Feminist Criticism," in Gloria T. Hull, Patricia Bell Scott, and Barbara Smith (eds), *All the Women Are White, All the Blacks Are Men, But Some of Us Are Brave* (New York: Feminist Press, 1982), pp. 157–75. Also see ch. 6 for further discussion of lesbian literary criticism.

77 See, for examples, Barbara Johnson, "Metaphor, Metonymy, and Voice in *Their Eyes Were Watching God*," in Henry Louis Gates, Jr (ed.), *Black Literature and Literary Theory* (New York: Oxford University Press, 1984), pp. 205–15, and "Thresholds of Difference: Structures of Address in Zora Neale Hurston," in Henry Louis Gates, Jr (ed.), *"Race," Writing, and Difference* (Chicago: University of Chicago Press, 1985), pp. 317–28. Also see Margaret Homan's "'Her Very Own Howl': The Ambiguities of Representation in Recent Women's Fiction," *Signs*, 9 (1983), pp. 69–79. For a review of some of the issues involved in white literary critics' reading Black women writers' texts, see Elizabeth Abel, "Black Writing, White Reading," *Critical Inquiry*, 19 (1993), pp. 470–98. For a more personalized statement about white feminist criticism of Black women writers, see Jane Gallop, *Around 1981* (New York: Routledge, 1992), pp. 143–76. For a fuller discussion of Black feminist literary criticism, see ch. 4.

78 Rich, *Of Woman Born*, p. 31.

79 Ibid., p. 31.

80 Adrienne Rich, *The Dream of a Common Language* (New York: Norton, 1978).

3

From Gynocriticism to Standpoint Epistemologies

If Adrienne Rich's *Of Woman Born* would urge women to recover the authority of their voices by sharing their experiences with each other, this method of recovery (often referred to as consciousness raising) also is conceived by Rich as a method to deconstruct patriochialism – that is, a method to counter the authorization of only men's experiences as the whole of culture. But while gynocriticism would revalorize women's experiences by focusing on women's writings, it only is with the development of a feminist or women's standpoint epistemology that a criticism of male-dominated culture is elaborated as a criticism of both the methods of science and the epistemology which grounds them. Proposed as an alternative way of knowing, a feminist or women's standpoint epistemology proposes to make women's experiences instead of men's experiences the point of departure. And if men's experiences long have been made to stand for the whole of culture, a feminist or women's standpoint epistemology based in women's experiences necessarily is conceived as a revolutionary practice of knowing and therefore, not surprisingly, is modeled on the revolutionary epistemology proposed by Marx.

Indeed, in constructing a feminist or women's standpoint epistemology, feminist theorists draw on Marx's analysis of ideology to elaborate the ways in which the exclusion of women from the public sphere affects the organization of knowledge, especially in academic disciplines. If, then, in *Money, Sex and Power* (1985), Nancy Hartsock draws on Marx's analysis of ideology to argue that it is the restriction of women to the private sphere which accounts for the typical treatment of domination in social science discourse on power, in *The Everyday World as Problematic* (1987), Dorothy Smith also draws on Marx to propose that it is the invisibility of women's work which accounts for the organization of sociological discourse – its complicity with what she describes as "the relations of ruling."

But, while both *Money, Sex and Power* and *The Everyday World as Problematic* move beyond what Heidi Hartmann called "the unhappy marriage of marxism and feminism," in which "Marxism and feminism are one and that one is Marxism,"[1] neither Hartsock nor Smith fully explore various historical developments other than feminism which also challenge marxism in the late twentieth century. That is to say, even though both a feminist and a women's standpoint epistemology shift the analysis of ideology from class to relationships of power/knowledge and therefore at least resonate with the conditions of late twentieth-century, postmodern capitalism, in which knowledge, including science, has become a primary productive force, they do not explore how the conditions of postmodern capitalism affect marxism – how these conditions have affected what marxist critics themselves describe as a "crisis in historical materialism."[2]

Indeed, by the early 1980s, marxist critics not only recognized a crisis in historical materialism brought on by changes in the relations of production and the meaning of labor; they also had begun to recognize the relationship of feminism to this crisis. Certainly, the development of a socialist feminist orientation was challenging both the substance and the method of marxist criticism. As Zillah Eisenstein would put it:

> Refocusing the Marxist method (as well as its content) via feminism necessitates a reordering of priorities, particularly the question of consciousness in relation to the conditions of society. Questions of consciousness become a part of the discussion of the social reality. . . . Along with this comes a focus on the importance of ideology. Thus, the dialectic will be self-consciously extended to the relations between consciousness, ideology, and social reality. This new way of viewing things – that society's ideas and people's consciousness are part of the objective social reality and that they operate out of the relations of sex, class, and race – is a product of the feminist assault on the inadequacies of the left, both in theory and practice.[3]

Indeed, by the mid-seventies, feminists had all but exhausted every effort to reduce women's oppression to capitalist exploitation; even the argument that women constituted an exploited class because the wife's housework reproduces the laborer and thereby contributes to the production of surplus value, had proven limited in explaining women's oppression. Thus, while it was recognized that the privatization of the domestic sphere in Western, modern, industrial capitalism had allowed for the exploitation of women as houseworkers and therefore also as an underemployed army of surplus labor, there nonetheless was a growing recognition that not only were more and more women working outside of the home but that the male's authority in the home increasingly was being replaced by corporate structures and the mass media communication technologies which maintain male domination in the corporations of which they are a part. In other words, it was becoming increasingly apparent that in late twentieth-century, postmodern capitalism, the separation of the private and public spheres functions primarily as an ideology, or to use Eisenstein's term, a matter of "consciousness."

Thus, if Smith and Hartsock would redress the male-dominated organization of knowledge by proposing an alternative form of knowing based on women's unique experience of the separation of the private and public spheres, other feminist theorists would take up the question of knowledge and power in relationship to mass media communication technologies. They would fashion a feminist materialism – that is, a materialist analysis of consciousness and ideology, that opens criticism to the collapse of the separation of the public and private spheres in late twentieth-century, postmodern capitalism. Thus, I would propose that Hartsock's *Money, Sex and Power* and Smith's *The Everyday World as Problematic* not only extend the criticism inaugurated with Marx's analysis of ideology to epistemologies based in women's experiences; they also open feminist criticism to a materialist analysis of ideology which challenges the very notion of the separate spheres and therefore the notion of women's experience, as well.

Reforming the Relationship of Marxism and Feminism

Since the focus of her critique of disciplinary knowledge is theories of power which originate in mainstream social science, especially political science, Nancy Hartsock draws on Marx to demonstrate how these theories are always already ideological constructions. Thus, Hartsock reviews the works of social scientists who explain power in terms of a market model of exchange. Beginning with the exchange theories of George Homans and Peter Blau and then turning to the theories of Harold Lasswell, Abraham Kaplan, Robert Dahl, Nelson Polsby, Talcott Parsons and even the critical theories of Peter Backrach, Morton Baratz, and Steven Lukes, Hartsock demonstrates the dependency of these theories on the market model of exchange. Hartsock's argument is that since the exchange model takes as its point of departure a focus on the participants only as they are engaged in the transaction of power, the transaction may in fact appear to be both egalitarian – as each participant appears to have something to exchange, and consensual – as each appears to come into the exchange of his own free will.

Thus, while each theorist more or less argues that domination in relations of power are inevitable, Hartsock emphasizes that each does so by arguing that a differentiated structure of domination develops over time; any condition of inequality prior to the "first" exchange is not considered relevant. As she puts it, "Social structure and its effects disappear from view."[4] Temporal and spatial relations are also held in abeyance, as the rational economic man is taken as the model; each man is imagined to be isolated from the other and their transactions appear to be out of time and space. As Hartsock puts it:

> The exchange abstraction, the epistemological form of human activity in commodity exchange, has marked theories modeled on the market in specific, though varied, ways. Thus they cannot be held to be entirely determined by the categories of commodity exchange, yet one finds that each theorist has to a large extent followed the implicit epistemological directions of commodity exchange in theorizing power. The influence of the qualitylessness of the commodity exchange led theorists of power to attempt to develop similarly qualityless but formally equivalent categories: Blau and Homans' category (commodity) of "social approval" (purchased with "help"); Lasswell, Kaplan, Dahl, and Polsby's "decisions" (purchased with expenditures of effort or exercises of power); Parsons' equation of power with money (to be spent for a variety of social commodities or invested at interest). All these represent what Marx termed the way a social relation between two persons can take the form of a relation between two separately produced commodities, a relation characterized by the dominance of abstract quantity.[5]

For Hartsock, then, the most salient feature of exchange theories of power is that they lead to a view of community as fragile, arbitrary, and false. That is to say, the image of community that develops through an application of the market model to power is one in which relationships can only be based on the compliance of most. After all, compliance is all that is left to those who have lost through the exchange of power; it is all that they have left to exchange. Hartsock puts it this way:

> Use of the market model, then, places a number of obstacles in the face of understanding either power or community. By claiming (falsely) that we live in a world of free and equal individuals interacting on the basis of self-interest, exchange theorists impoverish the theoretical understanding of community and present a deeply misleading account of reality. Theorization of the community in the form of a market results in the conclusion that the human community can only be fragile, instrumental, and ultimately false, composed of persons with no intrinsic connection with each other.[6]

However, if exchange theories give a false account of reality, Hartsock argues that it is because they are constructed in terms of the experience of the powerful. In arguing her case, Hartsock draws on Marx's general understanding that material life shapes consciousness. Therefore exchange theories of power, Hartsock proposes, only reflect the social activity of the powerful, just as economic theories based on exchange only reflect the social activity of the owning class.

To counter a view of reality which derives from the activity of the ruling, Hartsock follows Marx's proposal that only an epistemology rooted in production instead of exchange can ground a way of knowing that distinguishes reality from false appearances. Marx explains that the laborers' work or activity is erased in the production of the commodity, that is, the production of surplus value; thus, the commodity, which is the abstraction of use value in the service of exchange, hides within its abstractness the actual, sensuous activity of the workers. Thus, an "epistemology rooted in production, the one that defines the standpoint of the proletariat" not only would reflect the activity of the workers but, in that their activity actually produces surplus value, it also can reveal "the real relations of domination."[7]

Assuming Marx's labor theory of value and the analysis it permits of the exploitation of labor power as it is expended in space and over time, Hartsock then proposes that the standpoint of the ruling is "partial and perverse," while the standpoint of production is its "inversion" – full and liberating.[8] Yet, since the standpoint of the ruling rules or is one in which all must participate, the standpoint of production not only carries "a historical and liberatory role."[9] It also must be struggled for. The standpoint of production, therefore, requires "both science to see beneath the surface of the social relations in which all are forced to participate, and the education that can only grow from political struggle."[10] For Hartsock, marxism is both true science and political struggle.

Thus, Hartsock turns to the task of grounding a feminist analysis of power by way of an analogy to Marx's argument for an epistemology of production. That is to say, Hartsock argues that theories of power which employ the market model of exchange can only assume a community based on domination because these theories reflect the experiences of the dominators, that is, the experiences of men. Hartsock then proposes that only women's experiences provide a standpoint which can uncover the real relations of male domination.

Drawing on Robert Stoller's analysis of perversion and pornography, as well as Chodorow's revision of object-relations theory, Hartsock proposes that an "abstract masculinity" informs theories of power which assume domination. Hartsock rehearses Chodorow's argument that the male infant's precipitous separation from a mother who alone is responsible for his care, results not only in his learning masculinity through an identification "with an abstract, cultural stereotype . . . not attached to a well-known person."[11] But, therefore, the boy also develops a rigid and defensive sense of masculinity which leads to domination as the primary form of merging with others and as the primary way of structuring community.

If men's standpoint is both partial and perverse, a feminist standpoint is its inversion. Like the proletariat's standpoint, then, a feminist standpoint can expose the falseness of men's vision because a feminist standpoint derives from women's experiences – the experiences of the dominated rather than those of the dominators. In reproducing and nurturing others, women do the work of producing community. Thus, women's experiences can produce an understanding of the relationship between power, community, and what Hartsock refers to as "eros." Again drawing on Chodorow but also on Rich's descriptions of pregnancy and birth, Hartsock suggests that women's experiences can produce "a vision" not only characterized by a "valuation of concrete, everyday life" but also "a sense of a variety of connectednesses and continuities both with other persons and with the natural world."[12]

As gynocriticism tends to do, a feminist standpoint epistemology, at least as Hartsock constructs it, restricts unconscious desire to certain patterns of behavior which are assumed to be expressive of a division of labor due to the separation of the private and public spheres. Therefore, Hartsock dismisses the ongoing play of unconscious desire in the construction of the subject and experience; she assumes a fixed identification both between the male and masculinity and between the woman and femininity. The difference or division of unconscious desire within a man or a woman, within masculinity or femininity, is dismissed but so too are differences among women, differences of race, class, ethnicity, nationality, and sexuality. As Hartsock puts it:

> I propose to lay aside the important differences among women and instead to search for central commonalities across race and class boundaries. I take some justification from the fruitfulness of Marx's similar strategy in constructing a simplified, two-class, two-man model in which everything was exchanged at its value. Marx's schematic account in volume I of *Capital* left out of account such factors as imperialism; the differential wages, work, and working conditions of the Irish; the differences between women, men, and children; and so on. While all these factors are important to the analysis of contemporary capitalism, none changes either Marx's theories of surplus value or alienation. . . .[13]

But Hartsock's remarks are troubling not only because they make it seem that Marx himself reduced the analysis of domination to relations of exchange, and therefore a marxist analysis only can deal with questions of colonialism, gender, race, ethnicity, or sexuality in terms of exchange. Hartsock's remarks also are troubling because among marxists themselves, the theory of surplus value, that is, the labor theory of value, has long been in question, even in relationship to an international division of labor. That is to say, the development in the twentieth century of science and technology, as well as the growth of the state sector, have demanded a change in the conception of labor. As Stanley Aronowitz puts it:

> In the historical sense, the concept of "simple, abstract labor" no longer corresponds to the character of the labor process in the most advanced technological sectors. At the same time, it can no longer be maintained that industrial development (capital formation in primary and secondary production sectors) will be systematically denied the underdeveloped world. Thus, the central thesis of dependency theories that argue for the "development of underdevelopment" as a systematic imposition from the imperialist powers on the Third World has increasingly limited validity. Under these conditions, capital will require a new abstract quantitative principle to regulate exchange relations but it will not be labor.[14]

If, as Aronowitz suggests, the conception of labor needs to be readjusted in relationship to postmodern capitalism, when knowledge has become a main productive force, it also is in relationship to postmodern capitalism that Marx's insistence on the producing class as the historical agency of revolutionary change also needs to be readjusted. That is to say, it seems that since the conditions of historical agency can no longer be located simply in terms of labor and instead must be related to relations of power/knowledge, the question of historical agency increasingly needs to be addressed in terms that permit the discursive or ideological construction of subject-identity to be viewed not only as a process relatively autonomous of economic exploitation but as one which also does not erase the specificity of oppressions of race, gender, class, ethnicity, nationality, and sexuality.

Of course, Hartsock also recognizes limitations in Marx's thinking; she admits that "on the specific question of the ways power is gendered, I believe Marxian theory can be of little direct help."[15] But even though a shift to a feminist standpoint is Hartsock's response to the limitations in Marx's thinking, she does not fully explore the crisis in historical materialism brought on by late twentieth-century, postmodern capitalism; nor does she elaborate the relationship of feminism to that crisis. Therefore a feminist standpoint epistemology, at least as Hartsock constructs it, not only takes for granted the possibility of a woman's unified subject-identity in the category of historical agency. It also assumes that science is necessary for political change – that science can go beneath false images to the real relations of domination. Hartsock's criticism of the disciplines of social science, then, depends on an essentializing conception of woman and an unreflected ideology of scientificity, both of which would be questioned in a materialist feminist criticism – increasingly identified with a criticism of knowledge, science, and ideology in postmodern capitalism.

Laborers in the Fields of Knowledge

While Dorothy Smith's criticism of sociology also spares science from a postmodern criticism, her criticism cuts deeper into the assumptions of social science than Hartsock's does. That is to say, Smith's criticism not only is leveled at the abstractness that informs the social scientific misrepresentation of power; it is leveled at the abstractness that informs the social scientific misrepresentation of all human activity. Indeed, for Smith, it is the abstractness of social science which marks its complicity with "a mode of ruling," as she defines it:

> A mode of ruling has become dominant that involves a continual transcription of the local and particular actualities of our lives into abstracted and generalized forms. It is an extralocal mode of ruling. Its characteristic modes of consciousness are objectified and impersonal; its relations are governed by organizational logics and exigencies. We are not ruled by powers that are essentially implicated in particularized ties of kinship, family, and household and anchored in relationships to particular patches of ground. We are ruled by forms of organization vested in and mediated by texts and documents, and constituted externally.... The practice of ruling involves the ongoing representation of the local actualities of our worlds in the standardized and general forms of knowledge that enter them into the relations of ruling.[16]

But, while Smith's definition of the relations of ruling seems already to assume the conditions of postmodern capitalism by which knowledge, including science, has become a main productive force, it is not to promote a feminist understanding of postmodern capitalism that Smith engages marxist theory. Rather, just as Hartsock does, Smith turns to Marx for his argument that there are ruling ideas. Thus Smith argues that in class society, "mental production becomes the privilege of the class that dominates the means of production and appropriates the means of mental production."[17] Therefore, "ideas and social forms of consciousness may originate outside experience, coming from an external source and becoming a forced set of categories ..."[18] Indeed, these ideas "may dominate and penetrate the social consciousness of the society in general ... in ways that deny expression to the actual experience people have in the working relations of their everyday world."[19] Thus Smith argues that in class society, there is a "line of fault" between "the world as it is known directly in experience . . . and the ideas and images fabricated externally to that everyday world and provided as a means to think and image it."[20]

In making her argument that sociological discourse is complicitous with the relations of ruling, Smith starts at this line of fault, insisting on the distinction between the discursive and the actual experiences or the actual activities of actual persons. Arguing, then, that social scientific inquiry, sociology in particular, usually begins from a standpoint in a textually mediated discourse, Smith proposes that sociology is therefore distorted and distorting and that both experience and the subject of experience are beyond or behind the text, which itself mediates between the actual and the discursive.

If it is sociological discourse's abstractness, then, which makes it complicitous with the relations of ruling, it is because its abstractness only reflects the experiences of those who organize it, that is, men.[21] For Smith, it is men's experience of managing, administrating, organizing, and otherwise controlling situations that allows them to mistake abstraction or discourse for the actual. That is to say, from the standpoint of discourse or the standpoint of ruling, the actual activities which make abstraction possible remain invisible. For Smith, these activities can be made visible but only from the standpoint of women, since it is women who perform these activities. As Smith puts it:

> To a very large extent the direct work of liberating men into abstraction . . . has been and is the work of women. The place of women, then, in relation to this mode of action is where the work is done to facilitate men's occupation of the conceptual mode of action. Women keep house, bear and care for children, look after men when they are sick, and in general provide for the logistics of their bodily existence. But this marriage aspect of women's work is only one side of a more general relation. Women work in and around the professional and managerial scene in analogous ways. They do those things that give concrete form to the conceptual activities. They do the clerical work, giving material form to the words or thoughts of the boss. They do the routine computer work, the interviewing for the survey, the nursing, the secretarial work.[22]

For Smith, not only are women's daily activities "situated outside textually mediated discourses;"[23] women also maintain the relations of ruling, "articulating the local and particular existence of actors to the abstracted conceptual mode of ruling."[24] A women's standpoint, then, allows for an investigation of the way daily activities activate and maintain the relations of ruling. Thus without privileging women as knowers, in the way Hartsock does, Smith draws the same analogy Hartsock does between a proletariat standpoint and a women's standpoint. As Smith puts it:

> There is a difference between forms of consciousness arising in the experi-
> ence of ruling and those arising in the experience of doing the work that
> creates the conditions of ruling. Ideological forms of consciousness are
> definite practices of thinking about society that reflect the experience of
> ruling. From the standpoint of ruling, the actual practices, the labor and
> the organization of labor which makes the existence of a ruling class and
> their ruling possible are invisible. It is only possible to see how the whole
> thing is put together from a standpoint outside the ruling class and in that
> class whose part in the overall division of labor is to produce the conditions
> of its own ruling and the existence of a ruling class.[25]

While Smith recognizes that others also are outside the frame of ruling discourses – her examples, women and men of color, native peoples, and homosexual women and men, she nonetheless holds that "the standpoint of women is distinctive and has distinctive implications for the practice of sociology."[26] Thus, for Smith a women's standpoint specifically refers to a division of labor dependent on the separation of the private and the public spheres – a specifically gendered division of labor. That is to say, as no other standpoint can, the standpoint of women refers specifically to making the suppressed everyday world of work the entry point of inquiry.

It is in this sense, then, that a women's standpoint means to correct the abstractness of social science, sociology in particular; a women's stand-point means to organize both an analysis of and a resistance to the relations of ruling because it commits the researcher:

> to an exploration, description, and analysis of . . . a complex of relations,
> not conceived in the abstract but from the entry point of some particular
> person or persons whose everyday world of working is organized thereby.[27]

For Smith, then, the inquiry which a women's standpoint organizes is "comparable to consciousness-raising:"

> It is the individual's working knowledge of her everyday world that pro-
> vides the beginning of the inquiry. The end product is not of course,
> intended to be private. . . . Rather the approach . . . offers something com-
> parable to consciousness raising. Perhaps indeed it is a form of it, aiming
> to find the objective correlates of what had seemed a private experience of
> oppression. Like consciousness raising it is also to be shared.[28]

Thus, if the actual experiences of a particular person or persons is to be the entry point for inquiry, its end product is to be an analysis of "the extralocal determinations of our experiences," that is, the relations of ruling.[29] Smith, then, is not interested in reproducing the subject's actual experience, "substituting the analysis, the perspective and views of subjects, for the investigation by the sociologist."[30] She only is interested in demonstrating how the actual activities of actual persons activate the relations of ruling. Smith gives the example of walking her dog, explaining how she takes care to avoid some properties and not others.[31] She is able, therefore, to uncover certain property laws and community expectations which she takes account of in the appearance of lawns, houses, etc. Smith's point is that these laws and expectations are activated and maintained in her walking the dog; actual activities thereby "knit local lives and local settings to national and international social, economic, and political processes."[32]

Thus, like Hartsock, Smith turns to Marx for support for a women's standpoint. Drawing on *The German Ideology* in which Marx and Engels assert that consciousness is delimited by life, Smith proposes that inquiry need focus on the "world that actually happens and can be observed, spoken of, and returned to to check up on the accuracy of an account or whether a given version of it is faithful to how it actually works . . ."[33] Of course, for Smith, the question of accuracy is raised because although inquiry must begin with the everyday world of actual people's actual activities, these activities are nonetheless organized extralocally.

It is for this reason that Smith returns to empirical social science – turns from consciousness raising to sociology. As she puts it:

> Though women are indeed the expert practitioners of their everyday world, the notion of the everyday world as problematic assumes that disclosure of the extralocal determinations of our experience does not lie within the scope of everyday practices. We can see only so much without specialized investigation, and the latter should be the sociologist's special business.[34]

Like Hartsock, Smith finally returns to a specialized or scientific inquiry, albeit marxist; she finally turns to a professional or institutionalized knowledge, the location of which, if local, somehow also is extralocal, even beyond what women see from the standpoint of their everyday life.

Configurations of Authority

If Hartsock would construct a feminist standpoint epistemology first in the figure of the mother and then in the figure of the marxist-feminist social scientist, Smith would construct a women's standpoint epistemology first in the figure of the housewife, the homemaker, the secretary, the administrative assistant and then in the figure of the marxist-feminist social scientist. Both therefore raise the question of the production of knowledge, assuming the separation of the private and public spheres, or at least a division of labor derived from this separation that they maintain has been extended to the domain of knowledge and disciplinary discourses. But it is their assumption of the separation of the private and public spheres that prevents both Smith and Hartsock from dealing with questions raised by each other's arguments.

That is to say, if, as Smith argues, women maintain the relations of ruling and if their experience is thought and imaged in terms of the relations of ruling, how can "women's vision" simply be the "inversion" of men's vision, as Hartsock argues that it is? And if, as Hartsock argues, it is women's unconscious relational structure which differentiates women's knowing from men's, how can women figure a subject who knows consciously or directly from experience, as Smith would have it? Thus, putting together Smith's and Hartsock's discussions suggests that what allows for a notion like "women's knowing" is not so much a matter of women's actual exclusion from the public sphere or merely the difference between men and women's everyday activities. What seems to matter more is the way authority is figured in relations of power/knowledge and how men and women come to identify with hegemonic configurations of authority. In other words, how is discursive authority engendered and how does discourse engender differences that are different from the difference Marx elaborates between laboring and owning the means of production? How are differences engendered that have to do with an authorized production of "consciousness?"

It is not surprising, then, that in constructing a feminist or women's standpoint, both Smith and Hartsock need to bolster their analogies to Marx – Smith with her reference to consciousness raising and Hartsock with her reference to psychoanalysis. Thus, while Smith and Hartsock draw on Marx to insist on a subject agency – that is, a historically structured agency of change who knows the world directly through experience, nonetheless Smith's reference to consciousness raising and Hartsock's reference to psychoanalysis complicate the very consciousness of the subject for whom they claim historical agency, that is, women. After all, consciousness raising implies that interpretations cannot be separated from the particular political struggle which enframes them; nor can psychoanalytic interpretations be separated from the transference and countertransference of unconscious desire. That is to say, these ways of knowing, although counter to the abstract objectivity of social science, are nonetheless always already embedded in discourse and unconscious desire and, therefore, can only inform a subject with knowledge that is also embedded in discourse and unconscious desire.

Thus, while a feminist and a women's standpoint epistemology appropriately raise the question of the relationship of male domination and social science discourse as well as speak to the necessity of understanding the psychic structuration in and of authorized disciplinary discourses, neither Hartsock nor Smith develops an analysis of how text-mediated discourse is related to unconscious desire, subjectivity, and the production of the reality of experience; they instead continue to assume that feminist theory can offer a "truer" science of empirical reality. Thus, they fail to go beyond assuming that women can know differently from men or that women's experiences can be a starting point from which to more adequately represent the reality of experience.

Thus, because both insist on an agentic subject who directly knows reality through experience, neither Hartsock nor Smith draws on those feminist criticisms of historical materialism which open up to an analysis of ideology for which the subject and the reality of experience are taken together as the problematic. These feminists follow on Louis Althusser's revision of the marxist analysis of ideology,[35] especially Althusser's deconstruction of the base-superstructure model proposed by Marx in the "Preface to the General Introduction to a Contribution to the Critique of Political Economy:"

> In the social production of their life, men enter into definite relations that are indispensable and independent of their will, relations of production. . . . The totality of these relations of production constitutes the economic structure of society, the real foundation, on which arises a legal and political superstructure and to which correspond definite forms of social consciousness. The mode of production of material life conditions the social, political and intellectual life process in general.[36]

In contrast to what is implied by Marx's remarks, Althusser suggests that ideology be understood not as a mere reflection of the experiences of the ruling class or of the economic base. Rather, Althusser proposes that ideology be understood both to shape and be shaped by the contradictory developments of the political and economic forces; that is to say, ideology is constituted in relationship to the overdetermination of contradictions throughout the structure. For Althusser, then, the real is indefinitely enmeshed in contradictions so that ideology can be said to produce what counts as reality; ideology, therefore, produces what only can be described as a reality effect, that is, a reality-in-effect.

But, if ideology produces what can be seen, thought, or believed as the reality of experience, as Althusser suggests it does, then ideology also must construct a subject as the point or the position of intelligibility, as a figure of authority. To put it in terms Antonio Gramsci provides,[37] ideology refers to the processes of constructing hegemony and counterhegemonies. It refers to the struggles out of which hegemony or a coherent ideological discourse arises for which a form of subjectivity is constructed as author(ity). For Althusser, then, ideology is not a matter of consciousness but of the unconscious; that is, ideology is lived as reality through the workings of a subject's unconscious desire. Thus, the feminist materialism derived from Althusser's revision of marxism focuses feminist criticism on the relationship of ideology, hegemony, subjectivity, unconscious desire, and discursive authority.

Materialist feminists draw on Lacanian psychoanalysis, developing it beyond Althusser's often misleading references to it, in order to explore the way fantasy and unconscious desire are brought into play in reading and writing cultural productions that constitute hegemony and counterhegemonies. They especially elaborate the relationship of unconscious desire, sexual identity, and sexual difference. Arguing, as Lacan does, that a subject-identity is never unified and that the failure of sexual identity informs unconscious fantasy with a play of sexual difference, materialist feminists explore the relationship of unconscious fantasy and the notion of a subject-in-process, a notion which in the late 1970s was becoming a point of departure for a historical materialism informed with a psychoanalytically oriented semiotics influenced by Lacan's rereading of Freud. As Rosalind Coward and John Ellis would explain it:

> It may seem strange to situate the relevance of Lacan's work in a close connection with the philosophy of dialectical materialism and the problem of ideology in Marxism, but it is precisely in drawing these connections that his re-reading of Freud has most significance. For it provides the foundation of a materialist theory of the subject in the social process, a subject constructed as always already included by those social processes, but never simply reducible to being a support. Lacan's subject is therefore this new subject of dialectical materialism: a subject in process.[38]

The Return to Freud and the Literary Turn in the Analysis of Ideology

Thus, in 1975, when Laura Mulvey's now classic essay "Visual Pleasure and Narrative Cinema" was first published, it not only initiated what became known as "feminist film theory." It also opened up discussion of the relationship of unconscious desire, sexual identity, and discursive authority in the construction of hegemony. Indeed, Mulvey's essay would be recognized as "transdiscursive," as D. N. Rodowick describes it, for the way it "set theoretical agendas that inaugurate[d] whole fields of investigation."[39]

Drawing on Freudian and Lacanian texts, Mulvey argues that "psychoanalytic theory" can be appropriated "as a political weapon, demonstrating the way the unconscious of patriarchal society has structured film form."[40] Making use of psychoanalysis, then, Mulvey proposes "to discover where and how the fascination of film is reinforced by preexisting patterns of fascination already at work within the individual subject and the social formations that have molded him."[41] She especially focuses on the scenarios of fetishism and voyeurism for the way they project onto the reader or writer, while simultaneously eliciting from them, unconscious fantasies pertaining to knowledge, especially to the mastering of self and other through knowledge based in vision.

Thus while Mulvey describes the cinematic apparatus as an institutionalized mechanism able to reproduce again and again "an illusion cut to the measure of desire,"[42] Annette Kuhn argues that the illusion of film, especially of classic Hollywood films, is taken as reality because film texts unconsciously position the viewer (the reader or writer) as the point of intelligibility:

> One of the marks of classic Hollywood cinema is the invisibility of its devices of meaning construction: the audience is on the whole not aware of processes of signification. . . . Because in dominant cinema meaning presents itself as "already there" in the film text, the viewing subject is positioned as recipient of apparently preconstructed meanings. This is the ground of the argument that it is the work of ideology to produce an appearance of wholeness and "already there-ness" on behalf of the subject.[43]

Thus, a difference between standpoint epistemologies and a feminist materialist analysis of ideology quickly becomes evident. The latter shifts feminist criticism to the analysis of form; it takes as its point of departure the forming and shaping of the subject in reading and writing, that is, in meaning construction generally. And if the capitalist processes of commodification, abstraction, and the disavowal of production are always already assumed, it is because the focus is on how the readers or writers become or resist becoming subjects of these very processes – how they are or are not fascinated with and through the form.

Thus, another way in which a materialist feminist criticism differs from standpoint epistemologies is announced with the notion of patterns of fascination or fantasies of unconscious desire already at work in the individual and in the social formation. That is to say, rather than seeking the origin or cause of women's oppression, moving from women's experiences to the relations of ruling, materialist feminists instead focus on the ideological content of form, the way form continually engages the reader or writer in ideology through eliciting already existing fantasies of unconscious desire that are condensed both in the individual and in the social formation. Thus, a feminist materialism assumes that an individual's knowledge of the world and of self are always constructed in unconscious desire – that is, through unconscious fantasies or patterns of fascination. There is, then, no direct knowledge of the world in experience. There is no subject outside of unconscious desire and, therefore, discourse.

But if materialist feminists treat the subject as always inside discourse, it is to propose a certain understanding of the relationship of marxism, discourse, ideology, and subjectivity that draws on post-structuralism, while especially focusing on the feminine figure. As Gayatri Chakravorty Spivak explains:

> If I can talk about the critique of the subject in Marx, it seems to me that [it is] that particular insight, that the agent of history is not the individual as constituted by society . . . What we have seen in Marxism since then is a move toward collectivity as against the individual. The critique of the subject then has been understood in that way. At worst it has become a party line, at best it has become a genuine desire to mobilize. Whereas a post-structuralist reading would also say there is something on the other side of the individual. That is to say, not a collectivity which takes you to macrological solutions which in the end do not lead to the ends that had been prescribed, but in fact the subject has another side which is caught within the textuality of ideological or historical production. So we look at the female subject, at the subject in the margins of the periphery, the subject where you find it really, in terms of its place, of its constitution. . . . It exists within a certain kind of hegemonic ideological constitution which it shares with the makers of the rationalist narrative.[44]

In a materialist feminist analysis, discourse and textuality refer to the organization of ideological production which is understood to be related to but relatively autonomous of the economic determination of the mode of production. Materialist feminists, therefore, offer a treatment of discourse and textuality that connects ideological production to "the symbolic order" and to the oedipus complex's imposition of sexual identity through which the subject enters the symbolic order, at least in Western, modern capitalism. Thus, Kaja Silverman argues that in Western, modern capitalism, oedipus becomes the dominant narrative fiction meant to subjugate the individual to the symbolic order and to align the symbolic order with the mode of production. Oedipus becomes the dominant narrative logic through which the ideological coherency of hegemony is shaped.[45]

Silverman therefore proposes that in cultural productions, (post) oedipal fantasies are elicited from and projected onto the reader or writer not only to interpellate them again and again as subjects of hegemony, but in doing so, to authorize only certain modes of reading reality. Silverman describes these fantasies as unconscious scenarios of "authorial desire,"[46] which constitute both the political unconscious of the social formation of Western, modern capitalism and the fantasmatic of the modern subject; that is:

> ... that unconscious fantasy or cluster of fantasies which structures not merely dreams and other related psychic formations, but object-choice, identity, and "the subject's life as a whole." The fantasmatic generates erotic tableaux or *combinatoires* in which the subject is arrestingly positioned – whose function is, in fact, precisely to display the subject in a given place. Its original cast of characters would seem to be drawn from the familial reserve, but in the endless secondary productions to which the fantasmatic gives rise, all actors but one are frequently recast. And even the one constant player may assume different roles on different occasions.[47]

Thus, feminist film theorists suggest that in Western, modern capitalism, cultural productions, such as film, are intelligible to the reader or writer because they put the reader's and writer's fantasmatic into play; but they also seek to fix the reader's and writer's unconscious desire through an oedipal logic of narrativity that means to align the reader and writer's fantasmatic with projected fantasies that finally figure the unified subject of authority as masculine.

That is, the oedipal logic of narrativity usually constructs authority in cultural productions – not only in film but also in legal, scientific, economic, and political discourses – by figuring the feminine both as an obstacle to knowing and as a hindrance to the continuation of the narrative, while the masculine is made to figure the subject who masters the obstacle and thereby brings the narrative to closure in the realization of an authorized knowledge – that is, knowledge of himself in self-identity and knowledge of his experience as reality. As Teresa De Lauretis puts it:

> Much as social formations and representations appeal to and position the individual as subject in the process to which we give the name of ideology,

the movement of narrative discourse shifts and places the reader, viewer, or listener in certain portions of the plot space. Therefore, to say that narrative is the production of Oedipus is to say that each reader – male or female – is constrained and defined within the two positions of a sexual difference thus conceived: male-hero-human, on the side of the subject; and female-obstacle-boundary-space, on the other.[48]

But still, while feminist film theorists focus on projected fantasies that privilege masculinity in the construction of the authority of hegemony, it is to insist that hegemony must be obtained by eliciting the unconscious desire of readers and writers. Thus, the feminist materialist analysis of ideology, which feminist film theorists propose, not only insists on the impossibility of separating reality from fantasy or experience from discourse. It also insists that unconscious desire cannot simply be reduced to the imposition of ideology. That is to say, for ideology to function in the construction of hegemony, the reader or writer must be (unconsciously) complicitous, although the reader or writer therefore also can be resistant.

Thus, Silverman suggests that both the resistances and complicities elicited from readers and writers be understood in terms of what Freud referred to as the "positive" and "negative" resolutions of oedipus that inform the subject's fantasmatic. Although a positive resolution of oedipus represents an alignment with the dominant narrative fiction, a negative resolution does not; thus, a negative resolution of oedipus may permit counterhegemonic resistances. As Silverman puts it:

> Although I have characterized the positive Oedipus complex as the result of a normative interpellation into the dominant fiction, it by no means represents the only possible psychic response to the ideology of the family. . . . the psyche can exceed the constraints of the positive oedipus complex in a variety of ways. There is perhaps no subjectivity which does not escape the straightjacket of that complex to some degree, if only by simultaneously inhabiting its negative counterpart.[49]

Indeed, it is its insistence on both the unconsciously motivated complicities with and resistances to hegemony that enables a feminist materialist analysis of ideology to resist a treatment of ideology that reduces it to an economic determinism. But it also is through insisting on the complicities and resistances of unconscious desire that a feminist materialism makes trouble for a feminist or women's standpoint epistemology. That is, by proposing that both the feminine subject and the masculine subject are constructed in unconscious desire and that feminine identity as well as masculine identity are divided in unconscious desire, a division that cannot simply be reduced to oppression, a feminist materialist analysis of ideology profoundly troubles the notions of identity and experience, so often assumed in feminist theorizing. As Jacqueline Rose puts it:

> Thus feminism asks psychoanalysis for an account of how ideologies are imposed upon subjects and how female identity is acquired, only to find that the concepts of fantasy and the unconscious rule any notion of pure imposition or full acquisition out of bounds. . . . Perhaps even more diffi-cult, as feminism turns to questions of censorship, violence and sado-masochism, psychoanalysis hands back to it a fundamental violence of the psychic realm – hands back to it, therefore, nothing less than the difficulty of sexuality itself. For if psychic life has its own violence; if there is an aggression in the very movement of the drives; if sexual difference, because of the forcing it requires, leaves the subject divided against the sexual other as well as herself or himself . . . , then there can be no analysis for women which sees violence solely as accident, imposition or external event.[50]

If, then, a women's standpoint epistemology would propose an alter-native form of knowing grounded in women's experience, a feminist materialist analysis of ideology not only calls into question any empirical envisioning of experience; it does so by arguing that experience as well as the subject of experience are always already shaped in unconscious desire. The subject always is divided in unconscious desire. And if a feminist standpoint proposes an alternative form of knowing grounded in women's unconscious relational structure, especially its seemingly characteristic resistance to dominance, a feminist materialist analysis of ideology proposes that identifications with the dominant authorial mas-culine figure are possible for both men and women. Or to put it another way, sexual identifications must be obtained again and again; they must be elicited again and again in terms of the unconscious desires of both men and women. There is no psychic structure characteristic of men in general or women in general.

But, if a feminist materialism thereby complicates any proposal for a unified subject of experience as well as any argument for a knowledge based directly in experience by insisting instead on the productivity of unconscious desire in the construction of the subject and experience, it also profoundly complicates psychoanalytic discourse. That is to say, in arguing for an analysis of the relationship of unconscious desire and hegemony which at the same time means to question the oedipal privileg-ing of masculinity, a feminist materialism necessarily becomes a feminist counterpsychoanalysis which points to the ways both Freud and Lacan's psychoanalytic accounts are complicitous with the dominant fiction's privileging of masculinity. As Silverman puts it:

Freud consequently makes it impossible to conceptualize the incest taboo outside the context of a phallocentric symbolic order. It emerges as the guarantee that the paternal legacy will be transmitted in an orderly way from father to son. Although he is less concerned with phylogenesis than with the ontogenesis of the subject, Lacan also equates culture with the Name-of-the-Father.[51]

Freud's and Lacan's accounts are complicitous with the dominant fiction's privileging of masculinity because they universalize what is perhaps only characteristic of a Western, modern capitalism; that is to say, it only may be in Western, modern capitalism that the incest taboo is conflated with the privileging of phallicity (or masculinity) as the figure of discursive authority. It only may be as the dominant fiction of Western, modern capitalism that oedipus is the medium by which ideologies of class, race, gender, nationality, ethnicity, and sexuality also are projected and introjected.[52]

Thus, Freud's and Lacan's psychoanalytic accounts are complicitous with the functioning of the dominant fiction in the construction of a hegemonic subject that not only is figured as masculine but also as white, heterosexual, and propertied. In order to be able both to identify and criticize the deployment of the dominant fiction in the authorizing of hegemony, a feminist counterpsychoanalysis must keep distinct, at least theoretically speaking, what Freud's and Lacan's psychoanalytic accounts conflate. As Silverman puts it:

> It is consequently necessary to hold at some theoretical distance from each other not only the Name-of-the-Father and the symbolic order, the symbolic order and the dominant fiction, the dominant fiction and the oedipus complex but the oedipus complex and the psyche.[53]

Thus, a feminist counterpsychoanalysis turns psychoanalysis back on itself. In doing so, it uncovers what Mulvey describes as "the unconscious of patriarchal society."[54] It reveals how femininity functions as a category in the discourse of Western, modern capitalism – how, in that discourse, femininity is an effect of erasing from the figure of conventional masculinity all limitations or divisions of subjectivity; how these limitations or divisions are signified instead as feminine and castrated. Thus, a feminist counterpsychoanalysis reveals how femininity has been made to exist "within a certain kind of hegemonic ideological constitution, which it shares with the makers of the rationalist narrative," as Spivak would put it.[55] That is to say, psychoanalysis, which itself is part of the rationalist narrativization of knowledge, if only as its productive negation, is reoriented by a feminist counterpsychoanalysis so to retrieve what the rationalist narrative has made of the feminine figure. And if the construction of a feminist counterpsychoanalysis thereby culminates the psycho-analytic project, a feminist counterpsychoanalysis also is challenged to further elaboration; that is, feminist materialism is opened up to postmodernity.

After all, the intimate relationship of a feminist counterpsychoanalysis with the development of film theory indicates the limitation of a feminist counterpsychoanalysis to that period from the late eighteenth century to the 1960s in which the knowledge-formation characteristic of the cinematic apparatus both rises to and falls from dominance. Thus, as other mass media – television and computerization – come to dominate as mass media communication technologies, they also demand reformu-lations of the relationship of subjectivity, fantasy, and unconscious desire in the construction of hegemony and counterhegemonies. So too, psycho-biographies now circulating inside and outside the West seemingly necessitate the development of a variety of psychoanalytic approaches that might treat fantasy and unconscious desire in relationship to differ-ences other than sexual difference – differences of race, class, gender, ethnicity, and nationality.

Thus, a certain feminist project, originating with gynocriticism and culminating both in a feminist or women's standpoint epistemology and a feminist counterpsychoanalysis, is shown to have functioned as a revalorization of the feminine figure of the oedipal narrative, refinding her for a counterhegemonic criticism of Western rationalism – its episte-mological and scientific elaborations. Nonetheless, this feminist project is itself part of Western rationalism and its privileging of white, propertied, heterosexual masculinity.[56] It is for this reason that this project, as it comes to its ends, is referred to as white, middle-class feminism.

Indeed, since the publication of *Money, Sex and Power*, Nancy Hartsock also has recognized that "too much feminist theory was written from a perspective in which white middle-class women were seen as the norm and women of color were excluded and devalued."[57] Then, by way of a criticism of Michel Foucault and Richard Rorty, Hartsock suggests that rather than a postmodern criticism which seems to celebrate differ-ence, what is needed instead is to place a feminist standpoint epistemol-ogy in alliance with what she describes as the "epistemologies of marked subjectivities."[58] In doing so, Hartsock proposes to correct what she reads to be the "despair" of the postmodern critique.

For Hartsock, then, what an alliance between a feminist standpoint epistemology and the epistemologies of other marked subjectivities can provide is a way to recover, from beneath the surface of false appear-ances, the real determinations of domination. Referring to the use by Women of Color of marvelous or magic realism, as well as to Gloria

Anzaldúa's discussion of *la facultad,* Hartsock seemingly assumes a one-to-one relationship between these ways of knowing and science, even empirical science, which after all is for Hartsock the tool of grasping the real beneath false appearances. But it is precisely the difference between science and these ways of knowing which is foregrounded in figuring the subject as Women of Color, African-American feminists, Third World feminists, and queer theorists.

That is to say, when these subjects speak, the deconstruction of the opposition of fantasy and reality, fiction and history, polemic and academic discourse, literary criticism and social science is only furthered. The poetry of Gloria Anzaldúa's text of criticism and the magic realism of the writings by Women of Color, as well as "the ancient wisdom" of an Afrocentric consciousness in African-American women's writings, would be better read not as science but as a speaking in various tongues – something different from but related to what has been called unconscious desire.[59]

Afterwords

What should not go unrecognized about Dorothy Smith's and Nancy Hartsock's works is the enormous effort required of these theorists in taking on, as they do, their own academic training as social scientists – to take on, especially as Hartsock does, those mostly male theorists whom women social scientists for so long have been made to read, to study, to take to heart, and without being invited to notice how these theorists said nothing or something worse than nothing about women and their lives; to take on, especially as Smith does, those theorists whose authority has depended on the very ideology their theories install – the ideology of the separate spheres; to take on those theorists who imagine their theories to be public discourse simply because they eschew what they mark as feminine, that is: the emotional, the particular, the irrational, the domestic; to take all of this on, as Smith and Hartsock do, in the name of women, on behalf of women, and in the hope of ending all domination.

Thus, not only do a feminist and a women's standpoint epistemology uncover the ideological content of the separation of the public and private spheres; they also undermine the notion of disinterested disciplinary knowledges which the ideology of the separate spheres means to support. But in doing so, both a feminist and a women's standpoint epistemology open up to a feminist materialism, which extends feminist criticism to an analysis of ideology, when the separation of the private and public spheres has all but lost its force and when the oppositions between fantasy and reality, fiction and history, polemic and academic discourse, literary criticism and social science are further collapsed. Indeed, by treating all production and consumption of knowledge in terms of an unconscious authorial desire organized by an oedipal logic, a feminist materialist analysis of ideology not only furthers the reinvention of the social and the literary, letting loose a disavowed authorial desire. A materialist feminist analysis of ideology also brings a certain feminist theorizing to its culmination, that is a feminist theorizing that works within the hegemonic, ideological constitution of a Western rationalist narrative.

Perhaps it is not surprising, then, that at the very same time that a certain feminist theorizing comes to its ends, the notion of the separate spheres also would be criticized: not for the way it informs differences between men and women, but for the way it shapes differences among women. As Aida Hurtado puts it:

> The contemporary notion that "the personal is political" identifies and rejects the public/private distinction as a tool by which women are excluded from public participation while the daily tyrannies of men are protected from public scrutiny. Yet the public/private distinction is relevant only for the white middle and upper classes since historically the American state has intervened constantly in the private lives and domestic arrangements of the working class. Women of Color have not had the benefit of the economic conditions that underlie the public/private distinction. Instead the political consciousness of women of Color stems from an awareness that the public is *personally* political.[60]

And if the irrelevancy of the public/private distinction for Women of Color also seems to call into question white feminists' fascination with Freud and psychoanalysis, nonetheless, the writings of Women of Color, Third World feminists, and African-American feminists privilege fantasy, poetry, and unconscious desire. Indeed, there is a continued search for ways to secure a protection of what is "inside." Certainly, Zora Neale Hurston's character, Janie, in becoming a self-defined African-American woman by realizing finally that "she had an inside and an outside . . . and how not to mix them," resonates for Women of Color, African-American feminists, and Third World feminists, the dream of self-definition.[61]

Notes

1   Heidi Hartmann, "The Unhappy Marriage of Marxism and Feminism: Toward A More Progressive Union," *Capital and Class*, 8 (1979), pp. 1–2.
2   For example, see Stanley Aronowitz, *The Crisis in Historical Materialism: Class, Politics and Culture in Marxist Theory* (New York: Praeger, 1981).

3 Zillah Eisenstein, "Developing a Theory of Capitalist Patriarchy and Socialist Feminism," in Zillah Eisenstein, *Capitalist Patriarchy and the Case for Socialist Feminism* (New York: Monthly Review Press, 1979), pp. 41–2.

4 Nancy Hartsock, *Money, Sex and Power: Toward a Feminist Historical Materialism* (Boston: Northeastern University Press, 1985), p. 84.

5 Ibid., p. 101.

6 Ibid., p. 50.

7 Ibid., p. 116.

8 Ibid., p. 118.

9 Ibid., p. 118.

10 Ibid., p. 118.

11 Ibid., p. 238.

12 Ibid., p. 242.

13 Ibid., p. 233.

14 Aronowitz, *The Crisis in Historical Materialism*, p. 87.

15 Hartsock, *Money, Sex and Power*, p. 145.

16 Dorothy Smith, *The Everyday World as Problematic: A Feminist Sociology* (Boston: Northeastern University Press, 1987), p. 3.

17 Ibid., p. 55.

18 Ibid., p. 55.

19 Ibid., p. 55.

20 Ibid., p. 55.

21 Ibid., p. 56.

22 Ibid., p. 83.

23 Ibid., p. 107.

24 Ibid., p. 81.

25 Ibid., p. 80.

26 Ibid., p. 107.

27 Ibid., p. 160.

28 Ibid., p. 154.

29 Ibid., p. 161.

30 Ibid., p. 161.

31 Ibid., pp. 154–5.

32 Ibid., p. 154. Other examples of Smith's analyses of everyday activities can be found in her *The Conceptual Practices of Power* (Boston: Northeastern University Press, 1990), and *Texts, Facts, and Femininity* (New York: Routledge, 1990).

33 Smith, *The Everyday World as Problematic*, p. 123.

34 Ibid., p. 161.

35 Louis Althusser, *For Marx*, translated by Ben Brewster (London: NLB, 1971), and *Lenin and Philosophy and Other Essays*, translated by Ben Brewster (New York: Monthly Review Press, 1977).

36 Karl Marx, "Preface to a Contribution to the Critique of Political Economy," in Robert Tucker (ed.), *The Marx Engels Reader* (New York: Norton, 1978), p. 4.

37   Antonio Gramsci, *Selections From the Prison Notebooks*, translated by Quentin Hoare and Geoffrey Nowell Smith (New York: International, 1971).

38   Rosalind Coward and John Ellis, *Language and Materialism* (London: Routledge & Kegan Paul, 1977).

39   D. N. Rodowick, "Individual Response," *Camera Obscura*, 20 (1990), pp. 269–74.

40   Laura Mulvey, "Visual Pleasure and Narrative Cinema," *Screen* 16 (1975), pp. 6–18.

41   Ibid., p. 6.

42   Ibid., p. 17.

43   Annette Kuhn, *Women's Pictures: Feminism and Cinema* (London: Routledge & Kegan Paul, 1982), pp. 52–3.

44   Spivak's remarks are from a 1984 interview, republished in Gayatri Chakravorty Spivak, *The Post-Colonial Critic: Interviews, Strategies, Dialogues*, edited by Sarah Harasym (New York: Routledge, 1990), pp. 27–8.

45   Kaja Silverman, *Male Subjectivity at the Margins* (New York: Routledge, 1992), pp. 29–35.

46   Kaja Silverman, *The Acoustic Mirror: The Female Voice in Psychoanalysis and Cinema* (Bloomington: Indiana University Press, 1988), p. 216.

47   Ibid., p. 216. Silverman takes the notion of the fantasmatic from J. Laplanche and J.-B. Pontalis, *The Language of Psycho-analysis*, translated by Donald Nicholson-Smith (New York: Norton, 1973).

48   Teresa De Lauretis, *Alice Doesn't: Feminism, Semiotics, Cinema* (Bloomington: Indiana University Press, 1984), p. 121.

49   Silverman, *Male Subjectivity at the Margins*, p. 40.

50   Jacqueline Rose, *Sexuality in the Field of Vision* (London: Verso, 1986), pp. 15–16.

51   Silverman, *Male Subjectivity at the Margins*, p. 37.

52   Ibid., p. 34.

53   Ibid., p. 40.

54   Mulvey, "Visual Pleasure and Narrative Cinema," p. 6.

55   Spivak, *The Post-Colonial Critic*, p. 28.

56   For further discussion of the relationship of psychoanalysis, feminist theory, and homosexuality, see ch. 6.

57   Nancy Hartsock, "Postmodernism and Political Change: Issues for Feminist Theory," *Cultural Critique*, 14 (1990), p. 15.

58   Ibid., p. 25.

59   For a fuller discussion of the writings of African-American feminists and Third World feminists, see chs 4 and 5.

60   Aida Hurtado, "Relating to Privilege: Seduction and Rejection in the Subordination of White Women and Women of Color," *Signs*, 14 (1989), p. 849.

61   Zora Neale Hurston, *Their Eyes Were Watching God* (Greenwich, CT: Fawcett, 1969), p. 63.

4

Engendering African-American Criticism

Arguing that ideologies of race, class, gender, and ethnicity "are always imbricated in crucial ways with core elements of the dominant fiction," Kaja Silverman also notes that "sometimes the imbrication is so profound that elements drawn from these ideologies actually become peripheral components of the dominant fiction over an extended period of time."[1] That is to say, while the dominant fiction primarily produces authority through the opposition of masculinity and femininity, it may be impossible to separate the opposition of femininity and masculinity from other ideologically constructed oppositions. Indeed, in *Black Feminist Thought: Knowledge, Consciousness, and the Politics of Empowerment* (1990), Patricia Hill Collins not only elaborates a criticism of male domination that focuses on the way the ideologies of race, gender, and class function together in the authorizing of hegemony. She also draws together the scholarship, thoughts, and actions of African-American women in order to establish what she describes as "the Black feminist intellectual tradition" – a tradition that would stand as a revision of white feminist thought.

Indeed, revisiting US history from enslavement to postmodern capitalism, African-American feminists throughout the 1980s not only have insisted that the figure of the woman constructed in white feminist theory uncritically depends on ideologies of race and class. African-American feminists also have revised the history of the women's movement from suffragism to the second wave of feminism. Of course, Kate Millett had commented on the racist and bourgeois character of the suffragist movement, especially the second generation of suffragists who aligned themselves with Southern racists when white men refused to support women's struggle for the franchise while, however, supporting the enfranchisement of Black men.[2] Still, in *Ain't I a Woman* (1981), bell hooks returns to the conflict between Black women and white women over suffrage, suggesting that just as in the political discourse of the nineteenth century, in twentieth-century political discourse, "the term 'woman' is synonymous with 'white women' and the term 'blacks' is synonymous with 'black men.'"[3]

If hooks argues that a racism characteristic of the nineteenth century still is characteristic of the relationship between white feminists and African-American feminists, she also explores male domination within the African-American community. As Michele Wallace had in *Black Macho and the Myth of the Superwoman* (1979), hooks indicts civil rights leaders and leading twentieth-century Black male writers for their sexist, if not misogynist, attitudes toward Black women.[4] But unlike Wallace, hooks urges a revaluation of Black women's lives, suggesting that Black women's experiences can shape a consciousness that is counterhegemonic. In *Feminist Theory: From Margin to Center* (1984), hooks argues:

> This lived experience may shape our consciousness in such a way that our world view differs from those who have a degree of privilege (however relative within the existing system). It is essential for continued feminist struggle that black women recognize the special vantage point our marginality gives us and make use of this perspective to criticize the dominant racist, classist, sexist hegemony as well as to envision and create a counter-hegemony.[5]

If, then, in *Black Feminist Thought* Patricia Hill Collins develops what in 1986 she first described as a Black women's standpoint epistemology, she also redresses the hegemonic images against which Black women have struggled and which still inform the racism of white feminism. By using "the domestic" to figure a transformation of Black women's marginality into an epistemological stance of "the outsider-within," Collins also valorizes Black women's experiences. As she puts it:

> Afro-American women have long been privy to some of the most intimate secrets of white society. Countless numbers of Black women have ridden buses to their white "families," where they not only cooked, cleaned, and executed other domestic duties, but where they also nurtured their "other" children, shrewdly offered guidance to their employers and frequently, became honorary members of their white "families." These women have seen white elites, both actual and aspiring, from perspectives largely obscured from their Black spouses and from these groups themselves.[6]

> On one level this insider relationship was satisfying to all concerned. Accounts of Black domestic workers stress the sense of self-affirmation the

women experienced at seeing white power demystified. But on another level these Black women knew that they could never belong to their white "families," that they were economically exploited workers and thus would remain outsiders. The result was a curious outsider-within stance, a peculiar marginality that stimulated a special Black women's perspective.[7]

In making the domestic a figure of criticism, Collins deconstructs the totalizing tendencies of white feminist thought; the figure of the domestic especially undermines the separation of the public and private spheres – the primary assumption of a feminist or women's standpoint epistemology and of gynocriticism as well.[8] Not only does the figure of the domestic deeply trouble Dorothy Smith's generalizing assumption that all women as a group do the work that maintains the relationships of ruling at the same time that they are excluded as a group from ruling. The figure of the domestic also profoundly disturbs Nancy Hartsock's generalizing assumption of a uniquely feminine psychic orientation toward nurturing and against all domination.

But, in pointing to the totalizing tendencies of white feminist thought, Collins also recognizes that a Black women's standpoint can only provide a partial way of knowing. Indeed, in its recognizing the partiality of all knowledge, a Black women's standpoint epistemology further undermines the distinction of fantasy and reality, fiction and history, polemic and academic discourse, literary criticism and social science. Indeed, Collins draws without distinction on literature, art, music, as well as on the thoughts of ordinary women, friends, relatives, and acquaintances in order to inform a Black women's standpoint epistemology with what she, borrowing from Michel Foucault, refers to as the subjugated knowledges of Black women.

Thus, the figure of the domestic not only refers to the capacity of a Black women's standpoint epistemology to offer a more adequate description of the reality of experience. It also refers to the power of a Black feminist intellectual tradition to incite creativity in the celebration of survival. Often the mother, the grandmother, the aunt, or the sister of the African-American feminist, the domestic figures a desire to honor the labor of surviving, passed on as "wisdom," from mother to daughter, from woman to woman. As a figure of hope and desire, the domestic is a productive fiction to frame a tradition of survival which enables the struggle against oppression.

Thus, I would suggest that the figure of the domestic finally returns a Black women's standpoint epistemology to the difference of desire within a woman, to the way unconscious desire informs the construction of an intellectual tradition and thereby makes questionable the very assumption of a Black women's standpoint epistemology. That is to say, the question arises as to whether a politics of empowerment can or should be grounded in an epistemology of experience, even a relativized epistemology of experience. Thus, Collins's construction of a Black women's standpoint epistemology only instigates further debate over identity, experience, and postmodern criticisms of the production and consumption of knowledge, including disciplinary knowledges.

Politicizing Knowledge, Empowering Consciousness

In constructing a feminist or women's standpoint epistemology both Hartsock and Smith figure the knower first as a mother/housekeeper and then as a social scientist – a marxist-feminist social scientist; in constructing a Black women's standpoint epistemology, Collins figures the knower first as a domestic and then as a Black feminist – an academic who is an "organic" intellectual. Drawing on Gramsci, Collins puts it this way:

> Academicians are the intellectuals trained to represent the interests of groups in power. In contrast, "organic" intellectuals depend on common sense and represent the interests of their own group. . . . The outsider-within position of Black women academicians encourages us to draw on the tradition of both our discipline of training and our experiences as Black women but to participate fully in neither.[9]

In placing the Black woman academic in the stance already figured by the domestic, Collins means to explore the troubled and troubling relationship between academic knowledge and Black women's experiences, while investing the marginal position of the Black woman academic with the capacity for criticism already claimed for the domestic. Indeed, it is the relationship between academic knowledge and Black women's experiences as well as the marginal position of the Black woman academic which urges the reclaiming of a tradition of Black feminist thought – itself a tradition of marginalized intellectuals whose works have been suppressed by various institutions, perhaps most significantly the academy itself.

Thus, for Collins the construction of a Black women's standpoint epistemology necessarily involves recovering the subjugated knowledges of Black women.[10] This not only means "discovering, reinterpreting, and, in many cases, analyzing for the first time the works of Black women intellectuals who were so extraordinary that they did manage to have their ideas preserved through the mechanism of mainstream scholarly discourse."[11] It also means "searching" for Black feminist thought "in alternative institutional locations and among women who are not commonly perceived as intellectuals."[12] Thus, Collins would enlarge Foucault's understanding of subjugated knowledge as a "disqualified" knowledge owing its "force to the harshness with which it is opposed,"[13] by including among Black women's subjugated knowledges "the long-standing, independent" tradition of Afrocentric thought.[14]

Thus, following Barbara Christian's claim that "people of color have always theorized – but in forms quite different from the Western form of abstract logic,"[15] Collins looks for a tradition of Black feminist thought where Christian finds theory: that is, in the narration of stories, riddles, and proverbs through which Black women have "speculated about the nature of life through pithy language, that unmasked the power relations of their world."[16] If, then, the African-American feminist draws on the everyday experience of Black women, it is because their experience is one of story-telling; Black women, to use Christian's terms, "have always been a race for theory."[17] Thus, when the Black feminist says "we" or "our," as Collins explains she will do in referring to the experiences of Black women, it is a "we" of story-tellers, theoreticians, often located outside the academy – musicians, vocalists, poets, novelists, artists, activists, church-goers, and teachers.

As an academic, then, the Black feminist urges a Black women's standpoint epistemology not so much as a method for adequately explaining the experiences of Black women but more as a method of recovering a tradition of subjugated knowledges. Indeed, if the Black feminist is to draw on the experiences of Black women, it is because these experiences are always already framed in a story-telling seeking "wisdom."[18] Thus, when Collins turns to explore the various responses to the "core themes" which characterize Black women's experiences, she especially focuses on those responses which cultivate a wise resistance to hegemony. If, then, Collins valorizes responses that emphasize an "interdependence of experience and consciousness," an "interdependence of thought and action," as well as "a struggle for self-definition," while resisting both sexual oppression and what she describes as "controlling images," it is because, for Collins, it is these responses which give shape and support to Black feminist thought. Indeed, for Collins these responses become the very characteristics of a Black women's standpoint epistemology, thereby folding within a Black women's standpoint the reclaimed tradition of Black feminist thought.

Thus, by focusing only on particular responses to what is characteristic of Black women's experiences, Collins also can argue that a Black women's standpoint epistemology is not limited to Black women. Resisting essentialist biological categories of identity, as well as essentialist sociological categories of a uniform experience, Collins proposes that not only may anyone advocate a Black women's standpoint epistemology, but not every Black woman does or will.[19] Following on Donna Haraway's discussion of subjugated knowledges, in which Haraway argues that "the standpoints of the subjugated" are not "innocent positions" and therefore "the positionings of the subjugated are not exempt from critical reexamination, decoding, deconstruction, and interpretation," Collins recognizes that subjugation, in itself, is not "grounds for an epistemology."[20]

If, then, the point of a Black women's standpoint epistemology is to uncover the subjugated knowledges of Black women, the task of the Black feminist is not only to more fully articulate what Black women know but to become especially engaged with the critical aspects of their knowing. As the outsider-within, the Black feminist is critic not only of her academic tradition but of Black women's experiences as well. Thus, Collins takes a certain posture in the debates over Black feminist literary criticism, begun with what perhaps served as its "manifesto," Barbara Smith's 1977 essay "Toward a Black Feminist Criticism," in which Smith argues for a literary criticism that not only recognizes the specificity of Black women's writing but also treats it with intellectual seriousness.

Decrying the fact that both Black male critics as well as white feminist literary critics had ignored or dismissed Black women writers, Smith insists that "a Black feminist approach to literature that embodies the realization that the politics of sex as well as the politics of race and class are crucially interlocking factors in the works of Black women writers is an absolute necessity."[21] But if Smith proposes further that there are commonalities across the writings of Black women – that Black women writers, Black women characters, and Black women critics share a unique Black female language and a Black female experience which can ground a feminist criticism, still other critics insist on the historical specificity of the variation in Black women's experiences and language use.[22]

Thus, complaining that "black feminist criticism has too frequently been reduced to an experiential relationship that exists between black women as critics and black women as writers who represent black women's reality,"[23] Hazel Carby not only expresses her disagreement with Christian's version of a Black feminist literary criticism, she also indicates her preference for a materialist analysis, or a historically specific criticism oriented to the way societies are "structured in dominance" through struggles over ideologies of class, race, and gender.[24] Just as hooks, in *Ain't I a Woman*, documents the historically specific interplay of racism and sexism in conditioning the Black female slave's experience, in *Reconstructing Womanhood: The Emergence of the Afro-American Woman Novelist*, Carby explores the way race, gender, and class ideologies informed "the cult of true womanhood" in the antebellum period of US history. She therefore proposes that:

> Ideologies of white womanhood were the sites of racial and class struggle which enabled white women to negotiate their subordinated role in relationship to patriarchy and at the same time to ally their class interest with men and against establishing an alliance with black women.[25]

A materialist analysis, then, not only argues that Black women's experiences differ; it also suggests that their experiences are profoundly related to the dominant fiction constituting and reconstituting hegemony. Indeed, it is in relationship to hegemony that Black women's experiences may appear more similar than they are; certainly subjugated knowledges owe at least some of their shape to their repression in the construction of hegemony, that is, to the force with which they are opposed. Thus, if Collins too prefers a materialist analysis in her exploration of the core themes characteristic of Black women's experience, she also reveals Black women's ongoing concern with the inheritance of hegemonic constructions of womanhood.

That is to say, if Carby argues that to emerge as novelists, nineteenth-century Black women writers "had to define a discourse of black womanhood which would not only address their exclusion from the ideology of true womanhood but . . . would also rescue their bodies from a persistent association with illicit sexuality,"[26] Collins also shows again and again that Black women's experiences are still enmeshed in their confrontation with controlling images, with their struggle against them for self-definition. Collins's analysis of Black women's experiences, then, points, if at times inadvertently, to the intimacy of experience and discourse, as does any materialist analysis focused on a criticism of hegemony.

The Controlling Images in the Experience of Black Women

Thus, the political economic history with which Collins begins her treatment of the core themes characteristic of Black women's lives not only will have its counterpart in an analysis of the controlling images of the mammy, the matriarch, and the Jezebel. It also will be necessary for Collins to adjust the very images which inform political economic analyses, already established in male scholarship as well as in white feminist scholarship. Collins argues, then, that neither the class conflict model nor the status attainment model adequately addresses Black women's class position. Since Black women's families are often not two-parent nuclear and their labor is not always paid labor, the status attainment model, which usually focuses on the male family member's job, is insufficient. The conflict model also fails because it has not attended to the intersection of race and gender, while emphasizing paid labor in the shaping of class position.[27]

Collins also undermines feminist political economic analyses. Outlining a history of Black women's experiences of work and family, from enslavement to post-Second World War America, she calls into question the assumption of the separation of the public and private spheres that underlies much feminist theory. Not only does Collins reveal how the assumption of the separate spheres is more characteristic of the lives of middle- and upper middle-class white women, she also reviews various sets of data which show how both race and gender inform the ideological construction of the separate spheres, and therefore how race as well as gender also shape white women's experiences of work and family. Thus, Collins begins the history of Black women's work and family lives in the period of enslavement.

Indeed, it was enslavement which changed African women's work and family lives, since before enslavement, African women combined work and family life. But, with enslavement, women not only were made to work for the benefit of their owners but even their reproduction was harnessed for the increase of the slave population. In the period from emancipation to the migration of Blacks to cities of both the North and the South, Collins argues that women either continued to work as field hands or as domestics. With increasing urbanization, more and more women worked as domestics, although increasingly as day workers, and more and more men worked in manufacturing. Still, in contrast to white communities, which were shaped more quickly by the penetration of the exchange-based marketplace into everyday life, African-American communities, for the most part, remained places of collective efforts and communal child care, as women continued to work.[28]

But after the Second World War, with the loss to urban manufacturing and the shift to service occupations, the African-American community became more stratified by social class. Yet, as Collins argues, all classes continued to experience racism. Reviewing the conditions of everyday life for the middle and working classes as well as for those African-Americans living below the official poverty line – that is, one third of African-Americans, Collins notices that although the number of Black women in the professions increases, "the alternative open to past generations of Blacks – intact marriages based on reasonably steady, adequate paid jobs for Black men and reliable yet lesser paid jobs for Black women – is less available in the advanced capitalist welfare state."[29]

Thus, there is a growth of female-headed households, especially marked among the poor. And with the dismantling of the welfare state, Collins argues that more of the families headed by Black women are poor. What Collins finds most alarming, then, is the change in communal child care, especially among poor Black women, as the "networks of the slave era, the extended family arrangements of the rural South, the importance of grandmothers in child care, and even the recreation of Black community structures during the first wave of urbanization seem to be eroding . . ."[30] Thus, Collins brings the discussion of political economy to a close on an ominous note, recognizing that the differences of class have the potential to instigate "negative relations . . . among Black women."[31]

If once middle-class Black women worked "on behalf of 'race uplift' and fostered racial solidarity among all African-American women," Collins proposes that the challenge now is for Black feminists "to rearticulate these new and emerging patterns of institutional oppression that differentially affect middle-class and working-class Black women."[32] But, rather than further detailing the differences of lived oppression, Collins instead takes up the task of encouraging Black feminists to focus on racial solidarity through "race uplift;" she not only would turn to the ways in which the ideological construction of hegemony informs gender, racial, and class oppression but also to the ways Black women have countered hegemony in their struggle for self-definition. Thus, without a critical assessment of her own discursive construction of political economic "facts," Collins makes use of these facts to unsettle the ideology of the separate spheres, making possible a reformulation of the analysis of hegemony by installing a tradition of Black women's struggle against controlling images.

But if, in her ideological analysis of controlling images, Collins would draw upon, while underwriting, the strength and endurance of Black women, the difficulty she confronts is the contradictory position that historically has been fashioned for the Black woman in the hegemonic construction of white, propertied, heterosexual masculinity. That is to say, if the very notion of womanhood historically has been defined as Carby suggests it has, so that the strength and endurance of Black women would be the very condition of their exclusion from the definition of womanhood, then to valorize Black women's everyday lives requires something different from what white feminist theorists have done in making visible the privatized labor of white women in order to valorize their strength. Indeed, Collins suggests that Black women already suffer overexposure; the objectification of the Black woman, the insistence in making visible her sexuality as well as her strength and resilience, seem only to make her into a figure less human, animalistic or more "natural."[33]

Thus, what Collins makes central to her analysis of ideology is the contradictions which the figure of the Black woman historically has been made to contain in the construction of hegemonic masculinity. Starting with enslavement and the antebellum period of US history, Collins draws on Carby's analysis of this historical period and focuses on the way the interplay of images of Black and white women enabled an ideological imposition of "piety, purity, submissiveness and domesticity" as the seemingly natural characteristics of true womanhood. As Carby suggests, it is especially because white women's lives often were not in keeping with the ideology of true womanhood, that the comparisons between white and Black women were necessary to make the ideology a prism through which women understood their realities.[34] Thus, the imagined fragility of the white woman was contrasted with an image of the Black woman, whose strength and ability to bear fatigue was made to appear more masculine than feminine. Hooks, too, points out that "while black men were not forced to assume a role colonial American society regarded as 'feminine,' black women were forced to assume a 'masculine' role."[35]

Thus, Carby notices that even the slave narratives written by Black men did little to contradict convention about feminine sexuality. Focused on the denigration of their manhood, they figure the Black woman as a victim of the white patriarch's sexual abuse: "not just in her own right as a figure of oppression but . . . linked to a threat to, or denial of, the manhood of the male slave."[36] If slave narratives by women did show Black women as resisting but feminine, often horribly abused but surviving, the image which these narratives conveyed, of the strong, nonsubmissive Black female, eventually led to other condemning images, such as the black matriarch.[37] Collins argues that "From an elite white male standpoint, the matriarch is essentially a failed mammy, a negative stigma applied to those African American women who dared to violate the image of the submissive, hard-working servant."[38]

But, if the image of the mammy was made to figure the "part of woman that white southern America was profoundly afraid of," the matriarch also can be understood in terms of white femininity. Thus, Collins points out that the thesis of the Black matriarch "as an overly aggressive unfeminine woman" became a central controlling image in Black women's lives just at the same time white feminists were criticizing American patriarchy.[39] If for Collins, then, the Black matriarch was meant to image "what can go wrong if white patriarchal power is challenged," the image also obfuscated a complex political economic shift which afforded Black women "basic political and economic protections from a greatly expanded welfare state," allowing them to reject the subsistence-level exploitative jobs held by their parents and grandparents.[40] Thus, Collins argues that the images of the welfare mother and the Jezebel were joined to that of the matriarch in order to focus the images of Black women on sexuality, inciting the demand for its control. Altogether, then, the image of the mammy, the matriarch, the welfare mother, and the Jezebel have operated as a nexus of controlling images that blame Black women – their mothering and their sexuality, for all that threatens the lives and well-being of African-Americans. At the same time, this nexus of images shores up the hegemonic definition of white, heterosexual, propertied masculinity.

The Matrix of Resistance

But, if Collins reviews the images that historically have confined Black women's lives, it is to underscore how Black women's lives have been profoundly characterized by a necessity to resist these controlling images. As she puts it:

> The controlling images applied to Black women are so uniformly negative that they almost necessitate resistance if Black women are to have any positive self-images. For Black women, constructed knowledge of self emerges from the struggle to reject controlling images and integrate knowledge deemed personally important, usually knowledge essential to Black women's survival.[41]

Collins not only proposes that Black women's resistance to controlling images is essential to their self-definition but that Black women's self-definition, therefore, is essential to a Black feminist intellectual tradition. For Collins, then, the struggle for self-definition not only involves questioning "what has been said about African-American women but the credibility and intentions of those possessing the power to define."[42] Thus, the struggle for self-definition "reframes the entire dialogue from one protesting the technical accuracy of an image . . . to one stressing the power dynamic underlying the very process of self-definition, itself."[43]

But if deconstructing "the power to define" is one side of Black women's struggle for self-definition, Collins also argues that each woman must first want "to make the journey toward finding the voice of empowerment."[44] A Black women's standpoint epistemology, then, models a way of knowing that is itself characterized by the knower's struggle between "internally defined images of self" and her "objectification as the Other,"[45] a struggle in which "consciousness" is privileged as a "sphere of freedom."[46] For Collins this personal search for inner strength and self-identity involves returning Black feminist thought to the mother–daughter relationship and to re-envisioning Black women's relationships – a return to what hooks describes as the "homeplace."[47] Thus, Collins turns to a discussion of Black women and motherhood, beginning with June Jordan's words which bring Black feminists together with their mothers in the figure of the domestic:

> Just yesterday I stood for a few minutes at the top of the stairs leading to a white doctor's office in a white neighborhood. I watched one Black woman after another trudge to the corner, where she then waited to catch the bus home. These were Black women still cleaning somebody else's house or Black women still caring for somebody else's sick or elderly, before they came back to the frequently thankless chores of their own loneliness, their own families. And I felt angry and I felt ashamed. And I felt, once again, the kindling heat of my hope that we, the daughters of these Black women, will honor their sacrifice by giving them thanks. We will undertake, with pride, every transcendent dream of freedom made possible by the humility of their love.[48]

In "honoring our mothers' sacrifice," Collins would focus on what Black women describe as their mothers' efforts to protect their daughters from racial, sexual, and class oppression. Pointing to the specific struggle for survival that Black mothers and their daughters share, Audre Lorde for example remarks:

> All mothers see their daughters leaving. Black mothers see it happening as a sacrifice through the veil of hatred hung like sheets of lava in the path way before their daughters. All daughters see their mothers leaving. Black girls see it happening through a veil of threatened isolation no fire of trusting pierces.[49]

Thus, Collins also points to the way Black mothers, often "strong disciplinarians and overly protective," can complicate the mother–daughter relationship with their efforts.[50] Again Lorde gives an example of the complications that are enfolded in the daughter's relationship to her mother:

> My mother taught me to survive from a very early age by her own example. Her silence also taught me isolation, fury, mistrust, self-rejection and sadness. My survival lay in learning how to use the weapons she gave me, also, to fight against those things within myself unnamed. And survival is the greatest gift of love. Sometimes, for Black mothers, it is the only gift possible, and tenderness gets lost. My mother bore me into life as if etching

an angry message into marble. Yet I survived the hatred around me because my mother made me know, by oblique reference, that no matter what went on at home, outside shouldn't oughta be the way it was. But since it was that way outside, I moved in a fen of unexplained anger that encircled me and spilled out against whomever was closest that shared those hated selves. Of course I did not realize it at the time. That anger lay like a pool of acid deep inside me, and whenever I felt deeply, I felt it attaching itself in the strangest places. Upon those as powerless as I.[51]

If those mothers, who are focused on the survival of their daughters, often "have neither the time nor the patience for affection," there also are mothers troubled by addictions, as well as mothers "who lack preparation or desire for mothering."[52] Thus, Collins concludes that side by side, within the African-American community, there are women who "view motherhood as a truly burdensome condition that stifles their creativity, exploits their labor and makes them partners in their own oppression."[53] There also are others who "see motherhood as providing a base for self-actualization, status in the black community and a catalyst for social activism."[54] But, even while there are contradictory positions on mothering among Black women Collins emphasizes the nurturing aspects of Black women; she does so by drawing attention to "othermothers," a network of women who care for one another's children, even when they are not blood children but rather are what Carol Stack describes as "fictive kin."[55]

Just as hooks, in remembering her grandmother's house in the rural South, would describe a "homeplace" as a place of women – "their special domain, not as property, but as places where all that truly mattered in life took place – the warmth and comfort and shelter, the feeding of our bodies, the nurturing of our souls,"[56] Collins treats mothering in terms of a supportive community of women. But if, as Collins also suggests, the communal form of child care actually is eroding in urban areas and especially among poor Black women, then the figure of the othermother not only refers to the specific history of Black women's mothering; the othermother also is a figure of desire or "yearning," as hooks might put it.

Thus, if the figure of the othermother both expresses and fulfills the desire of Black feminists to honor the sacrifice of their mothers, the humility of their love, or what hooks describes as their "struggle in the midst of suffering,"[57] it also informs a vision of the future with a yearning for the homeplace. It is this vision and yearning which are at play, then, in the reclaiming of a Black feminist intellectual tradition, especially in founding a Black women's literary tradition – what Alice Walker describes as a search for "our mothers' gardens," thereby making grandmothers, quilt-makers, rootworkers, and gardeners into a literary matrilineage, othermothers-of-the-mind.[58]

Thus, while for hooks a yearning for the homeplace, especially when reminiscent of the folk of the rural South, is not a mere matter of nostalgia but rather a response to "extreme fragmentation and alienation,"[59] nonetheless, in a rereading of Nella Larsen's *Quicksand* (1928), Carby emphasizes the historical specificity of the construction of "the folk" in relationship to the establishment of literary traditions of Black writers generally and Black women writers in particular. As she puts it:

> But after World War I, the large-scale movement of black people into the cities of the North meant that intellectual leadership and its constituencies fragmented. No longer was it possible to mobilize an undifferentiated address to "the black people" once an urban black working class was established. This movement of masses of rural black southern workers destined to become an urban proletariat was not immediately represented in fiction but there was a distinct shift in who was represented as "the people." One possibility, in fiction, was that "the people" were represented as a metaphorical "folk," which in its rural connotations avoided and ignored the implication of the presence of black city workers.[60]

For Carby, then, the "search for a tradition of black women writers" also has followed the pattern of representing "the rural folk as bearers of Afro-American history and preservers of Afro-American culture."[61] Thus, Carby proposes that the literary tradition from Alice Walker back to Zora Neale Hurston not only privileges the folk but, in doing so, "has effectively marginalized the fictional urban confrontation of race, class and sexuality . . ."[62] And if Larsen's *Quicksand* is both precursor and representative of a marginalized tradition including Ann Petry, Dorothy West, Gwendolyn Brooks, and Toni Morrison, what seems especially important about this tradition is its representation of the female protagonist as "a sexual being," as a woman in a struggle over sexual desire, as well as race and class.[63]

For Carby, then, the marginalization of this tradition refers back to the nineteenth century, when Black women writers deflected the focus from female sexuality and desire in response to the hegemonic images of Black women's sexuality as excessive, even animalistic. Indeed, hooks even points to the limited treatment of sexual desire in Walker's *The Color Purple*. Offering different reasons than Carby might, hooks nonetheless argues that "Ultimately Walker constructs an ideal world of true love and commitment where there is no erotic tension – where there is no sexual desire or sexual pleasure."[64] As hooks explains:

Walker upholds the promise of an intact heterosexual bond with a relational scenario wherein the point of intimate connection between coupled male and female is not the acting out of mutual sexual desire for one another, but the displacement of that desire onto a shared object – in this case, Shug. Given such a revised framework for the establishment of heterosexual bonds, sex between Shug and Celie does not threaten male–female bonding or affirm the possibility that women can be fulfilled in a life that does not include intimate relationships with men.[65]

If by raising questions of eroticism in general and women's sexual pleasure in particular, hooks attempts to transfer the relationship of self-definition and sexual desire from a nineteenth-century context to a late twentieth-century one, Collins, however, would hesitate to explore the relationship of motherhood, sexual desire, and the inner struggle for self-definition or self-authorship. Instead, Collins treats sexuality primarily in terms of the sexual violation and the sexual exploitation of Black women, especially in pornography and prostitution. In doing so, Collins makes it less possible to critically reflect on the relationship of sexual desire, a tradition of Black feminist thought, and a Black women's standpoint epistemology of experience.

Sexual Desire and the Return of the Literary

Collins treats the sexuality of Black men and of Black women as a matter of the internalization of controlling images. Drawing a connection from the display of the enslaved Black woman on the auction block to the exhibition in the nineteenth century of Sarah Bartmann, the so-called Hottentot Venus, to the continued display in Paris of her genitalia and buttocks, Collins suggests that the racialization of sexuality has been central not only to science, anthropology for example, but also to pornography and advertising from the nineteenth century to the present. Thus Collins proposes:

> The alleged superiority of men to women is not the only hierarchical relationship that has been linked to the putative superiority of the mind to the body. Certain "races" of people have been defined as being more bodylike, more animallike, and less godlike than others. . . . Race and gender oppression may both revolve around the same axis of disdain for the body . . .[66]

Collins also treats homophobia, the mistreatment of lesbians, and the sexual abuse of Black women by Black men in terms of the internalization of controlling images. Thus, although Collins joins with other Black women in breaking "the conspiracy of silence," refusing to excuse "abuse as an inevitable consequence of the racism Black men experience,"[67] she nonetheless makes use of Audre Lorde's words in order to suggest that internalized structures of violence and domination are "that piece of the oppressor which is planted deep within each of us."[68] Therefore, Collins concludes that "sexuality and power on the personal level become wedded to the sex/gender hierarchy on the social structural level in order to ensure the smooth operation of race, gender, and class oppression."[69]

But without addressing how the internalization of controlling images is related to sexual desire "on the personal level" or how subjectivity or the personal are constructed in relationship to sexual desire, Collins risks reducing sexuality, particularly Black women's sexuality, to oppression, if not victimization. Collins enacts what Hortense Spillers proposes when arguing that the discourse on sexuality belongs to the empowered, that is, to white feminists who as women are relatively protected in comparison to Black women.[70] Thus, Spillers suggests that not only does the history of Black women's captivity continue to deny them a voice in the discourse of sexuality. But so does a subtle use of textual reference in the white feminist discourse on sexuality. As she puts it:

> My point is that the feminist analytical discourse that women engage in different ways and for different reasons must not only ascertain vigil over its procedures, but must also know its hidden and impermissible origins. I am remembering a folksay from my childhood, and to introduce it seems relevant to what I am driving at: "Mama's baby, papa's maybe." In other words, to know the seductions of the father and *who*, in fact, the father is might also help to set us free, or to know wherein we occasionally speak when we have least suspected it. Whether we are talking about sexuality, or some other theme we would identify this process of categorical aligning with prior acts of the text as the subtle component of power that bars black women, indeed, women of color, as a proper subject of inquiry from the various topics of contemporary feminist discourse.[71]

And yet, Spillers' own accounts of Black women's sexuality, like more recent readings of Black women's writings, Toni Morrison's especially, do play with "prior acts of the text," especially with psychoanalytic accounts of unconscious sexual desire, pushing psychoanalysis into contexts that can only deeply trouble it, even moving it beyond oedipal or anti-oedipal logics into relationship with what Spillers describes as a maternalism that does not reproduce mothering; that is, a maternalism still caught in a history of captivity which denied both Black women and men their parental rights, their parental function.[72] But, in *Black Feminist*

Thought, neither psychoanalysis nor a feminist counterpsychoanalysis are engaged, not even as objects for critical revision. While referring to Lorde's proposal that the erotic is a "replenishing and provocative force . . . , a measure between the beginnings of our sense of self and the chaos of our strongest feelings,"[73] Collins nonetheless does not elaborate the productivity of the erotic, its replenishing and provocative force. Collins emphasizes consciousness as a sphere of freedom but leaves underdeveloped the relationship of consciousness, the erotic, and unconscious desire.

Thus, in her treatment of the validity of knowledge in relationship to a Black women's standpoint epistemology, Collins returns to the authority of experience, leaving aside the relationship of a Black women's standpoint epistemology and the desire for a Black feminist intellectual tradition. And even though Collins differs with those standpoint epistemologies that are "rooted in a Marxist positivism," and that "suggest that the oppressed allegedly have a clearer view of 'truth' than their oppressors because they lack the blinders created by the dominant group's ideology,"[74] she nevertheless seems finally to privilege experience, especially the experience of oppression. Not only does Collins propose that "those individuals who have lived through the experiences about which they claim to be experts are more believable and credible,"[75] she even attributes a certain innocence to the subject of experience, if only inadvertently, with the autobiographical narrative with which she frames a Black women's standpoint epistemology.

Thus, in the preface to *Black Feminist Thought*, Collins introduces a Black women's standpoint epistemology with a personal story that employs the generic characteristics of the autobiographical narrative – from the loss of innocence in experience to the recovery of voice and self-definition in the authorization of one's own story. Collins, then, begins *Black Feminist Thought* by taking the reader to her childhood – "When I was five years old, I was chosen to play Spring in my preschool pageant. Sitting on my throne, I proudly presided over a court of children portraying birds, flowers, and the other, 'lesser' seasons."[76]

And if Collins's Spring would blossom with the love and support of the grown-ups, who told her "how vital my part was and congratulated me on how well I had done,"[77] the importance of her thoughts, feelings, and accomplishments in the eyes of these grown-ups soon was overshadowed. Starting "in adolescence," Collins increasingly was "the 'first,' or 'one of the few,' or the 'only' African-American and/or woman and/or working-class person in my schools, communities, and work settings."[78] Yet, as Collins's world expanded, she nevertheless felt herself "growing smaller," and therefore "became quieter and eventually was virtually silenced."[79] If for Collins, then, *Black Feminist Thought* reflects an "on-going struggle to regain my voice,"[80] the voice which is finally recovered is "the voice of Spring," an "honest, genuine, and empowering" voice.

Thus, Collins's autobiographical framing of a Black women's stand-point epistemology refers the voice of self-definition back to someone seemingly innocent, who knows nothing yet of racism, sexism, class oppression, or sexual desire and who only learns these in the post-adolescent world, beyond family, friends, and acquaintances – beyond the homeplace. But if Collins's autobiographical framing only oversim-plifies the very complexities which she actually puts into play in her construction of a Black women's standpoint epistemology, nonetheless, it is the autobiographical which troubles a Black women's standpoint epistemology with the question of desire: a question of the relationship of the desire for innocence and the reclaiming of a Black feminist intellec-tual tradition.

Indeed, in her discussion of autobiography, hooks proposes that auto-biography is not a matter of recapturing a lost innocence. It is a matter of returning to what was not innocent at all, that is, "the wounds and sorrows of my childhood."[81] Thus, for hooks, writing autobiography is not only a struggle against domination. It also is a struggle with family, "the remembered scoldings and punishments when mama heard me saying something to a friend or stranger that she did not think should be said."[82] There is, then, a tension in autobiography, between wanting to die and wanting to live – a division of desire in subjectivity itself. As hooks puts it:

> To me, telling the story of my growing up years was intimately connected with the longing to kill the self I was without really having to die. . . . I wanted to be rid of the girl who was always wrong, always punished, always subjected to some humiliation or other, always crying, the girl who was to end up in a mental institution because she could not be anything but crazy or so they told her. She was the girl who sat a hot iron on her arm pleading with them to leave her alone, the one who wore her scar as a brand marking her madness.[83]

If, for hooks, writing autobiographically finally means that "this death in writing was to be liberatory," a way "not to forget the past but to break its hold,"[84] nonetheless remembering her childhood gives to hooks's memories "a surreal, dreamlike style which made me cease to think of them as strictly autobiographical because it seemed that myth, dream and reality had merged."[85] As hooks explains it:

> Often I felt as though I was in a trance at my typewriter, that the shape of a particular memory was decided not by my conscious mind but by all

that is dark and deep within me, unconscious but present. It was the act of making it present, bringing it into the open, so to speak, that was liberating.[86]

Thus, hooks adjusts her definition of autobiography to one which accounts for the productivity of the psyche or unconscious desire: "autobiography is a very personal story telling – a unique recounting of events not so much as they have happened but as we remember and invent them."[87] And if what is dark and deep within her could be liberating for hooks, she nonetheless is left with the question as to "why childhood wounds become for some folk an opportunity to grow, to move forward rather than backward in the process of self-realization."[88]

If, then, self-definition is to be a central aspect of a Black women's standpoint epistemology, its autobiographical framing finally evokes the indeterminacy of unconscious desire and raises the question of the relationship of unconscious desire to the authority of experience. Thus, a Black women's standpoint epistemology is returned to its relationship to desire, elaborated as the desire for a Black feminist intellectual tradition, a desire for the return to the mother–daughter relationship, a desire for the return to the othermothers of the mind – to the domestic. A Black women's standpoint epistemology is thereby returned to the fictiveness of its subject, the fictiveness of the experiential subject, even though Collins is hesitant to recognize the subject of a Black women's standpoint as such – a hesitancy related to a resistance among some Black feminists to embrace a critique of essentialism without reservation.

Whereas the deconstruction of ideologies of race, class, and gender always involve some de-essentializing of categories, at least those of race, class, and gender, still Black feminists, for the most part, have been reluctant to embrace those postmodern criticisms of essentialism which generally call into question notions of identity and experience. As hooks explains it:

The unwillingness to critique essentialism on the part of many African-Americans is rooted in the fear that it will cause folks to lose sight of the specific history and experience of African-Americans and the unique sensibilities and culture that arise from that experience. An adequate response to this concern is to critique essentialism while emphasizing the significance of "the authority of experience."[89]

But, since the authority of experience usually is underwritten by an autobiographical accounting of the subject, hooks's own remarks about autobiography suggest that to articulate the authority of experience with a critique of essentialism can only be possible if, at the same time, the very forms of writing and representing the subject of experience are submitted to ongoing critical self-reflection. Indeed, when hooks finally does endorse postmodern criticism, it is in recognition of how it allows for a politically self-reflective aesthetics "that continually opposes re-inscribing notions of 'authentic' black identity."[90]

For hooks, a self-critical approach also allows for a shift of African-American feminist criticism to the study of popular culture, especially the mass-mediated forms of writing and representation. It offers an opportunity to recognize the differences among members of the Black community, while allowing "a critical exchange" between the Black feminist critic and "the uneducated poor, the black underclass." As hooks puts it:

> Much postmodern engagement with culture emerges from the yearning to do intellectual work that connects with habits of being, forms of artistic expression, and aesthetics that inform the daily life of writers and scholars as well as a mass population. On the terrain of culture, one can participate in critical dialogue with the uneducated poor, the black underclass who are thinking about aesthetics. One can talk about what we are seeing, thinking, or listening to; a space is there for critical exchange. It's exciting to think, write, talk about, and create art that reflects passionate engagement with popular culture, because this may very well be "the" central future location of resistance struggle, a meeting place where new and radical happenings can occur.[91]

Thus, hooks would orient the Black feminist intellectual tradition toward a criticism of the mass-mediated forms of culture and knowledge production. Criticizing white feminist film theorists for generally ignoring the question of race in their analysis of dominant forms of knowledge production and for specifically ignoring the way Black women are figured in the construction of white women's privilege,[92] hooks also notices that African-American critics "have made few, if any, revolutionary interventions in the area of race and representation,"[93] even though such interventions seem necessary. As hooks puts it:

> There is a direct and abiding connection between the maintenance of white supremacist patriarchy in this society and the institutionalization via mass media of specific images, representations of race, of blackness that support and maintain the oppression, exploitation, and overall domination of all black people.[94]

Thus, hooks urges Black feminists to intervene into the field of film studies particularly, and cultural studies generally, in order to ensure that "cultural studies be linked to a progressive radical cultural politics."[95]

But, orienting Black feminist thought to the criticism of hegemonic forms of writing and representation only makes the question of the relationship of writing or representational form to a Black women's standpoint epistemology even more pressing. That is to say, the necessity of grounding a politics of empowerment in an epistemology of experience is raised for question and specifically in terms of writing and representational form. Indeed, it is questions about representational form, the ethnographic form especially, which when raised by Third World feminists in the construction of a post-colonial criticism will move feminist criticism to a politics of form, that is, to the practical political and personal effects of being represented as "the other" of disciplinary discourses.

Afterwords

If already in the 1982 collection of essays *All the Women Are White, All the Blacks Are Men, But Some of Us Are Brave* both Patricia Bell Scott[96] and Elizabeth Higginbotham[97] would point to the racist and sexist categories of social science, especially focusing on sociology, in *Black Feminist Thought* Collins goes further; *Black Feminist Thought* challenges "the basic process used by the powerful to legitimate their knowledge claims" and thereby calls into question "the content of what currently passes as truth."[98] And if among the powerful, Collins, like other Black feminists, includes white feminist theorists, it not only is to indict white feminists who have failed to take the differences among women fully into account in their analysis of patriarchy. It also is to recognize the academy as a primary agency of power/knowledge in which white women have acquired privilege, albeit a relative one.

Thus, Black feminist theorists have urged white feminists to address the construction of "whiteness" in authorizing knowledge. But, as Mary Ann Doane argues, the task of understanding racial difference may be difficult for a white feminist critic, "when her social regime is constituted as the denial or evacuation of racial identity, when whiteness aspires to signify that it is color-less, absence, no race at all."[99] The task of deconstructing whiteness also may be distasteful because of the reprehensible characteristics of whiteness. As Doane puts it:

> There is nothing essential about the racial identity of the white woman, nor is there anything in it to embrace or to invest with pride. There are often compelling political reasons for the black's espousal of blackness, but this is not the case for the white's relationship to whiteness. To espouse a white racial identity at this particular historical moment is to align oneself with white supremacists.[100]

But then, deconstructing the notion of whiteness, no matter how difficult and distasteful, may be one of the primary ways for white women to resist white supremacy. Indeed, white feminists have begun to contribute to what Elizabeth Abel describes as "the racialization of whiteness,"[101] and to what Teresa De Lauretis calls a process of "dis-identification"[102] – a process which Biddy Martin and Chandra Talpade Mohanty suggest works on the "tension between the desire for home, for synchrony, for sameness, and the realization of the repressions and violence that make home, harmony, sameness imaginable, and that enforce it . . ."[103]

But, in questioning the relationship of white feminism to relations of power/knowledge, Black feminists increasingly have become more critical of their own discourse as well. Indeed, if in 1981 Lorde would argue that "Those of us who stand outside the circle of this society's definition of acceptable women; those of us who have been forged in the crucibles of difference; those of us who are poor, who are lesbians, who are black, who are older, know that *survival is not an academic skill*,"[104] four years later, Hortense Spillers points to the "new arrangements" connecting the construction of a tradition of Black women writers with the academy and the mass media:

> In short, the image of black women writing in isolation, across time and space, is conduced toward radical revision. The room of one's own explodes its four walls to embrace the classroom, the library, and the various mechanisms of institutional and media life, including conferences, the lecture platform, the television talk show, the publishing house, the "best seller," and collections of critical essays. These new arrangements, when perceived against the background of the Black Nationalist Movement and the most recent phases of the Women's Movement in the United States, give us striking insight into the situation of "tradition." The latter arises not only because there are writers there to make it, but also because there is a strategic audience of heightened consciousness prepared to read and interpret the work as such. Traditions are not born. They are made.[105]

Thus, not only is Black feminist thought located on the other side of the ideology of the separate spheres, it increasingly finds itself on the other side of the ideology of disinterested disciplinary knowledge. Therefore, Black feminist thought is articulated as an intellectual tradition, just at a time when disciplinary knowledge is losing its privilege, even its definition, in relationship to the mass media and when writing therefore refers to a network of mass media communication technologies of which academic discourse is only a part. Indeed, the articulation of Black feminist thought as an intellectual tradition only furthers the reinvention of the social and the literary, undermining the distinction of fiction and history, fantasy and reality, polemic and academic discourse, social science and literary criticism.

Thus, although feminist theorists – white feminist theorists especially but Black feminists theorists too, often refer to Black women's experience as a way to evoke the necessity for a experientially based knowledge, *Black Feminist Thought* actually brings feminist theory into the domain of social criticism and (dis)identity politics, focusing especially on the analysis of the hegemony of controlling images. It even suggests that the experience of racism, sexism, and class oppression are framed by the mass media communication technologies that make the hegemony of controlling images possible. The deconstruction of hegemony therefore requires a reflection on technologies of mass-mediated forms of representation; a criticism of relations of power/knowledge also must be a politics of form.

And if the post-colonial criticism of Third World feminists most insistently elaborates a politics of form, especially in the domain of the human sciences, Third World feminists also again raise the question of color. That is to say, they invite a recognition that the constructions of whiteness and blackness, rigidified in the context of colonialism and slavery, often cover over various ethnicities and cultural differences. It is these differences which would be put into play by Third World feminists, Women of Color.

Notes

1 Kaja Silverman, *Male Subjectivity at the Margins* (New York: Routledge, 1992), p. 34.
2 Kate Millett, *Sexual Politics* (New York: Ballantine Books, 1970), pp. 117–19.
3 bell hooks, *Ain't I a Woman: Black Women and Feminism* (Boston: South End Press, 1981), p. 8.
4 Michele Wallace, *Black Macho and the Myth of the Superwoman* (New York: The Dial Press, 1979).
5 bell hooks, *Feminist Theory: From Margin to Center* (Boston: South End Press, 1984), p. 15.
6 Patricia Hill Collins, "Learning From the Outsider Within: The Sociological Significance of Black Feminist Thought," *Social Problems*, 33 (1986), p. 14.
7 Patricia Hill Collins, *Black Feminist Thought: Knowledge, Consciousness, and the Politics of Empowerment* (New York: Routledge, 1990), p. 11.
8 In her address to the 1979 Second Sex Conference, Audre Lorde already had asked white feminists, "what do you do with the fact that the women who clean your houses and tend your children while you attend conferences on feminist theory are, for the most part, poor and third world

women?" This talk was first published in 1981 and then republished in 1983; see Audre Lorde, "The Master's Tools Will Never Dismantle the Master's House," in Cherrié Moraga and Gloria Anzaldúa (eds), *This Bridge Called My Back: Writings by Radical Women of Color* (New York: Kitchen Table, 1983), p. 100.

9   Collins, *Black Feminist Thought*, p. 18 n. 5.
10 Ibid., p. 10.
11 Ibid., p. 13.
12 Ibid., p. 14.
13 Michel Foucault, *Power/Knowledge: Selected Interviews and Other Writings 1972–1977*, edited by Colin Gordon (New York: Pantheon, 1980), p. 82.
14 Collins, *Black Feminist Thought*, p. 18 n. 3.
15 Barbara Christian, "The Race for Theory," in Gloria Anzaldúa (ed.), *Making Face, Making Soul, Haciendo Caras*, (San Francisco: Aunt Lute, 1990), p. 336.
16 Ibid., p. 336.
17 Ibid., p. 336.
18 Collins, *Black Feminist Thought*, p. 208.
19 Ibid., pp. 33–7.
20 Ibid., p. 234. Haraway's remarks are from Donna Haraway, "Situated Knowledges: The Science Question in Feminism and the Privilege of Partial Perspectives," *Feminist Studies*, 14 (1988), p. 584.
21 Smith's essay was republished in 1982; see Barbara Smith, "Toward a Black Feminist Criticism," in Gloria Hull, Patricia Bell Scott, and Barbara Smith (eds), *All the Women Are White, All the Blacks Are Men, But Some of Us Are Brave* (Old Westbury: Feminist Press, 1982), p. 159.
22 For a response to Smith's essay to which there is frequent reference, see Deborah McDowell, "New Directions for Black Feminist Criticism," in Elaine Showalter (ed.), *The New Feminist Criticism: Essays on Women, Literature and Theory* (New York: Pantheon, 1985), pp. 186–99.
23 Hazel Carby, *Reconstructing Womanhood: The Emergence of the Afro-American Woman Novelist* (New York: Oxford University Press, 1987), p. 16.
24 Ibid., p. 17.
25 Ibid., pp. 17–18.
26 Ibid., p. 32.
27 Collins, *Black Feminist Thought*, pp. 43–6.
28 Ibid., pp. 55–8.
29 Ibid., p. 62.
30 Ibid., p. 64.
31 Ibid., p. 65.
32 Ibid., p. 65.
33 Ibid., p. 69.
34 Carby, *Reconstructing Womanhood*, pp. 23–5.
35 hooks, *Ain't I a Woman*, p. 22.

36   Carby, *Reconstructing Womanhood*, p. 35.
37   Ibid., pp. 38–9.
38   Collins, *Black Feminist Thought*, p. 74.
39   Ibid., p. 73.
40   Ibid., p. 76.
41   Ibid., p. 95.
42   Ibid., p. 106.
43   Ibid., p. 106.
44   Ibid., p. 112.
45   Ibid., p. 94.
46   Ibid., p. 103.
47   bell hooks, *Yearning: Race, Gender, and Cultural Politics* (Boston: South End Press, 1990), pp. 41–9.
48   Collins, *Black Feminist Thought*, p. 115. Collins takes Jordan's remarks from June Jordan, *On Call* (Boston: South End Press, 1985), p. 105.
49   Audre Lorde, *Sister Outsider* (New York: The Crossing Press, 1984), p. 458.
50   Collins, *Black Feminist Thought*, p. 125.
51   Lorde, *Sister Outsider*, pp. 149–50.
52   Collins, *Black Feminist Thought*, pp. 119–29.
53   Ibid., p. 118.
54   Ibid., p. 118.
55   Ibid., p. 120. Collins is referring to Carol Stack, *All Our Kin: Strategies for Survival in a Black Community* (New York: Harper & Row, 1974).
56   Collins, *Black Feminist Thought*, p. 41.
57   Ibid., p. 43.
58   Alice Walker, *In Search of Our Mothers' Gardens* (New York: Harcourt Brace Jovanovich, 1983), pp. 231–43.
59   hooks, *Yearning*, p. 38.
60   Carby, *Reconstructing Womanhood*, p. 164.
61   Ibid., p. 175.
62   Ibid., p. 175.
63   Ibid., p. 174.
64   bell hooks, "Writing the Subject: Reading *The Color Purple*," in Henry Louis Gates (ed.), *Reading Black, Reading Feminist* (New York: Meridian Books, 1990), pp. 454–70.
65   Ibid., p. 457.
66   Collins, *Black Feminist Thought*, p. 171.
67   Ibid., p. 188.
68   Collins takes these remarks from Audre Lorde, *Sister Outsider*, p. 123.
69   Collins, *Black Feminist Thought*, p. 196.
70   Hortense Spillers, "Interstices: A Small Drama of Words," in Carol Vance (ed.), *Pleasure and Danger: Exploring Female Sexuality* (Boston: Routledge & Kegan Paul, 1984), pp. 73–100.
71   Ibid., pp. 88–9.
72   See, for examples, Hortense Spillers, "Mama's Baby, Papa's Maybe: An

American Grammar Book," *Diacritics*, 17 (1987), pp. 65–81; Helene Moglen, "Redeeming History: Toni Morrison's *Beloved*," *Cultural Critique*, 24 (1993), pp. 17–40; and Kathryn Bond Stockton, "Heaven's Bottom: Anal Economics and the Critical Debasement of Freud in Toni Morrison's *Sula*," *Cultural Critique*, 24 (1993), pp. 81–118. Spillers' remarks come from "Mama's Baby, Papa's Maybe: An American Grammar Book," pp. 77–8.

73 Collins takes her remarks from Lorde, *Sister Outsider*, p. 54.
74 Collins, *Black Feminist Thought*, p. 235.
75 Ibid., p. 209.
76 Ibid., p. xi.
77 Ibid., p. xi.
78 Ibid., p. xi.
79 Ibid., p. xi.
80 Ibid., p. xi.
81 bell hooks, *Talking Back, Thinking Feminist, Thinking Black* (Boston: South End Press, 1989), p. 155.
82 Ibid., p. 156.
83 Ibid., p. 155.
84 Ibid., p. 155.
85 Ibid., p. 157.
86 Ibid., p. 159.
87 Ibid., p. 157.
88 Ibid., p. 7.
89 hooks, *Yearning*, p. 28.
90 Ibid., p. 28.
91 Ibid., p. 31.
92 bell hooks, *Black Looks: Race and Representation* (Boston: South End Press, 1992), pp. 115–31.
93 Ibid., p. 2. The point hooks is making is not that African-American critics have failed to criticize mass media representations, but that the influence of their criticism has not yet brought about substantial change.
94 Ibid., p. 2.
95 hooks, *Yearning*, p. 9.
96 Patricia Bell Scott, "Debunking Sapphire: Toward a Non-Racist and Non-Sexist Social Science," in Gloria Hull, Patricia Bell Scott, and Barbara Smith (eds), *All the Women Are White, All the Blacks Are Men, But Some of Us Are Brave*, pp. 85–92.
97 Elizabeth Higginbotham, "Two Representative Issues in Contemporary Sociological Work on Black Women," in Gloria Hull, Patricia Bell Scott, and Barbara Smith (eds), *All the Women Are White, All the Blacks Are Men, But Some of Us Are Brave*, pp. 93–8.
98 Collins, *Black Feminist Thought*, p. 219.
99 Mary Ann Doane, *Femmes Fatales: Feminism, Film Theory, Psychoanalysis* (New York: Routledge, 1991), p. 247.
100 Ibid., p. 246.

101 Elizabeth Abel, "Black Writing, White Reading," *Critical Inquiry*, 19 (1993), p. 497.

102 Teresa De Lauretis, "Eccentric Subjects: Feminist Theory and Historical Consciousness," *Feminist Studies*, 16 (1990), p. 126.

103 Biddy Martin and Chandra Talpade Mohanty, "Feminist Politics: What's Home Got to Do With It?," in Teresa De Lauretis (ed.), *Feminist Studies/ Critical Studies* (Bloomington: Indiana University Press, 1986), p. 208.

104 Lorde, "The Master's Tools Will Never Dismantle the Master's House," p. 99.

105 Hortense Spillers, "Cross Currents, Discontinuities: Black Women's Fiction," in Marjorie Pryse and Hortense Spillers (eds), *Conjuring, Black Women, Fiction, and Literary Tradition*, (Bloomington: Indiana University Press, 1985), p. 250.

5

Formulating a Feminist
Post-colonial Criticism

If, in *Black Feminist Thought*, Patricia Hill Collins argues that Black women's survival is in part a matter of countering the legitimacy of hegemonic images of Black women, in *Woman, Native, Other: Writing Postcoloniality and Feminism* (1989), Trinh T. Minh-ha would turn feminist criticism to the deconstruction of the hegemonic images of the colonialized subject. But, whereas Collins challenges the legitimacy of hegemony without fully elaborating a criticism of the discursive construction of social science authority, Trinh proposes that "disrupting 'the grand narratives of the human sciences'" is not only necessary to a post-colonial criticism of hegemony; for the post-colonial subject, a criticism of the human sciences also is "a means to survival."[1] Thus, while some African-American feminists remain suspicious about "French theory,"[2] Trinh engages post-structural theory and deconstructive philosophy in order to inform feminist theorizing with a post-colonial criticism that deconstructs the authority of the human sciences. Indeed, the difference between a criticism of US racism and a post-colonial criticism is marked by the necessity in the case of the latter of a sustained effort to identify and criticize globalizing relations of power/knowledge.

In *Woman, Native, Other*, then, Trinh not only proposes that a post-colonial criticism necessarily is related to the deconstruction of the opposition in Western discourse of fiction and history, fantasy and reality, polemic and academic discourse, literary criticism and social science. She also suggests that the deconstruction of these oppositions requires a politics of form which places within the same space of theorizing a seemingly different practice of representation, so that each might bring the other into crisis. As Trinh puts it:

> I see theory as a constant questioning of the framing of consciousness – a practice capable of informing another practice, such as film production, in

a reciprocal challenge. Hence theory always has the possibility, even the probability, of leading the other practice to "dangerous" places and vice versa. I can't separate the two.[3]

Thus, if *Woman, Native, Other*, but also Trinh's film productions, *Reassemblage* (1982), *Naked Spaces – Living Is Round* (1985), and *Surname Viet Given Name Nam* (1989)[4] are composed of what she describes as "the irrespectful mixing of theoretical, militant and poetical modes of writing" and therefore enact a politics of form exemplary of post-structural theory and deconstructive philosophy, it is not only because "poetry," as Trinh notices, "is . . . the place from which many people of color voice their struggle"[5] and thereby "radically contribute to the questioning of the relationship of subjects to power, language and meaning in theory."[6] It also is because, for Trinh, "French theory" is part of her experience of the former colonization of Vietnam – one part of what she describes as "my hybrid reality."[7] Thus, while standpoint epistemologies assume the opposition of experience and discourse, thereby making it possible to take women's experience as the point of departure for a feminist criticism of discourse, *Woman, Native, Other* proposes that the post-colonial experience of the hybridization of reality makes both the notion of a uniform women's experience and the notion of a unified women's identity impossible. For Trinh, both the experience and the identity of the post-colonial subject are inseparable from their discursive constructions, thereby suggesting that a deconstructive politics of form be the starting point of a feminist criticism of discourse.

Indeed, post-colonial critics often draw a connection between a politics of form and the hybridization of reality derived from dislocations of identity and place. In the *Empire Writes Back: Theory and Practice in Post-Colonial Literatures*, Bill Ashcroft, Gareth Griffiths, and Helen Tiffin suggest that whether motivated by "dislocation resulting from migration, the experience of enslavement, transportation, or 'voluntary' removal for indentured labour," the treatment of place and identity in post-colonial writing is connected to the "alienation of vision and the crisis of self-image which . . . displacement produces;" there is a "gap which opens between the experience of place and the language available to describe it."[8] Thus, while colonization and de-colonization seem to urge the establishment of an identity and a homeplace, post-colonial critics instead reappropriate displacement: post-colonial criticism valorizes the hybrid rather than the unified subject-identity figured in the dominant fiction of Western discourse; it foregrounds the multicultural rather than the unified identity of the nation-state and it insists on locally

articulated criticisms of the globalization of relations of power/
knowledge.

In place of identity, then, there is a displacement – a refusal by post-
colonial critics to be identified and a questioning of the equation of
theoretical reflexivity with self-identity. Thus, while Trinh argues that
"identity remains necessary as a political/personal strategy of survival
and resistance,"[9] she also proposes that reflexivity is no longer simply a
matter of identity. As she puts it:

> The reflexive question asked . . . is no longer: *Who* am I? but *When, where,*
> *how* am I (so and so)? This is why I remain skeptical of strategies of
> reversal when they are not intricately woven with strategies of displace-
> ment. Here the notion of displacement is also a place of identity: there is no
> real me to return to, no whole self that synthesizes the woman, the woman
> of color and the writer; there are instead, diverse recognitions of self
> through difference, and unfinished, contingent, arbitrary closures that
> make possible both politics and identity.[10]

Thus, when identity is claimed, even essentialized, it is only as a point of
departure for criticism; it is a performative framing, what Trinh describes
as "a strategic claim."[11] Gayatri Chakravorty Spivak argues similarly:

> But it is not possible, within discourse, to escape essentializing some-
> where. The moment of essentialism or essentialization is irreducible. In
> deconstructive critical practice, you have to be aware that you are going to
> essentialize anyway. So then strategically you can look at essentialisms, not
> as descriptions of the way things are, but as something that one must adopt
> to produce a critique of anything.[12]

Even when post-colonial critics would claim an essential identity for
those of the Third World whom Spivak refers to as the subaltern classes
– among them, "subsistence farmers, unorganized peasant labor, the
tribals, and the communities of zero workers on the street or in the
countryside,"[13] the essential identity of the subaltern, as Spivak argues,
"is necessarily the absolute limit of the place where history is narrativized
into logic" – the oedipal logic of the dominant fiction of Western discourse.[14] In other words, the claim for the identity of the subaltern
subject favors anti-essentialism; it is a claim for the identity of groups,
which as Jenny Sharpe describes it, "appear only as a blank in the
historical record."[15]

Indeed, in her now classic essay "Can the Subaltern Speak?" Spivak
discusses the Subaltern Studies collective, whose project of writing the
history of the subaltern classes of India is defined by the collective's

distinguishing its work from an elite, colonial, and neo-colonial historiography; even the subaltern classes are defined only in terms of a difference from the elite population.[16] Spivak concludes that "since the 'subaltern' cannot appear without the thought of the 'elite,' the generalization is by definition incomplete – in philosophical language 'non-originary,' or in an earlier version of *'unursprunglick,'* non-primordial."[17]

And if Spivak, therefore, argues that "the subaltern can not speak,"[18] that the subaltern is not a unified subject-identity but an "identity-in-differential,"[19] it also is to suggest that when the post-colonial critic is confronted with the subaltern classes, what matters is "not to represent (*verstreten*) them but to learn to represent (*darstellen*) ourselves."[20] As Spivak puts it:

> This argument would take us into a critique of a disciplinary anthropology and the relationship between elementary pedagogy and disciplinary formation. It would also question the implicit demand, made by intellectuals who choose a "naturally articulate" subject of oppression, that such a subject come through history as a foreshortened mode-of-production.[21]

Thus, the search for self-definition and a homeplace is displaced in post-colonial criticism, as the relationship of knowledge, power, and academic discourse is reconfigured through what Trinh describes as "strategic and contingent struggles" at the limits of narrative – at the borderlines of definitions of language, place, history, identity, and representation. Neither a subaltern subject nor aligned with a Third World elite, the post-colonial critic enacts a politics of form that is a politics of (dis)identification. Even the identification of "Third World Woman" is deferred or displaced in the recognition and articulation of the differences and similarities between a colonization internal to the USA and the globalizing dislocations of post-coloniality.

If, then, Trinh sees a connection between her work and that of Gloria Anzaldúa, it is because of their different but similar struggles at borders.[22] Indeed, in *Borderlands/La Frontera* (1987), Anzaldúa articulates the experience of Third World women in terms of border fights that are always displacements of home and identity. In the figure of "the new *mestiza*," Anzaldúa also valorizes the hybrid. As she puts it:

> I want the freedom to carve and chisel my own face, to staunch the bleeding with ashes, to fashion my own gods out of my entrails. And if going home is denied me then I will have to stand and claim my space, making a new culture – *una cultura mestiza* – with my own lumber, my own bricks and mortar and my own feminist architecture.[23]

And if like *Woman, Native, Other*, *Borderlands/La Frontera* is composed of an "irrespectful mixing of theoretical, militant and poetical modes of writing," it is to show the bloody everyday experience at the border between the United States and Mexico as both a literal and a figurative struggle. The composition of *Borderlands/La Frontera* enacts a politics of form in order to dramatize the overdetermination of the colonized subjectivities of Third World women in the First World. Thus, the post-colonial criticism of Third World feminism shifts a feminist materialism even further from a crude economic determinism. It makes of feminist theorizing a criticism of hegemony which recognizes the discontinuities of the ideological, the political, and the economic, while looking for the interrelationship of oppressions of race, class, ethnicity, gender, and sexuality in both a national and a transnational frame.

Thus, while the global restructuring of the transnational division of labor, especially its effect on women, is a persistent provocation of Third World feminist theorizing,[24] nonetheless, the post-colonial criticism of Third World feminism is a criticism of hegemony which does not treat political economy only as a determinant or a cause. Instead, the question of political economy also incites a criticism of causality and determination, especially as they are and have been articulated in the Western discourse of the human sciences, including marxism and some versions of feminism. Therefore, the disciplining effects of political economy, globalized through anthropological interpretation especially, are taken as an object of criticism – a criticism of relations of power/knowledge.

Whereas Trinh reappropriates the ethnographic gaze in order to resist "the packaging of knowledge through a certain insistence on visual fascination and pleasure,"[25] Anzaldúa weaves together the artistic and the functional, the sacred and the secular in order to reappropriate the "ethno-poetics and performance of the shaman."[26] But neither simply provides an anthropology that more adequately describes the experiences of Third World women. Rather, *Woman, Native, Other* and *Borderlands/La Frontera* shift the ground of feminist theorizing from an epistemology of experience to an evaluation of strategies for publicizing local knowledges that might serve women at different times and in different places.

Thus, neither Trinh nor Anzaldúa search for a single and authoritative tradition of women's writings or women's experiences. Instead, they only make temporary and partial use of cultural artifacts in compositions that make legible the negations or erasures in Western discourse at the very same time that they make something positive out of the fractures and the pieces of what has been left behind in the West's appropriation of its colonized others. Yet, I would suggest that the desire for a tradition, although dispersed across surfaces of grafted cultural differences, nonetheless is asserted and speaks unconsciously. That is to say, taking up a politics of form or a politics of writing is not merely an intentional or conscious choice for either Trinh or Anzaldúa; rather, writing is a deeply troubled and troubling activity, driven by unconscious desire. Yet, how unconscious desire takes shape, or what its relationship to the dominant fiction of oedipus is, remain questions yet to be answered in feminist post-colonial criticism.

Naming and (Un)Naming the Great Master's Discourse

If *Woman, Native, Other* has at its centerpiece a criticism of both the ethnographic envisioning of the Other and the anthropological language of nativism, Trinh surrounds what is at the center of her text with beginning and ending chapters that explore story-telling and writing in the poetical mode. At the periphery, then, there is a place made for poetical writing and story-telling, even though the question of the authenticity of poetry and story-telling is indefinitely deferred. Thus, at the beginning and at the end of *Woman, Native, Other*, there is poetry and story-telling but there also is a displacement of authentic "native" origins.

Indeed, Trinh begins by displacing the usual autobiographical framing of the feminist text. In the first chapter of *Woman, Native, Other*, Trinh refuses the position of the autobiograph and instead takes up a position in what she describes as the "mirror-writing box," from which she claims:

> Writing necessarily refers to writing. The image is that of a mirror capturing only the reflections of other mirrors. When i say "I see myself seeing myself," I/i am not alluding to the illusory relationship of subject to subject (or object) but to the play of mirrors that defers to infinity the real subject and subverts the notion of an original "I." A writing *for* the people, *by* the people, *from* the people is, literally, a multipolar reflecting reflection that remains free from the conditions of subjectivity and objectivity and yet reveals them both. I write to show myself showing people who show me my own showing. I-You: not one, not two.[27]

But if this claim is difficult to voice, and it seemingly is for Trinh, it is because of what she describes as "the old master–servant's Guilt" – a guilt that is part of being identified as "writer of color, woman writer or woman of color."[28] There is the guilt "over the selfishness" of writing, guilt about family, friends, all others "less fortunate."[29] There is the authorial desire to be published, but "Why write? For Whom? What necessity? What writing?"[30] As Trinh puts it:

> Thus, it has become almost impossible for her to take up her pen without at the same time questioning her relation to the material that defines her and her creative work. As focal point of cultural consciousness and social change, writing weaves into language the complex relations of a subject caught between the problems of race and gender and the practice of literature as the very place where social alienation is thwarted differently according to each specific context.[31]

Even the Sartrean notion of *art engagé* or an art for the masses has become impossible; it no longer can assuage the guilt:

> Do the masses become masses by themselves? Or are they the result of a theoretical and practical operation of "massification?" From where onward can one say of a "free" work of art that it is written for the infinite numbers which constitute the masses and not merely for a definite public stratum of society?[32]

The guilt remains, hiding and revealing itself in the political commitment of Third World writers:

> In a sense, committed writers are the ones who write both to awaken to the consciousness of their guilt and to give their readers a guilty conscience. Bound to one another by an awareness of their guilt, writer and reader may thus assess their positions, engaging themselves wholly in their situations and carrying their weight into the weight of their communities, the weight of the world. Such a definition naturally places the committed writers on the side of Power. For every discourse that breeds fault and guilt is a discourse of authority and arrogance. To say this, however, is not to say that all power discourses produce equal oppression or that those established are necessary.[33]

Thus, Trinh resists a view of her writing as "giving voice" to Third World women, women, or Women of Color. Rather she writes against other writings, necessarily engaged with and in a struggle against hegemony, even while intimating a certain disinterest in any final overcoming. That is to say, even before she will desconstruct the anthropological language of nativism, uncovering its arrogance and authorial desire, Trinh refuses to promise a more authentic representation of the native or the native's actual experiences. Insisting that language does not express reality, Trinh is not seduced by the argument that clarity and directness are the characteristics of "good" writing. As she puts it:

Clear expression, often equated with *correct* expression, has long been the criterion set forth in treatises on *rhetoric*, whose aim was to order discourse so as to *persuade*. The language of Taoism and Zen, for example, which is perfectly accessible but rife with paradox does not qualify as "clear" (paradox is "illogical" and "nonsensical" to many Westerners), for its intent lies outside the realm of persuasion.[34]

Indeed, it is because she recognizes something like the paradoxical of Taoism and Zen in the writings of Hélène Cixous, Jacques Derrida, Roland Barthes, and Julia Kristeva that Trinh draws from both post-structural theories and Asian philosophies not only to unsettle the writing practices of the human sciences but also to displace rather than merely reverse the oppositions of Western discourse. Thus, Trinh deconstructs or displaces the oppositions of the subjective and objective, the universal and the narcissistic, the impersonal and the personal, especially focusing on the way these oppositions are configured in Western discourse in a crude or reductive opposition of masculine and feminine.

Trinh therefore draws on Cixous' discussion of writing in which Cixous privileges bisexuality as a position from which to displace the opposition of masculine and feminine. Trinh quotes from Cixous' "The Laugh of the Medusa" in which Cixous describes bisexuality:

Bisexuality: that is each one's location in self (*répérage en soi*) of the presence – variously manifest and insistent according to each person, male or female – of both sexes, nonexclusion either of the difference or of one sex, and, from this "self-permission," multiplication of the effects of the inscription of desire, over all parts of my body and the other body.[35]

Even though in her essay "French Feminism in an International Frame" Spivak criticizes French feminists not only for risking reducing writing to sexuality but also for their often unexamined privileging of avant-garde techniques of writing, nonetheless, Spivak also recognizes a certain usefulness for post-colonial critics of Cixous' writing – especially for the way it "stages plurality" in relationship to women.[36] Like Spivak, Trinh also finds Cixous' writing useful for the way it displaces oppositions in the insistence on plurality, even though Trinh too rejects any reduction of writing to sexuality, since this "does not, obviously, allow us to depart from a discourse directed within the apparatuses of sexuality."[37] Indeed, Trinh concludes that "Writing does not translate bisexuality. It (does not express language but) fares across it."[38]

Thus, if Trinh makes use of a notion like "writing bisexuality," it is to play with the Master's norms of clarity and accessibility; that is, it is to undermine the masculine figure of a unified subject of authority, especially in relationship to the authority of the human sciences. But, it also is to refuse any mere opposition of poetry and scientific discourse. Instead, Trinh recognizes that writing props or frames all knowledge, albeit elaborated in poetry and disavowed in scientific discourse. In other words, Trinh borrows from Cixous' writing what is most Derridean about it.

Indeed, like other post-colonial critics, Trinh finds Derrida's treatment of writing or textuality helpful to a post-colonial criticism. In an important sense, the colonial and post-colonial subjects are a production of texts – legal, political, and aesthetic. Thus, Spivak also points to a relationship between Derrida's treatment of textuality and post-colonial criticism, proposing that it is this relationship that corrects the common misreading of Derrida's treatment of textuality as reducing everything to a text, that is, to the verbal text. As she puts it:

> I think the notion of textuality was broached precisely to question the kind of thing that it is today seen to be – that is, the verbal text, a preoccupation with being in the library rather than being on the street. As far as I understand it, the notion of textuality should be related to the notion of the worlding of a world on a supposedly uninscribed territory. When I say this, I am thinking basically about the imperialist project which had to assume that the earth that it territorialized was in fact previously uninscribed. So then a world, on a simple level of cartography, inscribed what was presumed to be uninscribed. Now this worlding actually is also a texting, textualising, a making into art, a making into an object to be understood.[39]

If for Spivak, then, deconstructing the text is to recognize textuality as "something woven but beyond control,"[40] "a text/tissue/weave (politico-psycho-sexual-socio) of which the ends are not accessible to us,"[41] for Trinh, the grand narratives of the human sciences are motivated by a denial of textuality, a refusal to recognize this lack of control. Instead the human sciences are narrated to contain this lack, by worlding or textualizing the Other, in the figure of the woman/native. Thus, the anthropological language of nativism is shaped in the denial of writing and textuality, displaced onto the Other who is thereby made to figure the one in need of being controlled.

Thus, if Trinh treats anthropology as "a scientific conversation of Man with Man," it is to point both to men's infatuation with language and to how their infatuation differs from her own politicized self-consciousness about textuality. As she puts it:

> I have wondered time and again about my reading myself as I feel he reads me and my false encounter with the other in me whose non-being/being he

claims to have captured, solidified, and pinned to a butterfly board. Like any common living thing, I fear and reprove classification and the death it entails, and I will not allow its clutches to lock down on me, although I realize I can never lure myself into simply escaping it. The difference, as I sense it, is: naming, like a cast of the die, is just one step toward unnaming, a tool to render visible what he has carefully kept invisible in his manipulative blindness.[42]

Thus, Trinh retraces the history of the disavowed dream of anthropology to make the "native" in its own image, to make a perfect double, by defining the native as a human being, a specimen of the human species of Man. She argues that this dream also is a dream about language; it is a dream informed with a desire for the "neutrality" of language, thereby imagining language to be a transparent reflection of human nature, a human nature that the native has been made to figure. The materiality of words denied, words can bear the burden of reflecting the native's reality as the reality of human nature. But, in its own belief in language's capacity to lay bare the reality of the native, anthropology ironically increasingly would make visible the differences between Man and men. Indeed, Trinh suggests that while anthropology is concerned to make the native in the image of Man, difference becomes anthropology's very problematic, especially as anthropology is elaborated in the works of the Great Master – a title Trinh uses for Claude Lévi-Strauss, among others.

Not only would the Great Master notice the disturbing difference between Man and men. He would make every effort to recapture this difference in language; he would initiate an understanding of language as itself productive of difference, a difference internal to language, even while he encloses the play of difference in a totalizing (kinship) system of exchange in which Woman is the currency of exchange. That is to say, the difference between men, between their realities, always is contained in the opposition between Man and Woman. Thus, the Great Master shifts the orientation of anthropology to capturing the native's reality by studying his myths and the organization of reality they embed; anthropology is made a practice of what the Great Master refers to as the "total observation" of the native's everyday experience, only to find again and again its mythological or language-like structure – that is, the exchange of Woman.

But, just as the Great Master recognizes the productivity of language in the play of difference internal to it, and just as anthropology is itself recognized as a discursive production, what the Great Master calls "a mythology of myths," ethnography is made to blunt the more radical implications of these recognitions. The ethnographic narrative maintains a certain tension in anthropology between scientism and the recognition of the discursive construction of anthropological authority; the ethnography is formed around what Trinh describes as an unending oscillation between favoring the method of the *bricoleur* or that of the engineer. That is to say, the image of the ethnography becomes "either that of *bricolage* aspiring vainly after the engineer's scientism or that of an engineering constantly annulling itself through *bricolage* without being able to dispense with it."[43]

In other words, the ethnography becomes filled with the anthropologist's "longing for an impossible totalization which he sometimes claims and sometimes rejects as a 'grave mistake.'"[44] Hence, the ethnographic narrative becomes a displacement and projection of this unfulfilled longing onto the anthropologist's relationship to the native; that is, the ethnography narrates the ethnographer's impossible longing for a totalizing science in terms of the ethnographer's "heroic" (heterosexualized) struggle to come close to the native, woman, other, but not too close, preventing himself from going native, becoming woman, being othered. Indeed, the Great Master warns of the risk of total observation, the risk of "the complete absorption of the observer by the object of his observation."[45]

Having made visible anthropology's longing for an impossible totalization and the resulting eroticization of the ethnographer's relationship to the native, Trinh confronts the anthropologist with what he least wants to know. On one hand, Trinh reminds the anthropologist that for all the scientific jargon, anthropology only reproduces gossip, "gossip about gossip."[46] On the other hand, she insists that in this pursuit of gossip, anthropology gives form to a "legal voyeurism" that forces the native into a "personal identification" with the anthropologist.[47] The sexism and racism revealed in the Great Master's *Diary* is not the only mark of anthropology's "reluctant imperialism."[48] The ethnographic form also bears this mark.

Thus, for Trinh the treatment of difference in anthropology, and in the human sciences generally, erases differences and instead prescribes something more like an apartheid policy of separate development – "keep your way of life and ethnic values *within the borders of your homelands*."[49] It is in these terms that Trinh also criticizes white feminists. On one hand, there is the benevolence of white feminists in their taking "special care" to include a "representative" Third World woman, in insisting that Third World women be represented.[50] On the other hand, there is feminists' desire to enclose all women in the figure of the Woman – a desire complicitous with the human sciences' longing for totalization.

Hence, the preference for ethnography among some feminists, their insistence on the representation of the actual experiences of all women, is profoundly called into question – not only because the ethnographic form of the human sciences erases the differences of race, class, gender, ethnicity, nationality, and sexuality but also because in its longing for a totalizing science, ethnography denies the difference within – what Trinh refers to as the "Not-I:"

> Not One, not two either. "I" is, therefore, not a unified subject, a fixed identity, or that solid mass covered with layers of superficialities one has gradually to peel off before one can see its true face. "I" is, itself, infinite layers. Its complexity can hardly be conveyed through such typographic conventions as I, i, or I/i. Thus, I/i am compelled by the will to say/unsay, to resort to the entire gamut of personal pronouns to stay near this fleeing *and* static essence of Not-I.[51]

Thus when, in the final chapter of *Woman, Native, Other*, Trinh turns to discuss her practice of aesthetics, it is not to propose a method that more adequately or truthfully represents the actual experiences of the woman, the Third World woman, the Woman of Color. Indeed, even though the title of the last chapter is "Grandma's Story," Trinh's discussion of story-telling begins with a dislocation; that is, her story about story-telling starts when history separates itself from story-telling, when history "started indulging in accumulation and facts" and when, therefore, the questions of truth and accuracy first become relevant.[52] Thus, Trinh suggests that there is no simple return to a time before history, a pre-industrial, pre-modern, primitive time of story-telling. Instead, it is only by juxtaposing story-telling with scientistic history that the conformity and the uniformity of the categories of scientistic history are made visible; but it is only then that story-telling seems to have the force and power both to refresh and to freshly wound.

If, then, the very notion of Grandma's story raises expectations of a tradition passed from mothers to daughters, there also is the frustration of this expectation, a displacement of the origin of story-telling and the identity of the story-teller. After all, Trinh's practice of aesthetics is one of dislocation, of displacement in the juxtaposition of different practices of representation. If, then, history displaces story-telling, Trinh would return story-telling to that place, the place of a displacement, in order to again displace not only scientistic history but ethnography too.

Indeed, in her film productions, Trinh not only uncovers the disavowal of writing and textuality in the ethnographic or documentary form of the human sciences, anthropology in particular. She does so seemingly by producing documentaries of Vietnam (*Surname Viet Given Name Nam*), six countries of West Africa (*Naked Spaces – Living Is Round*), and five regions across Senegal (*Reassamblage*). Thus, Trinh places herself in the very position which she is criticizing, recognizing the weave of hegemony in which the film-maker always is caught, but the post-colonial critic too. As Spivak comments (about herself in conversation with Edward Said):

> We are post-colonials. We are in fact wild anthropologists. We, because of our class alliance, went out to do our field work . . . we went out to do field work in the West, not in the disciplinary sense, but pushed by class alliance and power lines, and we became successful, almost indistinguishable from them, unlike the disciplinary anthropologist. And we have now decided to look at the scandal of our production.[53]

As a "wild anthropologist," Trinh tries to work through the scandalous production of the post-colonial critic by both recognizing and problematizing a certain relationship between her experiences and those of others. As she puts it:

> These films are also strongly motivated by an experience that I lived through in formerly colonized Vietnam and that I clearly recognized, shared and re-lived in Africa; hence the necessity to make films that would always point to the process of constructing not truth, but meaning, and to myself as an active element in that process, both as a foreign observer of a specific culture and as a member of the general cultural zone and non-aligned bloc of countries known as the Third World.[54]

Thus, Trinh also works against the scandalizing production of Vietnamese or African peoples in mainstream cinema, deconstructing the hegemonic film techniques of documentary and classic Hollywood cinema. Manipulating sound and image, as well as their relationship, exploring line, space, and color in the context of various linguistic codes and languages, Trinh's films refuse viewers a certain or singular viewpoint. Viewers can never just see "Africa" or "Vietnam." Nor are viewers made only to see the productivity of the camera, that is, the film-maker's viewpoint at work. Rather, in being made to see both at once, viewers suddenly may not see at all; in other words, viewers may not know what they are seeing, may not know how to see it. Speaking specifically of *Reassemblage*, Trinh explains:

> I was mainly working with the look. How the West has been looking at other cultures, how these cultures look at themselves being looked at and how my own story as onlooker looked at is enmeshed in such a reflection. When you see an object, you are not seeing the look. Or in other words, you can't see the look when you look at the eye and vice-versa. That's why for many people it was impossible to understand the film because they were looking for the object and hence expecting some kind of packaging of the culture.[55]

But, if neither *Reassemblage* nor *Naked Spaces – Living Is Round* merely exploit Africa in order to deconstruct the very "look" which first was part of its colonization, it is because Trinh actually does show Africa but with such specificity that no one territorializing unit is operative, no one territorial unity is made possible. Indeed, in *Surname Viet Given Name Nam*, Trinh's exploration of Vietnam only produces a hybridization of place and time – even a space and time of not-knowing. Composed around a set of performed interviews seemingly with women in Vietnam but actually acted by Vietnamese women in the United States, who in a latter part of the film are interviewed about their performances, *Surname Viet Given Name Nam* returns to the disavowed fictionality of the interview, at the same time that it frustrates any view of an authentic Vietnam or an authentic Vietnamese woman.

Further frustrating viewers by refusing them a portrait of Vietnam in the terms of a simple opposition of communist and non-communist, *Surname Viet Given Name Nam* even proposes something of a complicity between non-alignment and the hybridization of reality. A connection also is made between the fixing of gender identities and the fixing of a national identity. Indeed, in *Surname Viet Given Name Nam*, Trinh works against the relationship of gender and nationalism at play in most mainstream cinema; Vietnam war films, especially those made in the United States, are exemplary. Thus, Trinh discusses *Surname Viet Given Name Nam* in terms of its resistance to the hegemonic construction of national identity through the fixing of gender identity:

> The question of nation and gender is opened up in a multiply layered way. For example, the name of Trieu Thi Trinh, one of the historical heroines who resisted Chinese domination, has at least five variations (heard and seen on screen); each of these is a different reading, a different emphasis of her attributes – her lineage . . . , her gender and age status, her leadership, or merely her simplicity. Similarly each of the numerous names used to designate Vietnam (also heard and seen on screen) relates to an historical period of the nation thereby to the diverse outside and inside influences that have contributed to what is viewed as the Vietnamese culture. So hybridization here refers to a negotiation of the difference not merely between cultures, between First World and Third World but more importantly within the culture.[56]

Thus, the post-colonial criticism of Third World feminism deconstructs both a unified subject-identity and a unified national identity, showing the engendering fiction which constitutes not only each entity but also their relationship. The notion of patriarchy also is shown only to have force in relationship to imperialism and colonialism; the same is implied for Western discourse's dominant fiction of oedipus that organizes unconscious desire in the construction of a hegemonic white, heterosexual, propertied masculinity. And if Spivak therefore urges a representation of the subject outside of the fiction of neo-colonial nationalism but also "outside of both psychoanalysis and counter-psychoanalysis,"[57] Trinh's repeated reference to the psychoanalytic and counterpsychoanalytic discourses in which the notion of bisexuality partly takes its meaning, instead suggests that post-colonial criticism focus on the relationship between "indigenous regulative fictions of psychobiography," to use Spivak's terminology, and the dominant fiction of oedipus which has been imposed with colonization and which still informs neo-colonial social science as well as mass-mediated cultural productions.

Thus, whereas a material feminist criticism suggests that the defensive and rigid opposition of masculinity and femininity in the context of a compulsory heterosexuality is not only shaped by, but is a vehicle for, ideologies of race, class, gender, and ethnicity, Trinh proposes the notion of bisexuality as a vehicle of criticism in the discourse of the hybridization of subject-identity and national identities. For Trinh, then, bisexuality informs what she describes as:

> [S]o many attempts at articulating this always-emerging-already-distorted place that remains so difficult, on the one hand, for the First World even to recognize, and on the other, for our own communities to accept to venture into, for fear of losing what has been a costly gain through past struggles. To unlearn the reactive language that promotes separatism and self-enclosure by essentializing a denied identity requires more than willingness and self criticism.[58]

While, for Trinh, the "more" that is required is a matter of seriously playing with the language of identity and separatism, for Gloria Anzaldúa, it is a matter of celebrating living "on the borders and in the margins." As Anzaldúa states it in the preface to *Borderlands/La Frontera*:

> [T]here have been compensations for this *mestiza* and certain joys. Living on borders and in margins, keeping intact one's shifting and multiple identity and integrity, is like trying to swim in a new element, an "alien" element. There is an exhilaration in being a participant in the further evolution of humankind, in being "worked" on.[59]

Although there is a troubling return in Anzaldúa's writing to an evolutionary language and to the notion of the raised or the new consciousness of the *mestiza*, it is a return that is juxtaposed with the multiplying of partial identities and the hybridization of nationality and ethnicity. Thus, the language of evolution which informs the unified subject-identity of Western discourse is displaced in being claimed for a subjectivity which never becomes unified and which speaks in many tongues.

Writing *Mestizaje* Theories

Indeed, *Borderlands/La Frontera* switches codes, as Anzaldúa puts it, "from English, to Castillian Spanish to the North Mexican dialect to Tex-Mex to a sprinkling of Nahuatl to a mixture of all of these." In this sense, *Borderlands/La Frontera* is an "invitation" from the new *mestizas* to those who do not live on borders or who live on different borders from the one between Mexico and the United States; it is an invitation to experience a reading and writing which also is a not-knowing – specifically, not knowing what might be said to or about you in another tongue. As Anzaldúa puts it in the closing lines of the preface:

> Presently this infant language, this bastard language, Chicano Spanish, is not approved by any society. But we Chicanos no longer feel that we need to beg entrance, that we need always to make the first overture – to translate to Anglos, Mexicans and Latinos, apology blurting out of our mouths with every step. Today we ask to be met halfway.[60]

But, of course, it is never clear just where halfway is; while it is always at a border, it is not clear which border. For Anzaldúa, the border of fantasy and reality is already the border of family and community which is already the border of one nation and another, which is already the border of masculine and feminine which is already the border of heterosexuality and homosexuality. There is only the movement back and forth, across the border. So that if there is a tradition of *mestizas*, it is "a tradition of migration, a tradition of long walks."[61]

Written as part of this tradition, *Borderlands/La Frontera* crosses the borders between poetry, autobiography, epic history, and mythology – grafting together bits and pieces of all the forms usually privileged in feminists' writings. And if finally *Borderlands/La Frontera* means to focus on what Anzaldúa describes as "her preoccupations with the inner life of the Self, and with the struggle of that Self amidst adversity and violation," the point of departure is a poetry which speaks of home and its loss, the home of the *Azticas del norte*, Aztlán (the US Southwest), which at the present moment is a "thin edge of barbwire."

I press my hand to the steel curtain –
chainlink fence crowned with rolled barbed wire –
rippling from the sea where Tijuana touches San Diego
unrolling over mountains
and plains
and deserts,
this "Tortilla Curtain" turning into *el rio Grande*
flowing down to the flatlands
of Magic Valley of South Texas
its mouth emptying into the Gulf.

1,950 mile-long open wound . . .

This is my home
this thin edge of
barbwire.[62]

From the edges of poetry and history, geography and mythology, Anzaldúa gives account of "the original peopling of the Americas" and of a great *mestizaje*, formed by "the continual intermarriage between Mexican and American Indians and Spaniards."[63] She also tells of Aztlán becoming the lost land as Anglos illegally invade and dominate. Thus, throughout the nineteenth century, the border is established separating native Mexican Texans from Mexico. By the end of the nineteenth century, a border culture emerges which exists today, shaped by a political economy which makes Mexico dependent on US dollars. As Anzaldúa puts it:

> Currently, Mexico and her eight million citizens are almost completely dependent on the U.S. market. The Mexican government and wealthy growers are in partnership with such conglomerates as American Motors, IT&T and Du Pont which own factories called *maquiladoras*. One-fourth of all Mexicans work at *maquiladoras*; most are young women. Next to oil, *maquiladoras* are Mexico's second greatest source of U.S. dollars. . . . The devaluation of the *peso* and Mexico's dependency on the U.S. have brought on what the Mexicans call *las crisis. No hay trabajo.*[64]

Half of Mexico's people are unemployed, leaving them little choice but to come north or starve. But, if 19,000 people without documents inhabit the border, crossing back and forth, so too does the Border Patrol; one out of three border crossers is caught and returned. Yet, it is not only at this border that there is "suffering, pain and ignoble death." There also are the borderlands of Chicago and other cities, where Mexicans, especially women, work as domestics, or in the garment industry, or in hotel work, living sometimes fifteen people in a room, in and out of various languages, beliefs, and cultures.[65]

It is this culture, "a shock culture," shaped by the experience of migration and an internal colonization, which informs Anzaldúa's struggle with the inner life of the Self. That is to say, the inner struggle also is one of leaving and being turned back and leaving again. As Anzaldúa explains:

> I was the first in six generations to leave the Valley, the only one in my family to ever leave home. But I didn't leave all the parts of me: I kept the ground of my own being. On it I walked away, taking with me the land, the Valley, Texas.[66]

Yet even while, from an early age, Anzaldúa had a strong sense of "who I was," the rebel in her, "the Shadow Beast," nonetheless made her feel "something was 'wrong' with me."[67]

For Anzaldúa, the Shadow Beast condenses all her resistances to limitations that seem unfair to her, those imposed not only by the dominant culture but by her own cultures as well – the culture of the Church and the culture which "our mothers" pass on, demanding "that women be subservient to males."[68] Selfishness is condemned. To stand out is to make others envious enough to "use witchcraft against you."[69] As Anzaldúa puts it:

> Alienated from her mother culture, "alien" in the dominant culture, the woman of color does not feel safe with the inner life of her Self. Petrified, she can't respond, her face caught between *los intersticios*, the spaces between the different worlds she inhabits.[70]

Thus, the Shadow Beast within Anzaldúa also is feared and idealized by others. As a lesbian of color, having "made the choice to be queer," Anzaldúa speaks of the "intimate terrorism of being sold out by her own people" – forced to be "*la Chingada*, the fucked one." The Shadow Beast becomes for others "the half and half," which is magical but deformed, both masculine and feminine, "the queer," who is "the mirror reflecting the heterosexual tribe's fear: being different, being other, and therefore lesser, therefore sub-human, in-human, non-human."[71]

Thus, Anzaldúa would reinvent her ethnicity, remake her culture, *una cultura mestiza*. Made of fragments of memory, criticism, unconscious fantasy, and mythologies of survival, *una cultura mestiza* returns to *Coatlalopeuh*, homophonous to the Spanish *Guadalupe*. That is to say,

Anzaldúa restores *Coatlalopeuh* to *Guadalupe* by retracing the division of the female deities – beginning with the separation in the Azteca Mexica culture of the good mother from "her dark guises," to the Church's desexing of *Guadalupe* and its defining all Indian deities the work of the devil. Thus, *Guadalupe*, "the single most potent religious, political and cultural image of the Chicano/*mexicano*," is reclaimed as *una mestiza.*[72]

Identified with Indian and Spanish cultures, conqueror and conquered, reality and spirit, *Guadalupe* also is made to disturb the rational modes of communication, including the human sciences of Western discourse. For Anzaldúa, then, reclaiming *Guadalupe* is a way to reclaim a mode of consciousness other than that of "white rationality." As Anzaldúa describes it:

> The other mode of consciousness facilitates images from the soul and the unconscious through dreams and the imagination. Its work is labeled "fiction," make-believe, wish-fulfillment. White anthropologists claim that Indians have "primitive" and therefore deficient minds, that we cannot think in the higher mode of consciousness – rationality. They are fascinated by what they call the "magical" mind, the "savage" mind, the *participation mystique* of the mind that says the world of the imagination – the world of the soul – and of the spirit is just as real as physical reality.[73]

But Anzaldúa not only rejects the opposition of fact and fiction, of the magical and the rational; she also speaks of this rejection as a process which the subject actually suffers, what she describes as "entering the *Coatlicue* state" – a returning to the dark aspects of *Coatlalopeuh,* that at the same time implies a withdrawal of allegiance to the modern nation-state, questioning the legitimacy of its violence. Thus, although Anzaldúa describes the process of entering the *Coatlicue* state as an experience of rupture in the taken-for-grantedness of the everyday world, it is not merely a matter of a bifurcation of consciousness that opens to a critique of the relations of ruling, to use the terminology of standpoint epistemologies.

It is more a matter of falling into "the underground aspects of the psyche,"[74] "the deep dark earth of the unconscious"[75] – something other, something else alongside the suffering of oppressions. Anzaldúa puts it this way:

> No, it isn't enough that she is female – a second-class member of a conquered people who are taught to believe they are inferior because they have indigenous blood, believe in the supernatural and speak a deficient language. . . . Why does she have to go and try to make "sense" of it all?

> Every time she makes "sense" of something she has to "cross over,"
> kicking a hole out of the old boundaries of the self and slipping under or
> over, dragging the old skin along, stumbling over it. It hampers her
> movement in the new territory, dragging the ghost of the past with her. It
> is a dry birth, a breech birth, a screaming birth, one that fights her every
> inch of the way.[76]

It is these dry births which give life to *la facultad*, a capacity for "instant
sensing, a quick perception arrived at by the part of the psyche that does
not speak."[77] *La facultad* informs the new *mestiza* consciousness, a
consciousness which refuses to "disown the white parts, the pathological
parts, the queer parts, the vulnerable parts."[78] The new consciousness,
then, returns to subjectivity its otherness disavowed and displaced onto
the Other in Western discourse. The new consciousness is so imbued with
the deep darkness of the psyche that consciousness loses the meaning it
has had in being opposed to irrationality or the unconscious. Indeed, for
Anzaldúa, the new consciousness is not a consciousness of being and
experience but a consciousness that is always already of the unconscious:
the unconscious of poetical writing, of *escritura y sabiduria*.

For Anzaldúa, then, writing is not opposed to living; it is a way to live:
"words, my passion for the daily struggle to render them concrete in
the world and on the paper, to render them flesh, keeps me alive." But
if writing keeps Anzaldúa alive, it is because writing "has a mind of
its own," "insisting on putting together the pieces of its own puzzle
with minimal direction from my will."[79] Thus, Anzaldúa describes her
self when writing as "I 'trance,'" allowing "scenes to be projected in
the inner screen of my mind,"[80] "gripped by a story which won't let me
go."[81]

> Gradually I become so engrossed with the activities, the conversations that
> I become a participant in the drama. I have to struggle to "disengage" or
> escape from my "animated story. . . ." Outside the frame, I am film direc-
> tor, screenwriter, camera operator. Inside the frame, I am the actors – male
> and female – I am desert sand, mountain, I am dog, mosquito.[82]

Anzaldúa struggles to direct her imaginary but can only fail. There is
an excess in the difference between the framer and the framed, between
the actor in the scene and the director of it; they are never identical. There
is an excess in subjectivity which is never fully caught in or outside the
frame, the excess of the unconscious, the Not-I. This excess always slips
representation, even those representations in which Anzaldúa seeks to
give this excess substance – in the imagery of writing as a painful birthing
or as a delightful flowering.

Living in a state of psychic unrest, in a Borderland, is what makes poets write and artists create. It is like a cactus needle embedded in the flesh. It worries itself deeper and deeper, and I keep aggravating it by poking at it. When it begins to fester I have to do something to put an end to the aggravation and to figure out why I have it. I get deep down into the place where it's rooted in my skin and pluck away at it, playing it like a musical instrument – the fingers pressing, making the pain worse before it can get better. Then out it comes.[83]

Picking out images from my soul's eye, fishing for the right words to recreate the images. Words are blades of grass pushing past the obstacles, sprouting on the page; the spirit of the words moving in the body is as concrete as flesh and as palpable; the hunger to create is as substantial as finger and hand. I look at my fingers, see plumes growing there.[84]

The language is excessive. It speaks excess: writing is as concrete, substantial, and palpable as fingers but fingers grow plumes. It is not so much that the psyche urges poetry; it is that the psyche cannot fully be represented and therefore every attempt fails. It is this failure which is the condition of possibility of poetical writing. Thus, poetical writing frames theory with this failure, thereby profoundly disturbing the seeming necessity of theory to be abstract, rational, academic. Poetical writing makes theory useful, makes it political, makes it beautiful. As Anzaldúa puts it:

Theorists-of-color are in the process of trying to formulate "marginal" theories that are partially outside and partially inside the Western frame of reference (if that is possible), theories that overlap many "worlds." We are articulating new positions in these "in-between," Borderland worlds of ethnic communities and academies, feminist and job worlds. In our literature, social issues such as race, class and sexual difference are intertwined with the narrative and poetic elements of a text, elements in which theory is embedded. In our *mestizaje* theories we create new categories for those of us left out or pushed out of the existing ones. We recover and examine non-Western aesthetics while critiquing Western aesthetics; recover and examine non-rational modes and "blanked-out" realities while critiquing rational, consensual reality; recover and examine indigenous languages while critiquing the "languages" of the dominant culture.[85]

Thus, not only does the post-colonial criticism of Third World feminism disarticulate Western discourse by writing the in-between of identities, ethnicities, languages, and discourses – "the in-between of all definitions of truth;"[86] it also attempts to write the otherness of subjectivity, the difference within, which is simply not reducible to cultural differences. And since the otherness of subjectivity will slip its representation, only a politics of form can mark its breath, its spirit, its coming and going, its being and non-being. Only a politics of form allows the post-colonial critic to uncover and recover from the disavowal of otherness in Western discourse. Thus, Anzaldúa writes of her thousand eyes, the infinite layers that is and is not the I:

> Something pulsates in my body luminous thin thing that grows thicker every day. Its presence never leaves me. I am never alone. That which abides: my vigilance, my thousand sleepless serpent eyes blinking in the night, forever open. And I am not afraid.[87]

Afterwords

In introducing two collections of writings by Women of Color, *This Bridge Called My Back* (1981, republished 1983) and *Making Face, Making Soul, Haciendo Caras* (1990), Anzaldúa argues that there are no bridges to the territory beyond the shadows; they must be built on the way. Like making face and making soul, the bridges are made with deeds, entangled in and with words.[88] Indeed, the bridges are new ways of reading and writing differences which simply cannot be incorporated into dominant forms or frames of reference, such as ethnography with its reductive impulse to capture the Other. For these feminists – Women of Color, the deconstruction of the "grand narratives of the human sciences" becomes a matter of politics, a matter of survival.

But still other feminist theorists have distanced themselves from a critique of representation and discursive authority, especially a critique of ethnographic authority. But, these feminists who would retreat from a politics of form usually only focus on a version of that politics that male critics of ethnography have offered in the name of postmodernism. Thus, Frances Mascia-Lees, Patricia Sharpe, and Colleen Ballerino Cohen (1989) have urged a rejection of the postmodern critique of ethnographic authority elaborated by James Clifford (1988), and George Marcus and Michael Fischer (1986), among others.[89]

Arguing that these male writers only re-establish insights already developed in feminist theory, Mascia-Lees, Sharpe, and Cohen suggest that feminist theory not only has elaborated "women's experience of otherness" but also it has uncovered "the inscription of women as other in language and discourse."[90] As they put it:

> This was particularly evident in feminist literary criticism, which moved from the cataloging of stereotypes to the story of female authorship as

resistance and reinscription. French feminists, notably Hélène Cixous and Luce Irigaray, playfully exploited language's metaphoric and polysemic capacities to give voice to feminist reinterpretations of dominant myths about women.[91]

While correctly insisting that male critics of ethnography have all but ignored the work of feminist critics of representation and discursive authority, Mascia-Lees, Sharpe, and Cohen themselves seem uninterested in critical works by feminist critics other than the gynocritics and French feminists to whom they only make brief reference. Instead, Mascia-Lees, Sharpe, and Cohen simply assert that "feminists speak from the position of the 'other.'"[92] They therefore not only assume that all feminists think alike but that they all think that all women experience otherness in the same way. They also assume that otherness is only a production of gender, as the gynocritics and the French feminists to whom they refer seemingly propose.

Thus, Mascia-Lees, Sharpe, and Cohen not only do not engage feminist criticism of representation and discursive authority very much more than male critics of ethnography do. They also fail to closely attend to the writings of African-American feminists, the writings of Women of Color, the post-colonial criticism of Third World feminists. Instead Mascia-Lees, Sharpe, and Cohen would reinvest anthropology with the privilege of being "'power brokers,' translating between the subordinate, disenfranchised group and the dominant class or power."[93] That is to say, while they paraphrase Nancy Hartsock's often referred to comment on the curiosity of the fact that the postmodern criticism of the subject and experience arises "precisely when women and non-Western peoples have begun to speak for themselves and, indeed, to speak about global systems of power differentials,"[94] Mascia-Lees, Sharpe, and Cohen nonetheless assume that anthropologists, if they are feminists, may speak for the subordinate, for the subaltern classes, due to the equality of otherness shared by all women alike.

Indeed, Mascia-Lees, Sharpe, and Cohen finally liken the feminist anthropologist to the post-colonial critic, whom they describe as "a Third World person who has been educated at Oxbridge."[95] They suggest that like post-colonial critics, feminist anthropologists are, at the same time, "the socially constituted 'other'" and speakers "within the dominant discourse, never able to place ourselves wholly or uncritically in either position."[96] Yet, Mascia-Lees, Sharpe, and Cohen refuse to recognize the practice of writing that post-colonial critics, Third World feminists, have elaborated precisely to recognize the scandal of their production, an effort, as Spivak puts it, "to unlearn our privilege," as well as to recognize that the human sciences are themselves global communication systems of power differentials.

Mascia-Lees, Sharpe, and Cohen rather imagine the feminist anthropologist, the post-colonial critic, and the subordinated or subaltern classes to equally share an alienation from their own cultures – an alienation first described by the Great Master, which Trinh argues made the anthropologist the Great Hero of modernity: "Gone out of date, then revitalized, the mission of civilizing the savage mutates into the imperative of 'making equal.' "[97]

Thus, in contrast to Mascia-Lees, Sharpe, and Cohen, Trinh suggests that while critics of ethnography like Clifford, Marcus, and Fischer have opened up the opposition of the literary and the social scientific, they have failed to problematize the literary enough, "making it quite easy for anthropologists to bypass, if not dismiss, the issues raised by confining them to the realm of 'literature:' "

> Not only is this literary consciousness viewed merely as "a new critical appreciation of ethnography" or as a preceding step to the reconceptualization and revalorizing of anthropological careers (as I have mentioned earlier, opening up "a self/other referential language-space where the observing-writing subject watches himself observe and write while foregrounding the specific instances of discourse involved in his own writing" has little in common with the moralistic self-knowledge and self-criticism aiming at "improvement"), but "literary" in Marcus's context does not constitute a site of discussion nor is the word problematized in its contemporary, controversial connotations.[98]

What cannot be made visible if the literary is not itself problematized is the transference of the authorial subject's otherness onto some Other, made possible for all narratives of Western discourse by the dominant narrative fiction of oedipus. What cannot be made visible if the literary is not itself problematized is how ethnography is a legitimizing form of voyeurism; how it is a narrative which deploys a rhetoric of sexual difference that erases differences – gender, racial, class, ethnic, sexual, and national differences.

What would be missed by not problematizing the literary is recognizing that the deconstruction of ethnographic authority proposed by post-colonial critics is a criticism of all social science, revealing that the disavowal of the literary, narrative, or discursive construction of social scientific authority is not only necessary to that authority but intimately connects that authority to a certain understanding of the nation-state and, therefore, to a certain mode of reading and writing the social. If, as Benedict Anderson argues, nations are imagined, then the ethnographic form has served as a narrative deployment of a national imaginary which means to manage both the multiculturalism produced by migration and the transnational produced by colonialism and neo-colonialism.[99]

In its criticism of the human sciences, then, post-colonial criticism furthers the reinvention of both the social and the literary, further collapsing the opposition of fantasy and reality, fiction and history, polemic and academic discourse, literary criticism and social science. By turning feminism to the task of criticizing the epistemological violence that has shaped the globalization of relations of power/knowledge, post-colonial criticism not only calls for approaches to knowledges that challenge inequality without erasing the local. It also therefore calls for reconceiving the transnational frame in terms of which identity, experience, and knowledge are configured – to reconceive the way in which the social is read.

Notes

1 These remarks are taken from a 1990 interview published in Trinh T. Minh-ha, *Framer Framed* (New York: Routledge, 1992), p. 155.
2 See Barbara Christian, "The Race for Theory," in Gloria Anzaldúa (ed.), *Making Face, Making Soul, Haciendo Caras* (San Francisco: Aunt Lute, 1990), pp. 335–45 and "The Highs and the Lows of Black Feminist Criticism," in Henry Louis Gates, Jr (ed.), *Reading Black, Reading Feminist* (New York: Meridian, 1990), pp. 44–51.
3 These remarks are taken from a 1989 interview published in Trinh, *Framer Framed*, p. 123.
4 The scripts for these three of Trinh's films appear in *Framer Framed*.
5 These remarks are taken from a 1990 interview published in Trinh, *Framer Framed*, p. 154.
6 These remarks are taken from a 1989 interview published in Trinh, *Framer Framed*, p. 122.
7 These remarks are taken from a 1990 interview published in Trinh, *Framer Framed*, p. 140.
8 Bill Ashcroft, Gareth Griffiths, and Helen Tiffin, *The Empire Writes Back: Theory and Practice in Post-Colonial Literatures* (New York: Routledge, 1989), p. 9.
9 These remarks are taken from a 1990 interview published in Trinh, *Framer Framed*, p. 157.
10 Ibid., p. 157.
11 Ibid., p. 157.
12 These remarks are taken from a 1986 interview published in Gayatri Chakravorty Spivak, *The Post-Colonial Critic: Interviews, Strategies, Dialogues*, Sarah Harasym (ed.) (New York: Routledge, 1990), p. 51.
13 Gayatri Chakravorty Spivak, "Can the Subaltern Speak?," in Cary Nelson and Lawrence Grossberg (eds), *Marxism and the Interpretation of Culture*

(Urbana: University of Illinois Press, 1988), p. 288.

14 Gayatri Chakravorty Spivak, "Subaltern Studies: Deconstructing Historiography," in Ranajit Guha and Gayatri Chakravorty Spivak (eds), *Selected Subaltern Studies* (New York: Oxford University Press, 1988), p. 16.

15 Jenny Sharpe, *Allegories of Empire: The Figure of the Woman in the Colonial Text* (Minnesota: University of Minnesota Press, 1993), p. 17.

16 Spivak, "Can the Subaltern Speak?," pp. 284–5.

17 Gayatri Chakravorty Spivak, *In Other Worlds: Essays in Cultural Politics* (New York: Methuen, 1987), p. 203.

18 Spivak, "Can the Subaltern Speak?," p. 308.

19 Ibid., p. 284.

20 Ibid., pp. 288–9.

21 Ibid., p. 289.

22 These remarks are taken from a 1990 interview published in Trinh, *Framer Framed*, p. 139.

23 Gloria Anzaldúa, *Borderlands/La Frontera* (San Francisco: Aunt Lute, 1987), p. 22.

24 For discussions of the international division of labor and Third World feminism, see especially Kathryn Ward's Introduction, in Kathryn Ward (ed.), *Women Workers and Global Restructuring* (Cornell: Cornell University Press, 1990).

25 These remarks are taken from a 1990 interview published in Trinh, *Framer Framed*, p. 163.

26 Anzaldúa, *Borderlands/La Frontera*, p. 66.

27 Trinh T. Minh-ha, *Woman, Native, Other: Writing Postcoloniality and Feminism* (Bloomington: Indiana University Press, 1989), p. 22.

28 Ibid., p. 6.

29 Ibid., p. 7.

30 Ibid., p. 9.

31 Ibid., p. 6.

32 Ibid., p. 12.

33 Ibid., p. 11.

34 Ibid., p. 16.

35 Hélène Cixous, "The Laugh of the Medusa," translated by Keith Cohen and Paula Cohen, *Signs*, 1 (1976), p. 884. Trinh also discusses the works of Cixous and other "French feminists" in her *When the Moon Waxes Red: Representation, Gender and Cultural Politics* (New York: Routledge, 1991).

36 Gayatri Chakravorty Spivak, "French Feminism in an International Frame," *Yale French Studies*, 62 (1981), pp. 154–84. Spivak has since returned to her earlier discussion of French feminism and still finds useful the work of both Cixous and Irigaray; see *Outside in the Teaching Machine* (New York: Routledge, 1993), pp. 141–71.

37 Trinh, *Woman, Native, Other*, p. 39.

38 Ibid., p. 39.

39 These remarks are taken from a 1984 interview published in Spivak, *The Post-Colonial Critic*, p. 1.

40 Ibid., p. 2.
41 These remarks are taken from a 1984 interview published in Spivak, *The Post-Colonial Critic*, p. 25.
42 Trinh, *Woman, Native, Other*, p. 48.
43 Ibid., p. 63.
44 Ibid., p. 63.
45 Trinh takes this remark from Claude Lévi-Strauss, *The Scope of Anthropology*, translated by S. Ortner Paul and R. A. Paul (London: Jonathan Cape, 1971), p. 26.
46 Ibid., p. 68.
47 Ibid., p. 69.
48 Ibid., p. 74. Here, Trinh is attributing the term "Great Master" to Bronislaw Malinowski and is referring to his *A Diary in the Strict Sense of the Term* (New York: Harcourt, Brace and World, 1967).
49 Ibid., p. 80.
50 Ibid., pp. 100–4.
51 Ibid., p. 94.
52 Ibid., p. 119.
53 These remarks are taken from a 1989 interview published in Spivak, *The Post-Colonial Critic*, pp. 166–7.
54 These remarks are taken from a 1987 interview published in Trinh, *Framer Framed*, p. 182.
55 These remarks are taken from a 1990 interview published in Trinh, *Framer Framed*, p. 163.
56 These remarks are taken from a 1990 interview published in Trinh, *Framer Framed*, pp. 142–4.
57 These remarks are taken from a 1987 interview published in Spivak, *The Post-Colonial Critic*, p. 71.
58 These remarks are taken from a 1990 interview published in Trinh, *Framer Framed*, p. 139.
59 Anzaldúa, *Borderlands/La Frontera*, the pages to the preface are not numbered.
60 Anzaldúa, *Borderlands/La Frontera*, the pages to the preface are not numbered.
61 Anzaldúa, *Borderlands/La Frontera*, p. 11.
62 Ibid., p. 2.
63 Ibid., p. 5.
64 Ibid., p. 10.
65 Ibid., pp. 11–13.
66 Ibid., p. 16.
67 Ibid., p. 16.
68 Ibid., p. 17.
69 Ibid., p. 18.
70 Ibid., p. 20.
71 Ibid., p. 18.
72 Ibid., p. 30.

73   Ibid., p. 37.
74   Ibid., p. 46.
75   Ibid., p. 47.
76   Ibid., pp. 48–9.
77   Ibid., p. 38.
78   Ibid., p. 88.
79   Ibid., p. 66.
80   Ibid., p. 69.
81   Ibid., p. 70.
82   Ibid., p. 70.
83   Ibid., p. 73.
84   Ibid., p. 71.
85   Gloria Anzaldúa, "*Haciendo caras, una entrada,*" in Gloria Anzaldúa (ed.), *Making Face, Making Soul, Haciendo Caras*, p. xxvi.
86   These remarks are taken from the script of Trinh's film *Naked Spaces* in Trinh, *Framer Framed*, p. 13.
87   Anzaldúa, *Borderlands/La Frontera*, p. 51.
88   Cherrié Moraga and Gloria Anzaldúa (eds), *This Bridge Called My Back* (New York: Kitchen Table, 1983); Anzaldúa, *Making Face, Making Soul, Haciendo Caras*.
89   See James Clifford, *The Predicament of Culture* (Cambridge: Harvard University Press, 1988) and George Marcus and Michael Fischer (eds), *Anthropology as Cultural Critique: An Experimental Moment in the Human Sciences* (Chicago: University of Chicago Press, 1986).
90   Frances Mascia-Lees, et al., "The Postmodernist Turn in Anthropology," *Signs*, 15 (1989), pp. 7–33.
91   Ibid., p. 12.
92   Ibid., p. 11.
93   Ibid., p. 24.
94   Ibid., p. 15.
95   Ibid., p. 33.
96   Ibid., p. 33.
97   Trinh, *Woman, Native, Other*, p. 59.
98   Ibid., p. 157n.
99   See Benedict Anderson, *Imagined Communities: Reflections on the Origin and Spread of Nationalism* (London: Verso, 1983). For a discussion of the narrative deployment of a rhetoric of sexual difference in the construction of a national imaginary see Andrew Parker, et al. (eds), *Nationalisms and Sexualities* (New York: Routledge, 1992).

6

Queer Embodiments of Feminist Theorizing

If both Trinh T. Minh-ha and Gloria Anzaldúa draw a connection between bisexuality or queerness and the hybridization of identity, it not only raises a question about the relationship of sexuality and (dis)identity politics; it raises the question specifically in terms of the relationship of feminist theorizing and what Judith Butler would refer to as "the hegemony of the matrix of heterosexual desire." Thus, whereas Trinh and Anzaldua trouble the human sciences with differences of race, class, gender, ethnicity, nationality, and sexuality, in *Gender Trouble: Feminism and the Subversion of Identity* (1990), Judith Butler specifically focuses her criticism of the human sciences on their deployment of the opposition of heterosexuality and homosexuality. In contributing to the development of what is referred to as "queer theory," Butler not only revises the relationship of lesbian criticism and feminist theorizing of gender and sexuality; she also challenges the heterosexism which queer theorists argue is constitutive of the epistemology of experience upon which the human sciences are grounded.

Indeed, throughout the late 1970s and the early 1980s, an intimate relationship between feminism and lesbianism often was assumed by feminist theorists.[1] That is, lesbianism was treated as a political choice, indeed the only political choice for feminists. Therefore, lesbian relationships usually were represented simply as relationships between women – not so much sexual but personal, emotional, nurturing, perhaps romantic. Indeed, when in 1980 Adrienne Rich proposed the notion of the "lesbian continuum," she extended the identity of lesbian to "woman-identified" women who both share "a rich inner life" and bond together "against male tyranny."[2] But even earlier, in 1973, the Radicalesbians already had identified the lesbian as "a woman-identified woman" who "acts in accordance with her inner compulsion to be a more complete and freer human being," unable "to accept the limitations and oppression laid on her by the most basic role of her society – the female role."[3] And in 1977 when Barbara Smith urged the establishment of a Black feminist literary criticism, she also proposed that all Black women's writing has an "innately lesbian" character:

> Not because women are "lovers," but because they are the central figures, they are positively portrayed and have pivotal relationships with one another. The form and language of these works are also nothing like what white patriarchal culture requires or expects.[4]

Whereas this view of lesbianism risked blurring all distinction of lesbian relationships from female friendships and women's political alliances, there also was a development throughout the late 1970s and the early 1980s of a lesbian literary criticism that did assume the uniqueness of the lesbian experience and the lesbian identity. After all, from the late 1970s through the early 1980s, a gay community was making itself visible, at the same time that gay-identified writers both outside and inside the academy articulated the specificity of gay identity and gay experience. Indeed, Bonnie Zimmerman argues that the lesbian criticism of this period usually proceeded from the assumptions "that one could (with difficulty perhaps) define a category called lesbian, that lesbians shared certain experiences and concepts and that discursive practices – literary texts, critical analyses, political theories – proceed from lived experiences."[5]

However, assuming the specificity of gay identity and gay experience only opened both to further specification and to the elaboration of their specific historical and cultural constructions, eventually undermining any sense of a uniform gay experience or a unified gay identity. For example, the equation of lesbianism with a feminist identity or with a woman-identified femininity was challenged in the so-called "sex debates" of the 1980s as some lesbian feminists defended sexual practices that had been criticized as male-identified, such as S/M and Butch-Femme.[6] Also throughout the 1980s, Women of Color increasingly refused notions of a unified lesbian identity or a uniform lesbian experience.

Thus, the privileging of a lesbian criticism which was meant to more authentically render both a lesbian identity and a lesbian experience already was being challenged, when lesbian critics entered what Zimmerman describes as "the current great debates" brought on by post-structuralism and deconstructive philosophy.[7] Indeed, these critical approaches would transform lesbian criticism into what Sally Munt refers to as "dkonstruction," that is, a deconstruction and reconstruction of "our own narratives of difference."[8] But, the shift to dkonstruction not only reflects the influence of post-structuralism and deconstruction on lesbian criticism, instigating the development of queer theory; it also indicates the effect queer theory would have on literary criticism and feminist theorizing generally. Indeed, queer theorists return literary criticism and feminist theorizing to sexuality – specifically to questions about the deployment of the opposition of heterosexuality and homosexuality in the construction of disciplinary knowledges and their underlying epistemology of experience. Queer theorists mean to trouble experience and identity, especially by problematizing the insistence on identifying the lesbian and the homosexual man.

Thus, following on archaeologies of sexuality like Michel Foucault's, queer theorists argue that by the nineteenth century, a discourse on homosexuality had developed that was not so much about the discovery of homosexual behavior but about the initiation of what Eve Kosofsky Sedgwick describes as "the crisis of homo/heterosexual definition" – a "world mapping by which every given person, just as he or she was necessarily assignable to a male or a female gender, was now considered necessarily assignable as well to a homo- or a hetero-sexuality."[9] By the nineteenth century, then, the homo/heterosexual definition not only informs the very shape of personal life; it also is central to the disciplining of knowledge.

Therefore, Sedgwick describes the epistemology of experience that, by the nineteenth century, grounds the human sciences as an "epistemology of the closet" in order to indicate how the opposition of homosexuality and heterosexuality was made the figure of other oppositions upon which an epistemology of experience depends and which it maintains – oppositions such as:

> secrecy/disclosure, knowledge/ignorance, private/public, masculine/feminine, majority/minority, innocence/initiation, natural/artificial, new/old, discipline/terrorism, canonic/noncanonic, wholeness/decadence, urbane/provincial, domestic/foreign, health/illness, same/difference, active/passive, in/out, cognition/paranoia, art/kitsch, utopia/apocalypse, sincerity/sentimentality, and voluntarity/addiction.[10]

To describe an epistemology of experience as an epistemology of the closet is to "out" epistemology, to expose it, suggesting that epistemology is not as it appears to be. It is to suggest that an epistemology of experience not only is a prescription to ground knowledge in the actual, the visible, the experiential; it therefore is as much about the constitution of a "plethora of ignorances." As Sedgwick puts it:

If ignorance is not – as it evidently is not – a single Manichaean, aboriginal maw of darkness from which the heroics of human cognition can occasionally wrestle facts, insights, freedoms, progress, perhaps there exists instead a plethora of *ignorances*, and we may begin to ask questions about the labor, erotics, and economics of their human production and distribution. Insofar as ignorance is ignorance *of* a knowledge – a knowledge that may itself, it goes without saying, be seen as either true or false under some other regime of truth – these ignorances, far from being pieces of the originary dark, are produced by and correspond to particular knowledges and circulate as part of particular regimes of truth.[11]

Indeed, it is the production and distribution of excusable ignorances and legitimated knowledges that makes possible what Foucault has described as subjugated knowledge – that is, knowledge about which some can without excuse simply claim ignorance, but which others are all but forced to embody. Thus, feminist standpoint epistemologies which make subjugated knowledges public and transform them into legitimate knowledges are relatively dependent on relations of the closet, and therefore feminist theorists who advocate standpoint epistemologies cannot critically engage questions about the ideological relationship of epistemology, identity, and experience – at least, not fully.

But, queer theory refuses to be a standpoint epistemology; it even calls into question the standpoint epistemology of the lesbian feminist criticism of the late 1970s and earlier 1980s. Instead, queer theory shifts the focus of a lesbian feminist criticism and of feminist theorizing generally from an epistemology of experience to the exploration of the practices of disciplining knowledge – asking "how certain categorizations work, what enactments they are performing and what relations they are creating rather than what they essentially *mean*."[12] For Butler, this shift from an epistemology of experience to locating "the problematic [of knowledge] within practices of *signification* permits an analysis that takes the epistemological mode itself as one possible and contingent signifying practice."[13] Thus, for Butler, as for Sedgwick, the deconstruction of the opposition of heterosexuality and homosexuality is intimately related to ejecting an epistemology of experience from its position of centrality in relationship both to knowledge and to politics.

Hence, queer theorists reject any radical disjuncture between heterosexuality and homosexuality and instead argue more along the lines of what Sedgwick describes as the "universalizing view" of homosexuality rather than the "minoritizing view." If the latter proposes that the homo/heterosexual definition only is important for a "homosexual minority," the former position suggests that the homo/heterosexual definition is of "determinative importance in the lives of people across the spectrum of sexualities."[14] It is in elaborating the universalizing view of homosexuality that Butler proposes that "there are structures of psychic homosexuality within heterosexual relations, and structures of psychic heterosexuality within gay and lesbian sexuality and relationships."[15]

For Butler, then, the universalizing view of homosexuality returns the deconstruction of the homo/heterosexual definition to an analysis of fantasy, the psyche, and unconscious desire. Thus, she criticizes the treatment of gender as a social construction of sexuality, for the way it naturalizes sexuality, especially anatomy, thereby denying its fantasmatic construction. Sedgwick even proposes that, quite likely, "a damaging bias toward heterosocial or heterosexist assumptions inheres unavoidably in the very concept of gender."[16] Thus, Sedgwick instead insists on a treatment of sexuality "that will respect a certain irreducibility in it to the terms and relations of gender."[17]

In returning sexuality to questions of the psyche, fantasy, and unconscious desire, queer theory, even more than a feminist counterpsychoanalysis, proposes that the treatment of gender as a social construction of sexuality not only fails to elaborate the fantasmatic construction of sexual identities. It also fails to treat the fantasmatic construction of what Freud defined as "the active and passive aims" of sexual desire – what Butler refers to as the "modalities" of sexual desire. The treatment of gender as the social construction of sexuality therefore fails to undertake a critical deconstruction of "sexual orientation." Even more than a feminist counterpsychoanalysis, queer theory proposes that the treatment of gender as the social construction of sexuality, indeed the notion of social construction generally, are articulated as defenses against the heterogeneity of unconscious desire in terms of both sexual aims and sexual identifications.

Thus, queer theory, especially Butler's articulation of it in *Gender Trouble*, not only deconstructs the opposition of sexuality and gender usually assumed in feminist theorizing. It also deconstructs the opposition of nature and the social, especially by reconceiving the body or anatomy – treating them not as nature but as screenings of unconscious fantasies, projected "performances of being," as Butler puts it. Thus, if *Gender Trouble* also calls into question the matrix of heterosexual desire in terms of which the psyche usually has been constituted in psychoanalytic accounts, the effect, I would propose, is not merely to dismiss the psyche but rather to make visible the play of unconscious fantasies on the surface of social constructions of reality – bodies or anatomies, Butler's prime examples. Queer theory, then, not only further collapses the distinction of fantasy and reality, fiction and history, polemic and academic discourse, literary criticism and social science; it does so by uncovering the intimate relationship of an epistemology of experience and heterosexism.

Troubling the Matrix of Heterosexual Desire

If Butler titles the first chapter of *Gender Trouble* "Subjects of Sex/Gender/Desire," she also immediately puts the title in trouble with the epigrams placed just beneath it. She draws from the writings of Simone de Beauvoir: "One is not born a woman, but rather becomes one;" from the writings of Julia Kristeva: "Strictly speaking, 'women' cannot be said to exist;" from the writings of Luce Irigaray: "Woman does not have a sex;" from the writings of Michel Foucault: "The deployment of sexuality . . . established this notion of sex;" and finally from the writings of Monique Wittig: "The category of sex is the political category that founds society as heterosexual."

Thus at the very start of *Gender Trouble*, Butler seems to suggest that if there are subjects of sex/gender/desire, they are not nor can they easily be identified as feminine. But it is not Butler's aim to define the conditions of possibility of identifying a feminine subject, but rather to challenge the very notion of a feminine subject-identity, especially the way feminist theorists have assumed the necessity of a unified feminine subject-identity as a precondition of a feminist politics. Although she is aware that other feminist theorists already have questioned the proposed unity of a feminine subject-identity both for the way it necessarily excludes the division of unconscious desire, as well as the differences of race, class, ethnicity, and nationality, Butler nonetheless argues that even most of these feminist theorists assume an already sexed body in their discussions of identity. It is this assumption that Butler calls into question in rereadings of the writings of Beauvoir, Irigaray, Foucault, Wittig, and Kristeva.

Thus, Butler suggests that although Beauvoir had argued that women are not born and that gender is socially constructed, still, the body to which socially constructed genders are imagined to adhere is uncritically assumed by Beauvoir to be the sexed body – a passive medium of culture. Indeed, Butler proposes that most feminist theorizing is sociological in this sense, treating gender as a socially constructed elaboration of the seemingly just-thereness of anatomy. It is in these sociological terms, then, that Beauvoir suggests that what is wrong for women is that their identities are socially constructed as the "Other" of masculinity.

But for Irigaray, both the subject and the other are masculine; that is to say, only masculinity can be produced again and again in a closed phallocentric signifying economy, which the dominant fiction of oedipus is. The feminine is not the other of masculinity; it is excluded altogether.

Thus, whereas Beauvoir would demand that women be represented as subjects, Irigaray argues that the symbolic order as a whole is inadequate to women's being represented. For Irigaray, then, the female is not always marked as "sexuality, itself" as Beauvoir and Wittig often imply. Instead femininity is absent, never marked in phallocentricism, although the erasure of the feminine leaves a trace.

Thus, Butler suggests that Irigaray "clearly broadens the scope of feminist critique by exposing the epistemological, ontological, and logical structures of a masculinist signifying economy."[18] Still, Butler rejects Irigaray's proposal for the elaboration of a feminine imaginary, finding it totalizing and essentialist but specifically because it does not make clear how female and male bodies are constituted, as such. Irigaray also assumes the sexed body.

And although Foucault insists that the category of sex is a production of a diffuse regulatory economy of sexuality, even he sometimes alludes to a pre-discursive natural libidinal multiplicity or heterogeneity outside the regulatory disciplines; Butler's example is Foucault's introduction to the journals he published of Herculine Barbin, a nineteenth-century hermaphrodite. Butler argues the same for Wittig's proposal that the deconstruction of the hegemony of heterosexuality would enable women to be universal subjects – just personal identities. Wittig not only assumes the already sexed body; as Foucault sometimes does, Wittig assumes a pre-discursive natural libidinal state, at least for women.

For Butler, then, while phallocentric discourse may deny women representation as subjects altogether or only represent them as masculinity's otherness, the question remains as to how phallocentric discourse constitutes "only" male and female bodies. Thus, Butler proposes that the very substance of the sexed body, in terms of which a personal identity or a natural libidinal heterogeneity usually are claimed, is itself an effect of a certain construction of identity that underwrites "the internal coherence of the subject, indeed, the self-identical status of the person."[19] Thus, Butler asks:

> To what extent is "identity" a normative ideal rather than a descriptive feature of experience? And how do the regulatory practices that govern gender also govern culturally intelligible notions of identity? In other words, the "coherence" and "continuity" of "the person" are not logical or analytic features of personhood, but, rather, socially instituted and maintained norms of intelligibility.[20]

Butler's remarks propose that discussions of identity always presuppose some regulatory practices governing gender and that these practices are not just about gender but are modes of reading the social – that is, socially instituted and maintained norms of intelligibility. Thus, Butler challenges all sociological discussions of identity because they "have conventionally sought to understand the notion of the person in terms of an agency that claims ontological priority to the various roles and functions through which it assumes social visibility and meaning."[21] She also challenges the philosophical account of the person, because it "almost always centers on the question of what internal feature of the person establishes the continuity or self-identity of the person through time . . ."[22] Both the conventional sociological treatment of roles and their functions, as well as the traditional philosophical treatment of the person, disavow the regulatory practices of gender which constitute intelligibility in the first place.

For Butler, then, "'intelligible' genders are those which in some sense institute and maintain relations of coherence and continuity among sex, gender, sexual practice, and desire."[23] That is, for Butler, gender identity cannot presuppose a sexed body; sexed bodies and gender identities are constructed at the same time. Genders and sexualities refer to prior norms of intelligibility, even while these norms function through aligning sex, gender, sexual practice, and desire. Thus, if Sedgwick argues that sexuality is irreducible to gender, Butler puts it somewhat differently; she suggests that sex does not precede gender. Instead, a regulatory fiction functions to converge sex, gender, and desire. Butler names this regulatory fiction "the heterosexual matrix of desire," by which she means something close to what Kaja Silverman describes as the dominant fiction of oedipus. But if Silverman emphasizes the way in which the dominant fiction functions to construct the hegemony of a propertied, white, heterosexual masculinity, Butler emphasizes how the dominant fiction necessarily defines as impossible certain identities of bodies, desires, genders, and sexual practices. As she puts it:

> The cultural matrix through which gender identity has become intelligible requires that certain kinds of identities cannot "exist" – that is, those in which gender does not follow from sex and those in which the practices of desire do not "follow" from either sex or gender.[24]

To deconstruct the matrix of heterosexual desire, then, Butler returns to psychoanalysis. Even though Butler argues that there are possibilities for not repeating the domination implied by a hegemonic heterosexual masculinity, she nonetheless recognizes what psychoanalysis proposes – that is, the impossibility of separating desire either from the matrix of heterosexuality or from phallocentrism. For Butler, then, psychoanalysis must be engaged because it is the discourse which problematizes the matrix of heterosexual desire, without simply denying it. But while Butler makes use of psychoanalysis to trouble gender identity, she also troubles psychoanalysis, even a feminist counterpsychoanalysis. That is, her criticism of the matrix of heterosexual desire focuses on "some aspects of the psychoanalytic structuralist account of sexual difference and the construction of sexuality with respect to its power to contest the regulatory regimes outlined here as well as its role in uncritically reproducing those regimes."[25]

Butler, then, begins her exploration of psychoanalysis with those feminist revisions of Lacan's reading of Freud which constitute a feminist counterpsychoanalysis and which treat the unconscious as the mark of the instability of a sexual identity. Indeed, these feminist theorists also point to the "illusion" of substance which a fixed sexual identity seemingly lends to identity generally; they focus on the fantasmatic as an effect of the very failure of the oedipal imposition of sexual identity. But while these feminist theorists follow Lacan in treating oedipus and its failure in terms of an enforced separation of the infant from the maternal body, Butler disputes the Lacanian claim that "the subject is constituted as a self-grounding signifier within language – only on the condition of a primary repression of the pre-individuated incestuous pleasure associated with the (now repressed) maternal body."[26] And although a feminist counterpsychoanalysis insists that the marking of primary loss as the maternal is a post-oedipal fantasmatic construction, Butler argues further that in focusing on the maternal body, a feminist counterpsychoanalysis glosses a repression of a homosexual aim. For Butler, it is this repression that enables post-oedipal fantasmatic constructions of the sexual aims or modalities of sexual desire.

Making an example of a discussion in Joan Riviere's 1929 essay "Womanliness as a Masquerade," about "intermediate types" between heterosexuality and homosexuality, that is, "types of men and women . . . who while mainly heterosexual in their development, plainly display strong features of the other sex,"[27] Butler proposes that this discussion only "makes plain . . . the classifications that condition and structure the perception of this mix of attributes."[28] Thus, Butler shifts the focus of a counterpsychoanalysis to the mix of attributes that trouble the classifications, especially those classifications which propose that certain attributes are expressive of a "naturalized" sexual orientation of the aims.

Butler deconstructs the notion of sexual orientation, suggesting that not only are the unconscious identities of subject and object of desire fantasmatically constructed, rather than naturally given. But the aims or modalities of sexual desire also are fantasmatically constructed. That is to say, the aims which Freud described as the acts toward which desire tends also are not naturally given. And if Freud already proposed that the aims are constructed – that they become masculine (or active) or feminine (or passive) only through a repression of "a naturally bisexual disposition,"[29] Butler suggests that the notion of the bisexual disposition already presupposes the matrix of heterosexuality. As she puts it:

> The "bisexuality" that is posited as a psychic foundation and is said to be repressed at a later date is a discursive production that claims to be prior to all discourse, effected through the compulsory and generative exclusionary practices of normative heterosexuality. Lacanian discourse centers on the notion of "a divide," a primary or fundamental split that renders the subject internally divided and that establishes the duality of the sexes. But why this exclusive focus on the fall into twoness?[30]

Thus, Butler turns the deconstruction of the heterosexual matrix of desire into a discussion of the psychoanalytic account of bisexuality. Starting with the argument that the oedipal imposition of sexual difference is initiated by the loss of an incestuous love object and that sexual identity is an effect of the internalization of the lost incestuous object choice, Butler suggests that there is another loss. Butler's argument is that if the father is renunciated by the girl and the mother by the boy, it might be noticed that the incestuous object is denied and internalized but the aim or modality of desire is not. Rather, the incestuous object is displaced onto other objects, without changing the modality of desire. Gender identity and heterosexuality seemingly cohere.

But Butler suggests that in the oedipal imposition of a heterosexualized sexual difference, there also must be a renunciation of the mother by the girl and a renunciation of the father by the boy. Butler suggests that in these cases, it is not so much a matter of a renunciation of an incestuous object choice; there is instead a denial of the very desire itself, a denial of the sexual aim or modality of desire. Indeed, for Butler, it is through this denial that sexual aims or the modalities of desire are first constituted. For example, for the boy not only is the father tabooed as object but the desire for the father itself is tabooed and precisely by being defined as feminine; thus feminine and masculine aims are constituted in the ongoing imposition of a homosexual taboo of the matrix of heterosexual desire.

Butler further argues that because the homosexual taboo effects a loss that is never avowed and therefore never grieved, the loss is not so much internalized as "melancholically incorporated;" that is to say, the loss is incorporated into the ego – the ego "taking on attributes of the other and 'sustaining' the other through magical acts of imitation."[31] If the melancholic incorporation allows the fantasmatic construction of the aims, as Butler suggests it does, then the sexual aims are the effect of what she describes as a "literalizing fantasy" that constitutes for the subject its sexed body or anatomy. As she puts it:

> Incorporation *literalizes* the loss *on* or *in* the body and so appears as the facticity of the body, the means by which the body comes to bear "sex" as its literal truth. The localization and/or prohibition of pleasures and desires in given "erotogenic" zones is precisely the kind of gender-differentiating melancholy that suffuses the body's surface.[32] . . . The conflation of desire with the real – that is, the belief that it is parts of the body, the "literal" penis, the "literal" vagina, which cause pleasure and desire – is precisely the kind of literalizing fantasy characteristic of the syndrome of melancholic heterosexuality.[33]

If, then, the syndrome of melancholic heterosexuality "encrypts" a denied homosexuality onto the body, Butler suggests that at the same time, an "inside" of the body is fantasmatically constructed, from which true sexuality is imagined to emanate.[34] Thus, the facticity of anatomy with its invisible interiority is exemplary of the forgetting of homosexuality – the forgetting not of the social construction of anatomical facticity but of its fantasmatic construction. As Butler puts it:

> Here we see the general strategy of literalization as a form of forgetfulness, which, in the case of a literalized sexual anatomy, "forgets" the imaginary and, with it, an imaginable homosexuality. In the case of the melancholic heterosexual male, he never loved another man, he *is* a man, and he can seek recourse to the empirical facts that will prove it.[35]

Thus, anatomy is the embodiment of the very operation that makes the outside appear as expressive of an inside. Indeed, in titling a collection of essays on lesbian and gay theories *inside/out* (1991), Diana Fuss means to make a similar point; that is, if the sexed body is constituted as an expression of an inside, it is because heterosexuality maintains its hegemony by creating both homosexuality as the outsider-within and identity as the internal struggle against homosexuality for heterosexuality.[36] For Butler, then, to turn the inside out means to reject any notion of a prediscursive homosexuality, heterosexuality, or bisexuality. Heterosexuality, homosexuality, bisexuality, and the body are fantasmatic constructions. Thus, when Butler turns to a discussion of practices which she describes as "subversive bodily acts," these also are psychic acts – given the outing of the inside.

After all, even though critical of the matrix of heterosexual desire in terms of which psychoanalysis has delimited the discourse of the psyche, Butler does not mean simply to be rid of the unconscious, the fantasmatic, or the psyche. As she puts it:

> To dispute the psyche as *inner depth*, however, is not to refuse the psyche altogether. On the contrary, the psyche calls to be rethought precisely as a compulsive repetition, as that which conditions and disables the repetitive performance of identity. If every performance repeats itself to institute the effect of identity, then every repetition requires an interval between the acts, as it were, in which risk and excess threaten to disrupt the identity being constituted. The unconscious is this excess that enables and contests every performance, and which never fully appears within the performance itself. The psyche is not "in" the body, but in the very signifying process through which that body comes to appear; it is the lapse in repetition as well as its compulsion, precisely what the performance seeks to deny, and that which compels it from the start. To locate the psyche within this signifying chain as the instability of all iterability is not the same as claiming that it is inner core that is awaiting its full and liberatory expression. On the contrary, the psyche is the permanent failure of expression, a failure that has its values, for it impels repetition and so reinstates the possibility of disruption.[37]

The "Agency" of the Lesbian Phallus

For Butler, then, identity is always a performance – a signification of being – that always is within "the orbit of the compulsion to repeat."[38] Indeed, signification is itself "a regulated process of repetition that both conceals itself and enforces its rules precisely through the production of substantializing effects."[39] For Butler, then, subversive bodily acts are acts of subverting signification, acts that engage the psyche in both deconstructing and reconstructing its own substantializing effects. Indeed, subversive bodily acts replace epistemologies of experience as the basis of politics.

Thus, while standpoint epistemologies would ground politics in the agentic subject of experience, Butler treats agency differently. She describes agency in relationship to the compulsive repetitiveness of the psyche: "'Agency' is to be located within the possibility of a variation on . . . repetition."[40] As Butler explains it:

> If the rules governing signification not only restrict, but enable the assertion of alternative domains of cultural intelligibility, i.e., new possibilities for gender that contest the rigid codes of hierarchical binarisms, then it is only

within the practices of repetitive signifying that a subversion of identity becomes possible.⁴¹

Butler does not figure agency as a person – the lesbian, the homosexual, the feminist. Like feminist post-colonial critics, she enacts a displacement in the place of identity. Instead of a personal agency, Butler figures agency in an act of bodily subversion. Thus, Butler offers "the bodily fiction of the lesbian phallus" which she erects by playing with the morphological imaginary of Lacanian psychoanalysis.⁴² Rereading Lacan's treatment of the phallus in "The Mirror Stage" (1977) and in "The Meaning of the Phallus" (1977), Butler notices that Lacan himself argues that both bodily contour and the shape of objects are not naturally given but derive from the projection of a *morphe* or form onto the infant's mirror image, transforming the infant's "body in pieces" into an imaginary unity; this, of course, is Lacan's now famous description of the construction of the infant's ideal ego in the spectacularization of the mirror stage.

What is unclear, however, and what Butler plays with, is whether the phallus is, as Lacan at least sometimes implies, an idealized and imaginary projection – itself an effect of the spectacularization of the mirror stage. Or whether the phallus is, as Lacan more often and finally insists, the privileged transcendental signifier of the *nom du père* that structures the symbolic order and distinguishes the symbolic order from the imaginary. In other words, although for Lacan no one ever has or is the phallus except in a fantasmatic construction, nonetheless he assumes and maintains the distinction between "having" and "being" the phallus. That is, by proposing that the phallus is the transcendental signifier of the symbolic order, the masculine figure becomes the signifier of "having" the phallus; the feminine figure becomes the signifier of "being" the phallus – a fetishized phallus disavowing the masculine subject's loss. Butler therefore offers the fiction of the lesbian phallus precisely because it collapses the distinction of being and having the phallus.

In doing so, the fiction of the lesbian phallus plays on and plays out the morphological imaginary of the dominant narrative fiction of oedipus.⁴³ It therefore also does the work of collapsing the difference between the symbolic order and the imaginary. After all, if the symbolic order supposedly is structured around the phallus as the privileged transcendental signifier, which is revealed instead to be an imaginary effect, then the symbolic order is shown to be dependent on a distinction from the imaginary that is itself imaginary – that is, ideological.

Thus, if Butler's elaboration of the fiction of the lesbian phallus seems like too much work to do just to establish the way the oedipal narrative privileges heterosexuality, it is because it is difficult work to realize that gender is not a literal reality, not even a socially constructed reality, but rather a literary reality. It is difficult work to realize that the literal effects of all social constructions of reality are fictionally or fantasmatically produced. It is difficult work to uncouple subjectivity and unconscious desire from a melancholic heterosexuality that forgets the imaginary and an imaginable homosexuality. Thus, Butler's fiction of the lesbian phallus not only figures agency differently; it also proposes a new mode of reading the social that collapses the distinction of fantasy and reality, fiction and history, polemic and academic discourse, social science and literary criticism – all figured in the opposition of homosexuality and heterosexuality.

Rewriting Autobiography/Reconfiguring Desires and Politics

If, in proposing a new mode of reading the social, queer theory figures agency differently, as a subversive bodily act rather than as a subject-identity, it also necessarily deconstructs the autobiographical framing of the agentic subject common to epistemologies of experience. Indeed, Butler offers no autobiographical framing for *Gender Trouble*; but Sedgwick, in the introduction to *Epistemology of the Closet*, refers the reader to her various attempts at an autobiographical statement of politics, the longest of which appears as "A Poem Is Being Written" (1987).

Arguing that feminist theorizing often conflates "identification as woman" and "identification with women" – a conflation autobiography promotes, Sedgwick proposes that "A Poem Is Being Written" troubles this conflation. It troubles the function of autobiography in feminist theorizing by making more explicit how "the relations implicit in *identifying with* are, as psychoanalysis suggests, in themselves quite sufficiently fraught with intensities of incorporation, diminishment, inflation, threat, loss, reparation and disavowal."[44] Thus, in "A Poem Is Being Written," Sedgwick superimposes unconscious fantasies on the surface of autobiography – unconscious fantasies through which she both identifies herself and identifies with other women.

About Sedgwick herself, "A Poem Is Being Written" nonetheless begins with Beatrix, the child that appears in one of Sedgwick's narrative poems. Sedgwick presents Beatrix taking a bath; she presents her as a figure in a family scenario described as the "space-making, space-marking chiaroscuro of their need and denial, centering on the nude child seen by coal-light in the cold bath."[45] Following Beatrix's bath, another family scene is presented – a scene involving Sedgwick's family, "an attentive,

emotionally and intellectually generous matrix of nurturance and peda-
gogy,"[46] a scene, nonetheless, in which a child is being spanked:

> Suddenly within the quiet and agreeable space ... of upwardly mobile
> assimilated American Jews in the 1950's there would constitute itself
> another, breath-holding space, a small temporary visible and glamorizing
> theater around the immobilized and involuntarily displayed lower body of
> a child. Of one of us.[47]

If, just before presenting the scene of spanking, Sedgwick announces,
"When I was a little child the two most rhythmic things that happened to
me were spanking and poetry,"[48] just following the presentation, there is
a reframing of the scene to the way Sedgwick always has imagined it; in
Sedgwick's imaginary, the child is spanked over a table rather than "the
parental lap." As a child, Sedgwick had made of the spanking a tableau
in which "the decontextualized, legless, and often headless figure of
display creates in turn a free switchpoint for the identities of subject,
object, onlooker, desirer. For, at the most schematic, active and passive,
but also for roles that far exceed those in resonance – the reactive, for
instance, and the impassive."[49]

Because the spanking and the imagination of it become indistinguish-
able for the subject of autobiography, the subject of autobiography
cannot be presented as an agentic subject. The subject of autobiography
is better understood as a switchpoint in fantasmatic tableaux and only
through these tableaux becomes the author(ity) but also the characters
and the form or body of poetry and narrative. As Sedgwick puts it:

> It is in this way, I think, that both the cropped immobilized space of the
> lyric and the dilated space around it of narrative poetry were constructed
> in and by me, as well as around and *on* me, through the barely ritualized
> violence against children that my parents' culture and mine enforced and
> enforces.[50]

Thus, an authorial desire takes shape within a writer who not only will
characterize herself as male-identified but who characterizes her male
identification in terms of a certain anal erotics. Indeed, Sedgwick speaks
in "A Poem Is Being Written" for a barely existing discourse of women's
anal erotics, the terms of which she imagines move her from the punish-
ing, humiliating, exciting spanking poetry to narrative poetry and finally
to academic criticism – terms with which she identifies herself as a gay
person, " 'as' a gay man."[51] Thus, while this identification informs the
authority of all of Sedgwick's writing, it is not because it provides an
epistemological standpoint. It is, as Sedgwick describes it, because "in

among its tortuous and alienating paths are knit the relations, for me, of telling and of knowing"[52] – relations of the closet.

Not so much the autobiographical accounting of the struggle to find a voice against the silencing of various oppressions, "A Poem Is Being Written" is more about that other struggle so often denied in autobiography – the struggle to find a way to identify with the voice that one's writing can suddenly reveal or (bring) out. There is then, a connection between the tortuous paths of telling and knowing and a style, Sedgwick's authorial style, about which she comments in this way:

> The visible marks of solicitous care and of self-repression, the scrupulously almost not legible map of exorbitance half erased by discipline, the very "careful [one might add very pleasurable] orchestration of spontaneity and pageantry" (the same with which one's parents took one over their lap): these stigmata of "decisiveness" in and authority over one's language are recognizable as such by their family resemblance to the power, rage, and assault that parents present to the child with a demand for compulsory misrecognition of them as discretion and love.[53]

And perhaps not only Sedgwick's style opens to the thickness of this particular elaboration. The writing of others connected to queer theory also has been made an object of attention, often being described as "erudite," "highly intelligent ... but steeped in a deliberate and needless obscurity," as Sherri Paris puts it.[54] Paris further proposes, "These are people who love words ... their own words most of all ... used lavishly, fashionably, inventively."[55] They love what Paris also describes as "obscure and tortuous formulations."[56]

And this love for words often is criticized for being "a-political" – especially indifferent to women's experiences. Thus, the tortuous paths of knowing and of telling are assumed to be chosen or intended, as if the writing style is a mere preference, an intended orientation and not a matter of an unconscious authorial desire, or a matter of the hegemonic discourse of heterosexist, white, propertied masculinity with which desire is entangled. But, of course, it may be precisely because the style seems so similar to those masculinist forms of canonical writing in science, literature, and criticism, that it seems even more inappropriate for feminism, especially an earlier lesbian feminism; indeed, the style may seem to suffer the pain of a male-identification with too much pleasure.

Indeed, queer theory is informed with desire which if, at one time, "could not speak its name," is now, in the naming, still caught in relations of the closet. In discussing "A Poem Is Being Written," Sedgwick comments that the focus on unconscious desire in relationship to the homo/heterosexual definition may lead, or perhaps inevitably leads, in two directions at once. Her example is "homosexual panic," which she would treat in relationship to a universalizing incitement of a defensive heterosexuality, but which in various legal situations also has been used as an argument for a pathological latent homosexuality and thus used to reduce moral responsibility for gay-bashing and other acts of prejudice and violence, enacted usually by male subjects against gay males. Thus, the style of queer theory is also fraught with the fear of "being misread;" it is defensively thick because of "the dangerous relationship of visibility and articulation around homosexual possibility."[57]

Indeed, queer theorists propose that there is no writing outside of the terms of the dominant fiction; nor can agency be articulated outside the orbit of repetition. The style of queer theory, then, is not a-political; instead, the style of queer theory suggests that all style necessarily is political. Fuss even suggests that queer theory is counterhegemonic in claiming a different kind of politics altogether. That is to say, not only does queer theory uncover the politics of the dominant fiction; it does so by displacing an epistemology of experience as the ground of politics. For Fuss, then, a view of politics as "the concealed motor which sets all social relations into motion" is displaced by a view of politics as "a set of effects" to be evaluated as such.[58] Justifying a "correct" politics with an epistemology of experience is called into question; the desire for change is imagined to be motivation enough for politics. As Shane Phelan puts it: "I do not need epistemology to justify my desire, my life, my love. I need politics; I need to build a world that does not require such justifications."[59]

Yet, displacing an epistemology of experience as the ground of politics does not entail abandoning all categorizations of identity and experience, since, as Phelan argues, "the realities of institutions and US politics require that we base common action on the provisional stability of categories of identity, even as we challenge them."[60] In other words, the categories of identity and experience are to be deeply embedded in a practice of (dis)identification and therefore cannot be deployed to privilege positions of knowledge. They instead are to be deployed as performative framings – invitations to political alliances and coalitions. As Butler puts it:

> Perhaps a coalition needs to acknowledge its contradictions and take action with those contradictions intact . . . It would be wrong to assume in advance that there is a category of "women" that simply needs to be filled in with various components of race, class, age, ethnicity and sexuality in order to become complete. The assumption of its essential incompleteness permits that category to serve as a permanently available site of contested

meanings. The definitional incompleteness of the category might then serve as a normative ideal relieved of coercive force.[61]

Thus, while Butler has been criticized for what Teresa Ebert calls a "ludic feminism" which "abandons the category of gender (as a materialist and historical construct, emphasizing the way the socioeconomic totality produces gender subjects),"[62] such a criticism assumes that a politics can only be serious if it deploys notions such as a unified subject-identity and a socioeconomic totality and if it also assumes a direct line of causality from socioeconomics to experience and identity. Such a criticism therefore misreads queer theory as ludic because it fails to treat queer theory in relationship to a materialist feminist analysis of ideology, which in developing a feminist counterpsychoanalysis, deconstructs the notion of a unified gender identity.[63]

And if a feminist materialist analysis of ideology does assume a socioeconomic totality, it also has made clear that that totality cannot be written without forgetting the otherness of the imaginary, a forgetting which queer theorists propose makes an imaginable homosexuality impossible. In other words, if there is to be a globalizing analysis of political economy, a feminist materialist analysis of ideology proposes that it must be represented as discontinuous with the psycho-analytics of psychobiography in order to problematize the autobiographical narration of authority and therefore to question the discourses of causality and economic determinism deployed in the human sciences. Thus, Ebert's view of historical materialism fails to problematize enough its relationship to the human sciences; it fails to problematize enough the authority of the human sciences – the assumptions and methodologies of both social science and literary criticism.

Afterwords

In 1984, nine years after its founding, the journal *Signs* published "The Lesbian Issue." In the introduction, the editors, Estelle Freeman, Barbara Gelpi, Susan Johnson, and Kathleen Weston, explain that because the focus of the issue – lesbian identity and survival of lesbians in homophobic cultures – is the same focus of most "fictional accounts and personal narratives," The Lesbian Issue may give the impression that the thinking on lesbianism is "most highly developed in the fields of literature and history."[64] The editors also note:

> Unquestionably, there is interest in the subject within the social sciences, but both research method and theory are hampered at present. One of the

methodological problems results from lesbians' need to remain "in the closet."[65]

But in 1984, there already was social science research; indeed, in 1982, *Signs* had published Susan Krieger's "Lesbian Identity and Community: Recent Social Science Literature," in which Krieger offered a reading of selected social science researches on the lesbian community and a lesbian identity.[66] And, in the 1984 Lesbian Issue itself, there not only is a review of Krieger's *The Mirror Dance*, an ethnographic report on her own research of a lesbian community (1983); there also are two responses to Krieger's earlier 1982 review essay on social science research. While the responses to Krieger's review essay do suggest that there are methodological problems with doing research on lesbians, the problems seem to be less about lesbians' need to remain in the closet and more about the relations of the closet that shape social science research methodology in the first place.

Respondents to Krieger's review essay, Chela Sandoval, Ann Ristow, and Pam Pearn all have complaints. Sandoval especially notices that not only did Krieger ignore what already was a body of work on and by lesbians of color, Sandoval also suggests that this exclusion allows Krieger to refer to "the" community, as well as to "a" lesbian identity. Thus, Sandoval questions what Krieger argues are the characteristics of "the lesbian community."[67] Sandoval especially is troubled by Krieger's characterization of lesbians as suffering more than heterosexuals do, an anxiety over a desire for merging and a need for separation given that "the community" all but demands a loss of ego boundaries, making personal differentiation nearly impossible. Indeed, it is this feature of the lesbian community that Krieger explores in *The Mirror Dance*. But Sandoval argues that what Krieger describes as the community's production of "a universalizing identity" that "levels all differences" is rather what Krieger produces in forcing this characteristic on all lesbians; Krieger, as Sandoval puts it, "does not flinch in identifying group dynamics that are similar for all lesbians across boundaries of time, class, race and geography."[68]

Eventually Krieger too would recognize the particularly personal orientation that shaped her own study of a lesbian community. Discussing *The Mirror Dance*, in "Beyond 'Subjectivity': The Use of the Self in Social Science" (1985), Krieger would propose that it was in becoming aware of her own struggle over a desire to merge and a need to separate that finally allowed her to get in "touch" with her data, what it was all about, and therefore to be able to recreate it as *The Mirror Dance*. Krieger's remarks suggest that *The Mirror Dance* is not just about a self-mirroring among women of a lesbian community but also between a lesbian community and Krieger herself; *The Mirror Dance* is a self-reflecting construction of others.[69]

But before "Beyond 'Subjectivity,'" in the appendix to *The Mirror Dance*, Krieger had described her study differently. Pointing to what seemed to her to be its "unusual" writing style, Krieger describes *The Mirror Dance* as an attempt to remove her voice and make only the voices of community members comment upon one another. As she put it in the appendix, "I added very little of my own wording to my text beyond crediting paraphrased passages to different speakers and identifying when speakers changed. I therefore became almost absent as a narrator. I was 'painting a picture' . . . rather than 'telling a story.'"[70] Krieger further explains that she was trying to write something more like a Virginia Woolf novel, what she describes as "a multiple person stream of consciousness narrative,"[71] that seemingly requires effacement of the narrator.

But if these two descriptions of *The Mirror Dance* differ, taken together they suggest that *The Mirror Dance*, in its heightened self-consciousness, only makes clearer what has been typical of social science research and writing. That is to say, on the one hand Krieger projects her own desires onto those she studies, and only later can recognize that "All the statements about others are, very significantly, also about ourselves."[72] But on the other hand, her writing is meant to efface her narration, making of herself a disembodied perceptual apparatus – painting, novel, moving camera. Thus, although it is the case that Krieger keeps her narrative voice out of *The Mirror Dance*, it also is the case that her voice is everywhere in *The Mirror Dance*, in every woman, perhaps instead of every woman.

Writing *The Mirror Dance* allows Krieger to fulfill her desire both to merge with every other woman of the community and to separate from the community, even transcend it. Like all social science research that "sees" from a transcendent position, *The Mirror Dance* assumes and deploys a certain distribution of who shall know and who shall be known, who shall see and who shall be seen, who shall be explained and who shall explain; *The Mirror Dance* is grounded in an epistemology of experience and, therefore, is caught in relationships of the closet. And yet, the peculiar effect of relations of the closet is that they cannot but transform every transcendence back into the oppositions of the homo/heterosexual definition.

Indeed, having shared with the reader that she was a member of the community she studied, Krieger, in the end, is the only one who is outed by *The Mirror Dance* – the anonymity of the other women is maintained.

Thereafter, Krieger can no longer transcend; she can only write herself into every text and in the self-conscious manner of the personal essay, an art form she will come to extol in her 1991 *Social Science and the Self: Personal Essays on an Art Form*. Krieger, therefore, moves from an ethnographic study written like a novel, in which the distinction of fiction and history, fantasy and reality, literary criticism and social science is problematized, to an art form of subjectivity, a making and unmaking of the self in writing.

Krieger's writings therefore move social science closer to the "fictional accounts and personal narratives" that the editors of "The Lesbian Issue" connected only with history and literary criticism. But in doing so, Krieger's writings unsettle not only social science research but literary criticism as well. Her writings uncover a problem shared by both literary criticism and social science, that is, how to find a way to collapse the distinction between them – a distinction that insistently promotes research methods and interpretive strategies that either urge making objects of research out of everyone or proffer from the writer, the scientist, or the critic heroic – or, better, anti-heroic – self-revealing autobiographical accounts.

The insistence on only these two alternatives suggests that the oppositions organized through the homo/heterosexual definition have been assumed by social science and literary criticism alike; indeed, these oppositions are their very condition of possibility. Therefore, it is no easy task imagining different methods of research and interpretation. But the effort to do so is what queer theory urges with its own effort to trouble the morphological imaginary of the dominant narrative fiction and therefore to further the reinvention of the social and the literary by making the play of unconscious fantasy and desire appear at the surface of social constructions of reality. In turning social science and literary criticism back onto each other, queer theory turns both inside out.

Notes

1   Of course the question of the relationship between lesbianism and feminism has not been raised only by lesbian and feminist theorists; it also has been raised by others against feminism. After all, as Lillian Faderman suggests, feminists often are and have been "accused" of lesbianism or bisexuality, in order to discredit feminism; Faderman takes as one of her examples the 1970 article in *Time*, "when *Time* magazine took it upon itself to discredit the new feminist movement by publicizing the bisexuality of Kate Millett, the woman that *Time* had earlier made a feminist leader." See Lillian Faderman, *Surpassing the Love of Men: Romantic Friendship and Love Between Women from the Renaissance to the Present* (New York: Morrow, 1981), p. 340. Indeed, in an article entitled "Women's Lib: A Second Look,"

Time did raise the question of Millett's bisexuality as a question of feminists' "maturity, morality, and sexuality." See "Women's Lib: A Second Look," *Time*, 96 (1970), p. 50.

2   Adrienne Rich, "Compulsory Heterosexuality and Lesbian Existence," *Signs*, 5 (1980), pp. 648–9.

3   Radicalesbians, "The Woman Identified Woman," in Anne Loedt, Ellen Levine, and Anita Rapone (eds), *Radical Feminism* (New York: Quadrangle Books, 1973), p. 240. The longer quote from which these remarks are taken is worth reproducing:

> What is a lesbian? A lesbian is the rage of all women condensed to the point of explosion. She is the woman who, often beginning at an extremely early age, acts in accordance with her inner compulsion to be a more complete and freer human being than her society – perhaps then, but certainly later – care to allow her. These needs and actions, over a period of years, bring her into painful conflict with people, situations, the accepted ways of thinking, feeling and behaving, until she is in a state of continual war with everything around her, and usually with herself. She may not be fully conscious of the political implications of what for her began as personal necessity, but on some level she has not been able to accept the limitations and oppression laid on her by the most basic role of her society – the female role. (p. 240)

4   Barbara Smith's 1977 essay was republished in 1982; see Barbara Smith, "Toward a Black Feminist Criticism," in Gloria T. Hull, Patricia Bell Scott, and Barbara Smith (eds), *All the Women Are White, All the Blacks Are Men, But Some of Us Are Brave* (New York: Feminist Press, 1982), p. 164.

5   Bonnie Zimmerman, "Lesbians Like This and That: Some Notes on Lesbian Criticism for the Nineties," in Sally Munt (ed.), *New Lesbian Criticism* (New York: Columbia University Press, 1992), p. 2. In this review of lesbian criticism, Zimmerman also includes a review of her own "What Has Never Been: An Overview of Lesbian Feminist Criticism" (1981, republished 1985), which throughout the 1980s, often was made to serve as an introduction to lesbian literary criticism. See Bonnie Zimmerman, "What Has Never Been: An Overview of Lesbian Feminist Criticism," in Elaine Showalter (ed.), *The New Feminist Criticism: Essays on Women, Literature and Theory* (New York: Pantheon Books, 1985), pp. 200–24.

6   For recent reviews of the "sex debates," see Steven Seidman, *Embattled Eros* (New York: Routledge, 1992) and Shane Phelan, *Identity Politics* (Philadelphia: Temple University Press, 1989).

7   Zimmerman, "Lesbians Like This and That," p. 2.

8   Sally Munt, "Introduction," in Sally Munt (ed.), *New Lesbian Criticism*, p. xiii.

9   Eve Kosofsky Sedgwick, *Epistemology of the Closet* (Berkeley: University of California Press; 1990), pp. 1–2.

10 Ibid., p. 11.

11 Ibid., p. 8.
12 Ibid., p. 27.
13 Judith Butler, *Gender Trouble: Feminism and the Subversion of Identity* (New York: Routledge, 1990), p. 144.
14 Sedgwick, *Epistemology of the Closet*, p. 1.
15 Butler, *Gender Trouble*, p. 121.
16 Sedgwick, *Epistemology of the Closet*, p. 31.
17 Ibid., p. 16.
18 Butler, *Gender Trouble*, p. 13.
19 Ibid., p. 16.
20 Ibid., pp. 16–17.
21 Ibid., p. 16.
22 Ibid., p. 16.
23 Ibid., p. 17.
24 Ibid., p. 17.
25 Ibid., p. 32.
26 Ibid., p. 45.
27 Ibid., p. 50.
28 Ibid., p. 50.
29 Of Freud's texts, the one that has been most influential in feminist discussions of sexual aims is *Three Essays on the Theory of Sexuality* (New York: Basic Books, 1962).
30 Butler, *Gender Trouble*, pp. 54–5.
31 Ibid., p. 57.
32 Ibid., p. 68.
33 Ibid., p. 71.
34 Ibid., p. 67.
35 Ibid., p. 71.
36 Diana Fuss, "Decking Out: Performing Identities," in Diana Fuss (ed.), *inside/out: Lesbian Theories, Gay Theories* (New York: Routledge, 1991), pp. 1–12.
37 Judith Butler, "Imitation and Gender Insubordination," in Diana Fuss, *inside/out*, p. 28.
38 Butler, *Gender Trouble*, p. 145.
39 Ibid., p. 145.
40 Ibid., p. 145.
41 Ibid., p. 145.
42 Judith Butler, "The Lesbian Phallus and the Morphological Imaginary," *Differences*, 6 (1992), pp. 133–71.
43 See also Elizabeth Grosz's elaboration of the notion of "lesbian fetishism" in "Lesbian Fetishism." *Differences*, 3 (1991), pp. 39–54.
44 Sedgwick, *Epistemology of the Closet*, p. 61.
45 Eve Kosofsky Sedgwick, "A Poem Is Being Written," *Representations*, 17 (1987), p. 111.
46 Ibid., p. 114.
47 Ibid., p. 114.

48 Ibid., p. 114.
49 Ibid., p. 115.
50 Ibid., p. 115.
51 Ibid., p. 133.
52 Ibid., p. 133.
53 Ibid., p. 117.
54 Sherri Paris, "A Lure of Knowledge," *Signs*, 18 (1993), p. 985.
55 Ibid., p. 985.
56 Ibid., p. 986.
57 Sedgwick, *Epistemology of the Closet*, p. 18.
58 Diana Fuss, *Essentially Speaking: Feminism, Nature and Difference* (New York: Routledge, 1989), p. 106.
59 Shane Phelan, "(Be)Coming Out: Lesbian Identity and Politics," *Signs*, 18 (1993), p. 777.
60 Ibid., p. 779.
61 Butler, *Gender Trouble*, p. 15.
62 Teresa Ebert, "Ludic Feminism, the Body, Performance, and Labor: Bringing Materialism Back into Feminist Cultural Studies," *Cultural Critique*, 23 (1992), p. 37.
63 In a work that initiated much discussion about homophobia and literature, Sedgwick discussed historical materialism, the analysis of ideology, and feminist criticism; see *Between Men: English Literature and Male Homosocial Desire* (New York: Columbia University Press, 1985).
64 Estelle Freeman, et al. (eds), "Editorial," *Signs*, 9 (1984), p. 554.
65 Ibid., p. 554.
66 Susan Krieger, "Lesbian Identity and Community: Recent Social Science Literature," *Signs*, 8 (1982), pp. 91–108.
67 Chela Sandoval, "Comment on Krieger's 'Lesbian Identity and Community: Recent Social Science Literature,'" *Signs*, 9 (1984), p. 727.
68 Ibid., p. 727.
69 Susan Krieger, "Beyond 'Subjectivity': The Use of the Self in Social Science," *Qualitative Research*, 8 (1985), pp. 309–24.
70 Susan Krieger, *The Mirror Dance: Identity in a Women's Community* (Philadelphia: Temple University Press, 1983), p. 191.
71 Ibid., p. 187.
72 Susan Krieger, *Social Science and the Self: Personal Essays on an Art Form* (New Jersey: Rutgers University Press, 1991), p. 166.

Afterwords

While reviews of feminist thought often focus on the effects of feminist theorizing on the lives of women "beyond" the academy, or on the political movements which organize women's resistance to oppression, domination, and exploitation, I have focused my readings of various feminist texts on the relationship of feminist theorizing and academic discourse. My readings even propose a view of feminist thought as an intertextual production that is itself dependent on the academy, that is itself profoundly engaged with academic discourse in a struggle for authority. But, this view of feminist thought is not meant simply to ignore the relationship of feminist theorizing, women's lives, and the political movements organizing women's resistance. Rather, it is meant to argue that because feminist theorizing is dependent on the academy, feminist theorists necessarily have become engaged in revising academic discourse, reconfiguring its relationship to desire and power.

Thus, while recently there has been much concern voiced about the retreat of feminists into the academy and the resulting development of a postfeminism that, it is claimed, undermines the very goals of feminist politics,[1] I have suggested that feminist theorizing might better be understood in terms of its radical reformulation of the distinction of inside and outside the academy – of feminist theorizing and political movements. Indeed, the debates among feminist theorists which often are characterized as instigating postfeminism – debates over essentialism versus anti-essentialism, over the unconscious construction of subjectivity versus the empirical self, and over discursive criticism versus epistemologies of experience – all have double readings. That is to say, from a perspective that maintains the distinction of inside and outside the academy, these debates seem overly academic. But from the perspective I have been elaborating, which treats the distinction of the academy and the world beyond it with suspicion, these debates seem to function as vehicles for transforming this suspiciousness into a reconfiguration of the academy, social movements, and theorizing in terms of relations of power/knowledge.

Thus, the debate over essentialism versus anti-essentialism is seen as overly academic only when it is assumed that there is a need to establish identity in order to maintain a connection between theory and the political movements beyond the academy. The debate over the empirical self versus the unconsciously constructed subject also is found objectionably academic only when it is assumed that politics needs a unified subject of social agency and therefore the recognition of the instability or division of subjectivity makes political movements impossible. Similarly, the debate over discursivity, and experience is dismissed as academic only when it is assumed that the legitimacy of political movements against oppression rests on establishing both the objectivity and the validity of representations of the actual experiences of the oppressed.

But then there is the other reading of these debates, the one I have been elaborating, which suggests that they result from feminist theorists' efforts to turn the academy outward to political movements at the same time as they struggle to bring political movements to bear on the academy, resulting in making the academy itself a site of feminist politics. From this perspective, the debates over essentialism, subject-identity, unconscious desire, discursivity, and experience are viewed in terms of the way they reconfigure desire, power, and academic discourse and therefore profoundly disturb the assumption that the forces of power are outside the academy and that therefore academic knowledge can offer a disinterested judgement of politics.

From this perspective, the debate over essentialism versus anti-essentialism is seen as a vehicle by which to turn the disciplines to questions of identity and difference so that sexuality, post-coloniality, race, gender, class, and ethnicity might be delivered from a social science of deviance and instead be brought to bear in identifying and reformulating the relationship of predicating normalcy and legitimizing the authority of knowledge. The debate over the unconsciously constructed subject versus the empirical self is seen in terms of feminist theorists' efforts to uncouple sexuality, post-coloniality, race, gender, class, and ethnicity from minoritizing cultural histories in order to instigate genealogies of fantasmatic and ideological constructions of excluded others that have functioned in the establishment of scientific authority and the canonization of literary texts, cultural traditions, and interpretive methods. Similarly, the debate over a discursive criticism versus epistemologies of experience is seen to derive from and further provoke the questioning of disciplinary authority and its insistent opposition of reason and desire, knowledge and power, disinterest and passion.

Indeed, from this perspective, the debates that currently characterize feminist theorizing not only evidence that academic knowledge is not disinterested; they also demonstrate that the forces of power are not external to the academy and disciplining knowledges. Instead the differing among feminist theorists points to the way the academy actively produces the relationships of power/knowledge in which it is embedded. Thus, feminist theorizing not only reformulates the distinction of inside and outside the academy; it suggests that the disciplines function to distribute persons, places, events, and perspectives in relations of power/ knowledge. Indeed, the debates that currently characterize feminist theorizing suggest that oppressions of race, class, gender, ethnicity, sexuality, and colonialism are the effect of disciplinary deployments of relations of power/knowledge.

Of course, this view of the academy and the disciplines makes a disciplinary approach to feminist theorizing untenable. It unsettles feminist theorizing itself, demanding a self-consciousness about the position of feminist thought in relations of power/knowledge – a self-consciousness that refers feminist theorizing again and again to its fantasmatic and ideological construction. Certainly the specific challenges posed to feminist theorizing by African-American feminists, feminist post-colonial critics, Third World feminists, and queer theorists suggest that since there is no uniform experience that characterizes all women's lives, nor is any woman's identity uniformly feminine, then any construction of a feminist subject that is based on a totalizing theory of women's uniform experience or a woman's unified subject-identity is informed by and deploys a relationship of desire, power, and knowledge that is relatively unexamined. That is, totalizing theories are fantasmatic and ideological constructions.

Thus, in pointing to the blindness of some totalizing feminist theories to the differences among women and to the difference of desire within a woman, African-American feminists, feminist post-colonial critics, Third World feminists, and queer theorists only complicate the debates over essentialism, subject-identity, unconscious desire, discourse, and experience, and not least because they also make these debates a means to authorize themselves as subjects of knowledge. Indeed, in their demands for authority, African-American feminists, feminist post-colonial critics, Third World feminists, and queer theorists not only uncover and further aggravate sibling rivalries that have and still divide the desire for a universal sisterhood; they therefore also propose a revision of the relationship of feminist theorizing and social movements. The writings of

African-American feminists, feminist post-colonial critics, queer theorists, and Third World feminists document the way in which social
movements are struggles over the resources for establishing authority –
struggles over the values that shape both what counts as reality and
which subjectivities are to be viewed as normal, authentic, even desirable.
Social movements are struggles over legitimizing modes of reading the
social – contentions over hegemony and counterhegemonies.

The debates among feminist theorists, then, sharpen the critical edge
of feminist thought by insisting on an ongoing self-reflection in feminist
theorizing focused on the interrelationship of organized demands for
authority. Thus, feminist theorizing gives shape to a social criticism that
necessarily is discontinuous with the disciplines – that is, which takes
disciplinary authority as its object of criticism. As such, feminist theorizing not only treats literary canons and cultural traditions as a means of
promoting and suppressing modes of reading the social; it also redresses
the terms by which social science frames theoretical perspectives and
research methodologies. That is to say, the debates in which feminist
theorists are presently engaged are reconfiguring the relationship of
identity, subjectivity, experience, desire, and discourse by rewriting nationalism, sexuality, ethnicity, race, class, and gender – by rewriting the
terms of the modernist reading of the social.

Thus, I have treated feminist theorizing as a development of
disciplinarity but to the point of its undermining the very distinctions
that the disciplines both deploy and authorize as constitutive of a legitimate form of reading social relations. Especially in transgressing the
border between literary criticism and social science, feminist theorizing
uncovers what has been the disavowed narrative or fictional production
of authority necessary to social science and to which literary criticism has
attributed value in relationship to the promotion and suppression of
various other narrative fictions. Feminist theorizing therefore suggests
that social science theory and literary criticism as well as social movements might better be understood as parts of a network of mass-mediated practices of communication – mass-mediated technologies of
reading the social that are productive of hegemony and counterhegemonies.

Therefore, the debates engaging feminist theorists, although not resolved, nonetheless do indicate what the future relationship of the academy, criticism, theory, and political movements might well be. That is to
say, increasingly social criticism will treat political movements in terms
of relations of power/knowledge; recognizing the academy as part of
these relations, social criticism will treat theory as much for its form as
for its content – the form by which the authority of the content is

constituted. The debates engaging feminist theorists thereby give shape to a social criticism in which, increasingly, experience will be treated as inseparable from discourse and discourse inseparable from unconscious desire.

Thus, as I already have suggested, even in feminist theorizing which advocates standpoint epistemologies of experience, there is a hesitancy in deploying the notions of experience and the empirical self. That is, in standpoint epistemologies, the notions of experience and the empirical self never simply are treated with the taken-for-grantedness that had been or still is obtained for them in the deployment of the dominant narrative fiction of oedipus. After all, feminist theorists who advocate standpoint epistemologies at least distance themselves from the dominant narrative fiction both for the way it figures the subject as masculine, propertied, white, and heterosexual and for the way it authorizes "his" experience as reality.

Standpoint epistemologies therefore depend on a prior discursive criticism of hegemony and its constitutive disavowed fantasy of a unified masculine subject – prior, that is, to their grounding a counterhegemonic knowledge in women's experiences. Thus, whereas standpoint epistemologists recognize the masculine subject as a desiring, ideological, discursive construction, they often do not recognize the female subject as such. Yet, as I have proposed, the autobiographical framing of the woman as knower – as feminist subject – functions, usually in an unexamined manner, as a discursive construction of the subject of feminist standpoint epistemologies.

Thus, social criticism increasingly will necessitate methods for articulating and disarticulating the autobiographical framing of writing in order to understand if and how it functions as a regulative narrative fiction of the subject as author; not only will the dominant fiction of oedipus installed with Western, modern capitalism continue to be a focus of criticism but those narrative fictions now circulating inside and beside Western dominance, inside and beside late capitalism, also will be articulated and disarticulated. Thus, as I already have suggested, the criticism of psychoanalysis both for its connection to the rise to dominance of a patriarchal, heterosexist, white, bourgeois class in Europe and for its deployment by that class in the constitution of a world-system of colonization and neo-colonization, is not, however, a mere dismissal of unconscious desire, the psyche, or fantasy.

Indeed, the writings of feminist theorists, including African-American feminists, feminist post-colonial critics, Third World feminists, and queer theorists, suggest that in the future, various psychoanalytic approaches will be necessary for articulating and disarticulating psychobiography.

Thus, the articulation and disarticulation of psychobiography will remain central to elaborating not only how the personal is political but also how the political is personal. That is, feminist theorists will continue to shape a social criticism that reinvents the social and the literary, precisely in refusing to reduce the personal to the political or the political to the personal.

Perhaps the most striking effect of the debates engaging feminist theorists, then, is the way in which they are rearticulating the political in terms of relations of power/knowledge. Particularly noteworthy is the way in which feminist theorizing is giving shape to a social criticism that is discontinuous with a marxist analysis of political economy – especially an economically deterministic marxist analysis. Indeed, a feminist materialist analysis of ideology most clearly represents the ongoing struggle of feminist theorists to shape a social criticism of relations of power/knowledge that refuses an economic determinism but which recognizes that discourse is in part shaped by a capitalist world system.

Thus, the debates in which feminist theorists are presently engaged also can be understood in terms of feminist theorists' efforts to treat the material effects of a globalizing political economy, when from the perspective of a subject there is no grasp of the effects of political economy outside of their discursive construction, that is, outside the ideological production both of subjectivity and of the authority of knowledge. Hence, feminist theorizing is returned again and again to the questions: is there a standpoint from which a globalizing political economic analysis can be made? How can various political movements be articulated in terms of globalizing effects of political economy; how can the difference within the subject and differences among subjects be articulated in these terms?

If standpoint epistemologists answer these questions by insisting on the nondiscursive materiality of experience, at least of women's experience, other feminist theorists suggest that what standpoint epistemologists necessarily neglect is their dependency on the human sciences for authorizing the experiences of others as a position from which to theorize. Feminist theorists, among them feminist post-colonial critics, Third World feminists, queer theorists, and African-American feminists, suggest that efforts to establish nondiscursive elements of political economy often reinscribe the disavowal of otherness in the human sciences onto social criticism.

Thus, the effort of some feminist theorists to articulate a politics of form which disrupts the grand narratives of the human sciences also can be understood as an effort to write about the globalizing effects of political economy which neither reduces psychobiography to an economic determinism nor treats psychobiography in terms of a bourgeois individualism, thereby urging theories that elaborate how analyses of political economy and psycho-analytics of psychobiography are both discontinuous with each other while both are conditions of possibility of a social criticism of postmodernity.

Thus, the way in which feminist theorists align their theorizing with various political movements while resisting ongoing reappropriation by academic disciplines not only allows feminist thought to continue to exert a profound influence on academic discourse. It also necessitates that feminist theorists focus on articulating strategies for judging and evaluating knowledge which are not disciplinary, but rather transdisciplinary, which are about a globalizing political economy but which refuse to reduce psychobiography to an effect of economics, and which focus on differences but in order to keep in mind the often painful difficulties of coming to terms with each other, even in alliances and coalitions against oppression, domination, and exploitation.

In the closing chapter of *The Science Question in Feminism* (1986), Sandra Harding concluded that the subject matter of feminist theory can not be contained "within a single disciplinary framework or any set of disciplines."[2] She then suggested that feminist theory at least must cross the border between "two worlds," the world of science and "another world hidden from the consciousness of science:"

> [T]he world of emotions, feelings, political values; of the individual and collective unconscious; of social and historical particularity explored by novels, drama, poetry, music and art – within which we all live most of our waking and dreaming hours under constant threat of its increasing infusion by scientific rationality. Part of the project of feminism is to reveal the relationship between these two worlds – how each shapes and forms the other. Thus in examining the feminist criticisms of science, we have had to examine also the worlds of historical particularity and of psychic repressions and fantasies that constantly intrude, only to be insistently denied in the scientific world.[3]

I have been suggesting that the project of revealing the relationship between these two worlds has been the project of feminist theory since the early 1970s; but especially in the late 1980s and early 1990s, feminist theorists, while not finding it easy to resolve their differences, nonetheless are furthering the project of reinventing the social and the literary. Indeed, it is precisely in bravely differing with each other that feminist theorists have made their differences into a social criticism of relations of power/knowledge. Feminist theorizing thereby has made of the academy a site for both issuing and critically examining invitations to coalitions and alliances against oppression, exploitation, and domination.

Notes

1 For a provocative discussion of postfeminism and academic discourse, see the introduction to Tania Modleski, *Feminism Without Women: Culture and Criticism in a "Postfeminist" Age* (New York: Routledge, 1991).
2 Sandra Harding, *The Science Question in Feminism* (Ithaca: Cornell University Press, 1986), p. 245.
3 Ibid., p. 245.

Index